MY HIDEO
STORIES OF SU

CONFESSIONS
OF A
HOLIDAY
REP

CY FLOOD

JOHN BLAKE

Published by John Blake Publishing Ltd,
3 Bramber Court, 2 Bramber Road,
London W14 9PB, England

www.johnblakepublishing.co.uk

www.facebook.com/Johnblakepub   facebook

twitter.com/johnblakepub   twitter

First published in paperback in 2002 as *It Shouldn't Happen
to a Rep* and subsequently in 2004 as *Sun, Sea and Sex*.
This edition published in paperback in 2012.

ISBN: 978 1 85782 668 5

British Library Cataloguing-in-Publication Data:

A catalogue record for this book is available from the British Library.

Design by www.envydesign.co.uk

Printed in Great Britain by CPI Group (UK) Ltd

1 3 5 7 9 10 8 6 4 2

Papers used by John Blake Publishing are natural, recyclable products made
from wood grown in sustainable forests. The manufacturing processes
conform to the environmental regulations of the country of origin.

Every attempt has been made to contact the relevant copyright-holders,
but some were unobtainable. We would be grateful if the
appropriate people could contact us.

For Helen, Charlotte, Lola and Daniel

ACKNOWLEDGEMENTS

THIS BOOK WOULD never have seen the light of day without the encouragement and expertise of my friend Nigel Bowden, who alas is no longer with us. I owe him a big thank you and will never forget his encouragement. The world is a dimmer place without 'slippery of the Costas'.

I'd like to acknowledge all of the brilliant reps and guests I worked with during my ten years in the job – you were all brilliant.

A big thank you to my wife, Helen, who has lived with this project for far too long. She has been my impromptu editor and critic, and she is the only one I really listen to.

To all the people who have been forced to sit and listen to the raw script – Allan Mclean, Angie Jones, Malcolm, Julie and Sofia and all those who I have forgotten – I can't thank you enough.

I reserve a very special thanks for Niel Roberts, who had the kindness to lend me a laptop that he never got back! That laptop was the very tool that helped me to transform my hand written scripts into a typed, ready-to-read manuscript – a massive thanks to you and also your brother, Mike, who is forever alive in this book.

Thanks must go to my parents, John and Theresa, for all their unwavering support. Also Mary, Greg, Lorraine, Suzannah, Chris, Rob, Carolyn, Jenna, Ruby and Faye. Ian and Val also deserve a mention for their continued labour, and Geoff and Sue, who now live a life of luxury after a lifetime of hard work – you too are in some way responsible for inspiring and encouraging me to finish this work.

CONTENTS

INTRODUCTION

THE LIFE OF A REP is a privileged existence. If you ever get the chance to live overseas, and get paid for it, grab it with both hands because it's a wonderful experience. To be a rep working for thousands of British holidaymakers is amazing, and anyone lucky enough to experience it will get a lifetime's worth of wonderful memories. I've been very lucky in my life, and I am truly grateful for having the opportunity to be a rep.

I have moved on nowadays but I cherish the memories of working in the holiday industry. I miss the people I worked with; they were all brilliant and very different. Many of them, in their own individual way, gave me the inspiration to write this memoir, so I wish to thank the teams from Ibiza, Lanzarote, Tenerife, Kos and, of course, the Austrian Alps – you really were the best. I'd love to get you all back together again but over the years I've learnt the past is best left in the past, where it belongs. Thanks to you all.

CONFESSIONS OF A HOLIDAY REP

I started this diary before I had even left the UK; I somehow knew that one day it would end up in print. The life of a rep is just too good not to be recorded. I have done the best I can to put my memories down on paper, and I apologise if I have offended anyone at all – it was never intended. The views I express are mine and mine alone. I've tried to be as accurate as possible, but at times my memory may have altered the story.

I have tried to include all of the places I've had the privilege of working in, even the winter destinations, but I am sure I may have sometimes mixed up personalities and destinations; however, the main points are all there. Should you by any slim chance think you recognise yourself, it's probably not you. I have tried to be discreet where possible and never set out to offend anyone, so please forgive me if I have strayed over the line. And, whilst I mostly remember and indeed only write about the guests that caused me problems – or the dickheads and numpties – I have to stress that the majority of people I came across were fantastic, happy people, but they are the ones I have forgotten.

My final thanks must go to you, the reader – thank you. Before you continue to read my story, try to put aside your preconceptions because my story will probably turn out to be very different from what you are imagining. I hope you enjoy the read.

Lastly, and one final thought, I think the role of the rep has changed over the years – with the advent of cheap flights and the adventurous spirit of the British holidaymaker, people have been led away from traditional package tours –

but the golden days of repping may well come back again. I certainly hope they return, because even though the reps had great fun, I think most of the people we worked with had a fantastic time, too.

Cy Flood, 2012

REPPING: WHAT'S IT ALL ABOUT?

I PUSHED OPEN the bathroom door. There before me was a naked man on all fours in an empty white bath. He had been there for some time, trying not to move. His face was contorted with pain and embarrassment. A toilet brush was protruding from his backside. The business end of the implement stuck out of his rear as if it was a porcupine's tail. Most of the ten-inch-long, white plastic handle was wedged deep in his rectum.

A wave of uncontrollable laughter began to sweep over me, but twelve years as a tour rep instantly subdued any wisp of a smile. Instead, I gave the usual cheery greeting:

'Hi, Mr Brown. Is everything OK?'

He winced and managed to say, 'Actually, no.'

Tour rep training teaches you to be positive whatever the circumstances. 'Have you tried giving it a good tug?' I blurted out, in an attempt to be helpful.

'Of course I have,' groaned Mr Brown.

Standing next to me in the small bathroom was Mrs Brown. The causes of her tears and worry were many. She had failed in her attempts to deliver her husband from his anal agony and was now forced to seek my help. She expected me to conjure up an instant remedy and, at the same time, ensure that none of the other hotel guests, or the management, or the company I worked for, ever got to hear of the family's shame. Mr Brown's two young children sat on the sofa in the next room and watched their father with concern.

There was little I could do. I was not a doctor. I had no training in how to remove the hook from the tip of the handle of the toilet brush that was now dug into the lining of Mr Brown's lower colon. A wrong move and he could have bled to death in front of his loved ones. The company's guardian angels – Responsibility, Loyalty and Cover-Up – hovered over me, reminding me that, no matter how ludicrous the situation, it had to be treated as routine. I picked up the phone and calmly asked the receptionist to call an ambulance.

Mr Brown was eventually removed from the bath and, like a large pink suckling pig stuck on a stretcher, he was carried, grimacing, through the hotel's maze of green and white corridors and along cacti-lined paths. With its orange lights flashing, but the siren off, the ambulance drove ever so slowly to the island's only hospital.

I made my way to my windowless office in the hotel complex. Part of my job as the resort manager for the whole of Fuerteventura was to make out a daily report of what happened on this rugged, spectacular Canary island, which is well down the company's list of top destinations. On Fuerteventura, nothing out of the ordinary was supposed to happen.

Incident forms are in triplicate and designed for idiots to fill out, with just the spaces to be filled in. *One up the bum,* I thought. *Brush up ends in clean out,* I wondered. No. This particular company was not known for its humour. My report about Mr Brown's unconventional use of a lavatory brush was sent back to headquarters labelled simply as 'anal accident'.

I needed a beer, and left my office for one, slamming the awkward glass office door shut. The vicious Saharan winds that sweep the island filled my ears, eyes and hair with sand once more. The blast furnace heat soon had the sweat running down my back to form a large damp patch round my waist. By the time I reached my local, The Wobbly Dog, my company issue shirt was stuck to me and my tie clung round my neck like a nylon noose.

As the beer had its desired effect, I reflected on the anal accident and how I had come to witness it. And that started me thinking about how I had ended up on an island that resembles the moon with goats and is frequented by hordes of people who would never dream of living there and don't seem to enjoy themselves much when they are there anyway. It had all started when I was a child.

As a kid, I had been fascinated by stories of people who ran away to sea, joined the Foreign Legion, the circus or simply travelled the world. But by the time I was thirty, I believed that all those romantic notions had passed me by. The most adventure I would get would be a fortnight somewhere hot where millions of like-minded lemmings went. Although I was on the verge of marriage at the time, I was having an attack of nerves. I was scared of the thought of settling down; the idea of comfortable routine made me jittery. Before I was too old, I fancied running off to play for six months.

The holiday brochures I had constantly flicked through stirred my imagination. For a few weeks, I wrestled with my conscience and my fears. Finally, temptation won out over security and, convinced that I was on the doorstep of a life of sunny hedonism, I applied for a job as a tour rep. I confidently looked forward to dealing with throngs of happy holidaymakers and working alongside diligent colleagues to make a package holiday worth every hard-earned penny. So, one damp April afternoon in 1992, Cy the sandpaper salesman became Cy the sun, sea and sand man. The prospect of dealing with car accidents, death, suicide, rape and violence had never entered into my calculations. Neither had the fact that holiday-makers get involved in as much sex, drugs, corruption and criminal activity.

On my last day at work, I went for a drink with my mate Steve at The Railway Tavern next to Liverpool Street station. We had joined the sandpaper company at the same time and were leaving on the same day, but for entirely different reasons. We were both feeling a trifle melancholy, as the firm had been good to both of us. And we were apprehensive about our futures, which were to be poles apart. Steve was going to a better-paid job with more money and security to provide for his family. I was desperate to shag all the girls I had drooled over in holiday brochures. We downed our beers, wished each other good luck, shook hands and disappeared down different tunnels to very different destinies.

During the weeks before I was called up to do my holiday rep training course, my emotions see-sawed. I wanted all that sex; I wanted to get drunk, live in the sun and get paid to do it. But I still could not satisfactorily work out why a sane, logical, thirty-year-old would harbour ambitions to become a lunatic, unhinged twenty-year-old.

I suppose the seed had been sown in the summer of 1988, when I went on the ultimate in sun, sea and sex holidays – a youth holiday to Ibiza. It was the biggest mistake in holiday terms I have ever made. I went with my cousin Mike. We were opposites: he was a mollycoddled mummy's boy who always had money; I was playing in a rock and roll band churning out the old standard, waltzing through the working men's clubs of Bristol. His parents loathed me, but could do little to stop us going away on holiday together. We decided to take Ibiza by storm, just as we did Bristol most weekends. We arrived on the island expecting to spend the fortnight in an alcoholic blur interspersed with frequent exchanges of body fluids with all those heavenly bodies the travel agent had mentioned – nudge, nudge, wink, wink.

We arrived early in the morning and the coach took us to San Antonio, the Sodom and Gomorrah of the Mediterranean, where shagging, clubbing and losing it on drink and drugs were the norm. We could barely contain our excitement – until, that is, we arrived at our hotel. The concrete and breezeblock structure looked as though it had only just survived an earthquake; the food was the stuff that starving refugees would turn their noses up at. But worst of all, there were no available women. Nine out of ten of our fellow fun-seekers were either hardened Estuary boys or dullard Jocks. Both breeds were dangerous and obnoxious when in drink, which was most of the time. There was little scope for two pleasant lads from the West Country to have a good time. As the gloom set in, Mike and I predictably downed bottle after bottle of San Miguel, argued, ogled and took the mickey out of the two tribes from the north–south divide – providing they couldn't hear us. At the welcome party, the rep smoothly relieved us of half our spending money to pay for trips to the water park, the bucking bronco barbecue, the hillbilly hoe-down, the hypnotist show and a boat trip. The captain's cruise sounded enticing: a trip to a secluded beach, packed with scantily clad women, water as clear as gin, a feast ashore and bottles of champagne to be dived for on the seabed. A perfect day was in the making.

The trouble was, Mike and I had stayed up until dawn the night before, drinking and arguing about the girls we hadn't shagged. We were woken at 8am by the sprightly rep and, with hangovers that would have put George Best to shame, we climbed aboard the boat. The sun rose; the heat increased and our heads started to feel like they were being drilled open from the inside.

'Go and get some water, or a Coke, or something,' I murmured to Mike – the one with the money.

'Shit,' he exclaimed. 'I've left the fucking bum bag in the room.'

'Don't worry,' I replied, very calmly all things considered. 'I'll get a loan off one of the reps.'

The promises of help and understanding they had expounded at the welcome party were still fresh in my fuzzy brain. I found a male rep leaning over the stern, guzzling a cold Coke and feeding a fat sandwich to the seagulls, and explained the situation. He surveyed me with the same revulsion Mike and I had used when we'd tripped over a dead dog on the side of a road outside San Antonio.

'Tough luck, pal. You'll have to grin and bear it,' he chortled. With that, he pushed past me, headed to the bar and bought another Coke. A red mist came down over my red eyes.

The cruise around the delightful island of Formentera was obviously well known in the perfect bay we were headed for. As our boat approached, all other shipping upped anchor. The beach cleared in seconds as around fifty of Britain's finest examples of yob culture disembarked, shouting, swearing and being sick over each other.

By now our thirst was of biblical proportions as we fried on the shimmering sands. My tongue, I decided, was definitely stuck forever to the roof of my mouth; my lips were like the sandpaper I used to sell. Our heavenly surroundings had become a thirsty hell. Then it was Mike's turn to have a bright idea. Being a good swimmer, he decided to end our purgatory by diving for a couple of those bottles of chilled champers. He disappeared down into the azure waters and I sat back and started imagining how I would feel when he surfaced, a green bottle in each hand. I had mixed feelings as to how I felt about him when he didn't. He swam ashore and lamely told me he had his contact lenses in and couldn't open his eyes in the water. I wanted to kill him.

Then I saw a female rep coming towards us through what seemed like a mirage. I explained our predicament and, mercifully, she took pity on us and gave us two bottles. Out popped the corks and we thrust the cold necks straight down our throats.

It was like drinking bubbly battery acid. It stripped the enamel from my teeth and tore at my tonsils. I spat it out. Blistered and delirious, Mike and I sat on the burning sand watching the male rep down more cold Cokes. Until it was time to leave paradise, we discussed in hoarse tones how we would take it in turns to torture him to death.

On the plane home, I couldn't get over what an interesting, albeit demanding, job those reps had. And how bad they were at it. The genie was out of the bottle now. I knew that I wanted to be a rep – and a good one. I drew up a well-embellished CV as bait and sent it off. One company called and, in March 1991, I found myself on a ten-day training course held on Majorca.

I enjoyed every second of that course, even though it was a bit like what I imagine basic training in the army to be. You are stripped down to your basic parts to see what you are made of and then rebuilt the way the company wants you. I passed muster and was offered a job but, after much heart-searching and tears from my fiancée, I turned it down at the time and went back into sandpaper. But as I went from dry shop to ironmongers, I found myself brooding about the life I could have been having in Majorca. The genie wouldn't go back in the bottle.

So in October 1991, I revamped my CV and tentatively sent it off to another tour operator. I was summoned for an interview. I explained my motives and reasons – though, of course, not the ones to do with drinking and shagging – and told them why I thought I'd shine as a rep. I also mentioned that I had languages (a friend had given me some Spanish tapes – that's what I thought they were, anyway – and had spent some time talking back at the tape recorder). When the girl who was interviewing me asked me to tell her about my family in Spanish, she looked baffled as I spluttered on for about a minute, then said she had heard enough. She confided in me that her Spanish wasn't up to much, but said that mine sounded OK. It was only later, when I did learn Spanish, that I found out that those tapes I had been given were, in fact, Brazilian Portuguese.

There followed an intimidating group interview with other likely candidates, a sudden-death multi-choice questionnaire – fail that and you are out – and then the part everyone dreads, the presentation. Each of us had to sell a trip to the rest, who were sitting round in that tight circle. One woman droned on for forty-five minutes about the wonders of Coventry, handing out pamphlets and pinning pretty pictures on the walls, until the exasperated examiner told her to sit down. We applauded politely and then it was my turn.

I had rehearsed my merry tale of a wild Wild West night out time and again. In my head I could hear the laughter and the excitement as my captive audience lapped it up. I got all my lines right and my delivery was perfect. But not a sound emanated from those sitting in front of me. They stared past me, their faces as blank as fused television screens. Halfway though my show, the examiner put his head in his hands. I was unsure as to whether the gesture was caused by amusement or despair. I returned to my seat to tepid applause and went back to my fiancée resigned to a life selling sandpaper and taking our future offspring to see Bristol City play.

When a big envelope flopped on to the lino three weeks later, I had trouble opening it, such were my nerves. But there it was: my chance of a new life, a passport to debauchery and general misbehaving. I was among the ten per cent of the 6,000 applicants to be invited on the training course – the toughest of them all.

When some of the chosen few gathered at a hotel in Essex on a frosty February morning, I was primarily worried about two things: my name and my age. In the 1930s, Cyril was among the nation's favourite names, but by the time I was born – in the Sixties – it was reserved for hamsters or tortoises, fluffy toys and other objects of ridicule. My father was unaware of this when he came across the name in a book he was reading, liked the sound of it and informed my mother that the lad was going to be called Cyril. My mother protested, but the old man insisted and so Cyril I became. I was the only Cyril on the Hartcliffe council estate in Bristol, where I grew up. Matters were made worse by my parent's Irish brogue, which meant they pronounced my name as 'Cerril', which came out sounding like 'Sarah'. Some of our neighbours were mightily bemused by the eccentric Irish family that lived at the end of the street and had a son called Sarah. Being called Cyril pronounced Sarah was also the cause of a few scuffles in the school playground. Even now the name is likely to provoke fits of giggles. And, of course, everyone knows the rendition of the song 'Nice One Cyril', written in honour of the only famous Cyril I've ever heard of – the Tottenham Hotspur player Cyril Knowles.

And that wasn't all. Being a good ten years older than the rest of my course companions made me feel like I was a sly old fox let loose amongst a flock of young chickens. For them it was their first or second job. I sensed they thought I was only doing the course as a last desperate attempt to make something of myself. Maybe they were right.

Some of my suspicions were confirmed when I approached the door of the room where we would all meet formally for the first time and I caught the faint strains of 'Nice One Cyril'. *Not very original*, I thought, and strode in. Our names were on labels: Andrew, Malcolm, Robert and a collection of sensible girls' names. I thought of sitting down in front of any of them, even a Sarah if there had been one. Instead I sat down behind my tag; the oldest bloke with the silliest name.

Courses always begin with trainees introducing themselves to the group. The teeth-grinding strategy serves a dual purpose: to give the course tutors an instant idea of

11

the new recruits' potential to cause trouble, and to give the trainees their first opportunity to make fools of themselves. Telling total strangers a brief history of yourself tends to result in a tale of woe, intertwined with lies and pathetic attempts to raise a laugh. One bloke announced, 'Hi! My name's Darren. I'm twenty-three, from London. I used to be plumber, but all the pipes got fixed. I wanted to be a chicken, but I couldn't pluck up the courage. So now I want to be rep, as it's gonna be sun, sea and sex, but this time I'm gonna get paid for it.' There was a cringing silence, briefly broken by one of the tutors deliberately letting her biro clatter on to the floor.

After Darren came Liz, a wardrobe of a Welsh girl with a voice that must have put sheep to flight as it echoed round the valleys. In her previous job she had sold sex aids and she was an expert on the subject, so she told us with a knowing smile. Liz expounded on her sales techniques, but just when it looked as though she was about to whip out a contrivance and demonstrate its purpose, one of the tutors told her sharply to sit down. The atmosphere was one of collective shock.

Now it was my turn. 'Hi! My name's Cyril and I used to be a sandpaper salesman and I support Bristol City.' The howls of laughter caught me by surprise. 'No, really. I am called Cyril and, well, someone's got to sell sandpaper,' I twittered above the rising tide of hysteria. One girl had slipped off her chair. 'And I want to be a rep because anything's better than watching Bristol Rovers. And that's it really.' I sat down feeling silly. I glanced at the tutor who had dropped her biro. The bottom half of her face had all the humour of a bulldog eating stinging nettles, but I thought I saw the merest glint in her eyes that made me think I had made the right career move.

Nice one Cyril, I thought.

Our course tutors were Malcolm and Tracy. An efficient and well-worn pair; they played the roles of good cop, bad cop. Malcolm was friendly and could be approached. The way round him was to ask him to reminisce. He would oblige with wondrous tales of times in Benidorm or Greece, neglecting the coursework, his mind out there somewhere in the Mediterranean, a long way from the stuffy classroom in Essex.

Tracy, though, was not for turning. Her view was that the course was not meant to be fun, and that knowledge should be acquired through fear and diligence. We joked that she only smiled when she broke wind. I christened her Miss Prissy Knickers, a nickname that I believe stuck with her for a while.

The week's course was intensive and gruelling. We laid on welcome parties, did role plays, paperwork practicals, boring but essential theoretical work and endless presentations about even the most mundane minutiae of package tour holidays. To counteract the wealth of information being hurled at us, we socialised and drank copious quantities of Guinness.

No one has ever satisfactorily explained to me why, but the job of a tour rep was particularly attractive to women and gay men and my course reflected this. My pal for the week was Andy, an affable sort, who had had a career carved out at a big high street retailer. He was the same age as me, and had joined the company for most of the same reasons as I had. On the first night at the bar, he let it be known he wanted to be a rep so as to turn himself into a shag monster. We hit it off immediately.

The girls on the course outnumbered the boys. There was Liz, of course, who made instant friends with another Welsh wench called Julie. Both were of the same build – short and wide – with masses of wild blonde hair, giant chests and an obsession with willies. Standing together at the bar, from behind they resembled the back row of a rugby scrum. They developed the tiresome habit of kissing you, hugging you and grabbing you at the slightest pretence. Their intentions were blatant, but Andy and I – the two budding sex machines – wimpishly turned them down with, 'Nah, not my type.'

Michelle, another of the girls in our group, was a no-nonsense Mancunian, and was destined to be a rep from the day she was born. She bore a startling resemblance to the Simply Red singer Mick Hucknall and was duly dubbed Mick. It came as no surprise that she sailed through the course and went on to shine.

The other girl I recall on that course was Karen, who was about as out of place as a rep as a camel in a garage. She was from somewhere in the Home Counties and had a cut-glass accent and a way of putting people down that made you feel you were something nasty stuck to her shoe. I'd figured that she'd doubtless do well in up-market resorts. The company thought otherwise and sent her to Ibiza, to get a bit of experience of the other side of life.

The only other bloke of record from that time was Quentin. He shared a room with Andy and shared his thoughts with us chaps on the kind of men he fancied. After one heavy night at the bar, Andy returned to their room, to be confronted by a fretting Quentin.

'Where've you been all night? I've been worried sick,' he trilled. Andy pushed past him and crashed on his bed. He awoke the next morning to find himself in the bed with his pyjamas on and Quentin at his bedside with a welcome cup of tea. Andy was strangely quiet for a couple of days afterwards, and drank noticeably less.

Quentin never made the grade. But the rest of us did. There we were, the class of '92, ready for an exciting future, serving the travelling British public. I was gripped by a tinge of sadness and much foreboding as we rookie reps stood in the drizzle and said our farewells. And Liz tried to stick her tongue down my throat for the last time.

WELCOME TO IBIZA

I WAS AT the front of the crowd, leading it through the streets of San Antonio towards the next bar. This was the first pub crawl of the year, but we had still managed to get about eight hundred people booked up, and we were now marching them towards the third bar of the night. The atmosphere was electric; they all seemed to be chanting in unison some song about travelling: 'Here we go, here we go, here we go!' Everything was good-natured and fun. I had to pinch myself to be absolutely sure that I was really doing this. Just a few short weeks ago I had been selling sandpaper to boring old carpenters. Here I was today leading a large group of British youth on a bar crawl in Ibiza. I knew where I preferred to be, and it wasn't sniffing sawdust. I jumped along with the crowd, feeling tipsy – not only because of the free drinks I had just helped myself to in the last bar, but because of the fantastic atmosphere. The free drinks bit was a real godsend. I was learning fast that the name badge with the company logo pinned to your left breast was more than just a name tag. It could be a bloody credit card. A credit card that came without any bills dropping to remind you of your sins. *Brilliant! I've really landed on my feet here*, I thought to myself.

Bar crawls were a very common sight in Ibiza when I worked there. Ours was mainly a family company, but we seemed to have a lot of youth arriving at the start of the season, so we had no trouble getting our own crawl up and running. The companies who specialised in the youth market had eyed our arrivals with envy; they would not be happy with our crawls starting before their own. Rumour had it that day that the competitors were going to combine their guests so as not to lose face and get their own bar crawl on the street that night as well. This kind of collaboration between competitors was apparently unheard of before, so we didn't take it too seriously and set off earlier in the evening without checking with the bar owners whether anyone else was going to be in, and if so at what time. This all seemed a distant irritation as we led the group around the corner on to the sea-front in San Antonio town.

My mate Chris grabbed my arm and I tried to push him away. I was having such fun. This repping stuff was truly wonderful. Chris grabbed my arm again, this time more forcefully. I looked at him; he was staring straight ahead. I followed his gaze. There before us, fifty yards away, were one gang of youth reps with the other boys, and about five hundred of their youths all drunk, singing and full of beans. *No problem*, I thought to myself, *we can just walk around them*. Chris, however, being a veteran of two years' service in this business already, had quickly realised this could be trouble. Any youth rep worth his salt knows that when Brits get together in groups, violence is never far away. It's one of the reasons that bar owners are always reluctant to let groups of lads into bars unless they are firmly under control. What looks like good fun one minute can quickly turn nasty. Our group of lads had begun to notice the group of British lads in front of them with their own reps and they started to chant: 'Who the fuckin' hell are you? Who the fuckin' hell are you?' Quite a good question under the circumstances. What we really needed now was a group of Germans to walk past, so the entire group could unite in their antipathy for the German nation. Where are the bloody Germans when you need them?

We realised we were going to have to act fast if we were going to avert a potentially nasty situation. A bottle came sailing through the air in the direction of the other group. It smashed somewhere in the crowd. Then, all at once, both groups broke ranks and started to race towards each other. Within minutes there was skin and hair flying in all directions. I suddenly began to think that selling sand-paper was not such a bad proposition after all.

Chris grabbed me by the arm and taught me the first lesson for every rep in crowd control. Self-preservation. We ran like hell to the safety of a nearby bar; the doorman quickly ushered us in and shut the door behind us. Within minutes the police had arrived in force. They seemed to be enjoying the baton practice this opportunity afforded them. Arrests were few; bruised ribs were plentiful. Within half an hour ambulances had arrived and the paramedics were quickly sorting the drunk from the injured.

We emerged from the bar to find several of our colleagues had done exactly the same thing that we'd done, in other nearby establishments. Now our work would really begin. 'Pick an ambulance,' shouted Chris. 'We'll have to go with the gits to hospital now, just to make sure they're all right.'

I took his advice without question, as he had already saved my bacon once that night. I jumped into an ambulance with a young bloke who had managed to cut his head open, either on a bottle or from a fall. Either way, he looked pretty miserable as he sat meekly on the seat of the ambulance. His girlfriend, very obviously the worse for alcohol, was lying on the floor in front of him, laughing. At least she had had the wherewithal to notice me climb into the ambulance and sit opposite her stricken boyfriend. She opened her eyes as the ambulance doors slammed shut and we began our twenty-minute journey to the hospital in Ibiza town. 'Cy!' she screamed as she hauled herself up and tried to sit beside me. She looked at me blankly. 'My mate fancies you,' she gibbered, 'but I think you are an ugly bastard.' Then she slumped down with her head resting in my lap and fell asleep. Good start to the season, really. If I had known it was going to be like this, I'd have joined years ago.

*   *   *

One thing that inspired confidence in me that I had made the right decision when joining this company as opposed to all the other tour operators – apart from the fact they had been the only ones to offer me a job that summer – was that they offered thorough training. I had already been through the mill before I left the UK and, on arriving in Ibiza in late April 1992, I soon discovered that the guests didn't actually start arriving for another two weeks. We were there to face another gruelling training course. That, coupled with the time spent learning the ropes in a hotel in England, certainly adds up to a lot of training before you even see a punter.

I was not alone; there were another hundred recruits as well for this season in Ibiza. We all arrived together in the middle of the night in a very quiet Ibiza airport. As soon as we walked through the arrival doors into the eerily quiet arrival lounge, we were each given an agenda for our latest training course for the next couple of weeks. We were then whisked to waiting buses and onwards to the resort of Playa den Bossa. On arrival at our home, one of the hotels in the resort (home for the next two weeks, anyway), we were handed our room keys. My worst fears had come true. I would be sharing a room. It turned out that my room-mate had arrived earlier that day from Manchester. He was already in the room. My room.

I hadn't actually shared a room with anyone since I was six years old but, even way back then, I knew I wasn't cut out to share my sleeping quarters with anybody. It was tough then, and the room-mate in question had been my brother. Now it was going to be a complete stranger. You get used to your own company in bed. I like the privacy to daydream about the day gone by or the day to come. I like the privacy to pick my nose, or even – if the need arises – to scratch my arse or fart or both, or even to read, and many other things that I dare not mention. Wrist exercises and the like. This is always difficult if you are sharing. I've always found that you quickly get used to your own bodily noises, functions and smells. You become quite tolerant of your own shortcomings. Yet when you witness the same smells and noises coming from a bed a couple of feet away, it's incredible how disgusted you can become.

This was a bad start, but I had no choice: it was a case of share or go home. I decided to share. I just had to hope that this would not be the permanent arrangement for the whole season.

The hotel was quite expansive and judging by the number – 2353 – my room was quite a way off from reception. I don't quite know how I worked that out; I just had this sixth sense about it. I was right, though. It was bloody miles away from reception. If you walked it in your shorts and T-shirt, it would take maybe just a couple of minutes at a brisk pace: up the stairs and past the pool and the entertainment area outside, up another two flights of stairs, along two more corridors, and you were there. No problem. It's a different story when you're laden down with heavy suitcases containing enough luggage for the next six months. My suitcases were heavy – dangerously heavy. Heart-strainingly heavy. This severely compounded the difficulty to the task in hand. After a long, tiring journey, which had begun that morning in Bristol, I dreaded this final thrust.

I decided there was only one way to approach it. I summoned all my last reserves of energy in an attempt to get the cases to my room as quickly as possible. This went OK for a while. First I attacked my hand luggage, taking it straight to the room so I could familiarise myself with the geography of exactly how to get there. When I arrived, I decided to knock on the door in case my room-mate was taking any midnight wrist excursions. I knocked politely. After waiting for a few minutes, I started to reach into my pocket for my own key. Just as I did so, the door handle turned and the door opened slightly. I pushed my head through the gap, just in time to see a figure climbing back into bed. This was my first encounter with my new room-mate, Martin. The time in Ibiza was 11pm. Going to bed at 11pm where I came from was unheard of. I figured he was either upset about something or a boring bastard. I later learned neither of these assumptions was true, but more of that later.

Back in reception, there was a general hive of activity as other nervous trainees were scuttling to and from rooms with gigantic suitcases filled with God only knows what. I saw my largest suitcase sitting in the corner of reception, looking menacing, with its outsize zipper grinning at me defiantly, like a row of silver teeth, saying, 'Come on, have a go.' I summoned all my strength and lunged at the case. I figured that once I got this heavy one out of the way, the rest would be a cake walk.

At first the case was stubborn. It seemed heavier than before. I went as quickly as I could with my cumbersome load – through the reception hall itself and out towards the courtyard and past the pool. The doorway to the staircase proved tricky, but with an even sterner effort I managed to drag it through. The stairs required superhuman stamina, but I didn't stop. I pressed along through the corridor, and with one last effort I grounded the defiant bundle at my door. I rested before opening the door and giving it the final push home. In truth, I was tempted to break into a mad bout of laughter in celebration of my first conquest on foreign soil. Small as it was, I was jubilant.

Then a squeaky voice piped up from behind me. 'I think you've got my suitcase there,' it said. I turned around to see a small, pretty blonde girl, with the biggest blue eyes, looking accusingly at me.

'Oh no,' I replied confidently, 'it's definitely mine.'

'No,' she said. 'It's definitely mine, look at the tag.'

I looked at the tag, expecting to see 'Cy' written soberly in the corner. But when I turned it around, there to my utter horror was written the name 'Monique'. In crayon.

'See,' said the girl. 'Thanks.' She dragged the case to her room, two doors away. The last I saw of her case as she disappeared into the room was the grinning zipper. I was mortified. All that effort, to carry someone else's case to their room. My immediate thoughts were to run after the girl, grab the case and take it straight back to reception, whatever the effort involved, but she was just too quick for me. If only I could have got my hands on her case, I could have beaten it up, disfigured it in some way so I could never mistake it for my own again. I consoled myself by reflecting that mistakes can happen to anyone. I returned to reception to see my cases where I had left them; they were grinning at me defiantly. Half an hour later they were in my room, where I resolved to leave them untouched until the morning, when I could thrash them relentlessly.

I prodded my room-mate to see if he wanted to join me in the bar for a quick drink. He refused with a grunt, and off I went alone for a solitary nightcap. As I sat alone in the bar supping a well-earned beer, I felt no small amount of anxiety about the future. In essence this was just another training course, but whereas the last one was still in the UK, things now suddenly seemed very real. I was here in Spain, and there was no going back. I had given up everything I had at home for a moody room-mate and heavy suitcases.

Not surprisingly, I was feeling a little lonely and nervous about the future. Dotted around the bar were others huddled together in little groups for security – there is safety in numbers. It was a low-key start to the greatest adventure of my life to date. I sat there contemplating the world and was down to my last sip of beer and about to retire to bed when from around the corner came my old friends, Liz and Julie, from my training course back in England. I was very glad to see them charging towards me. They hugged me together; it was a bit like being in a scrum down with the England pack, but it was very welcome to know that I had friends here after all. A few more drinks were imbibed, and suddenly it didn't seem such a bad place after all.

Some time later, my mood had lightened as I made my way to my room for a good night's sleep. But my plans took a severe beating when I opened the door of my room. I was nearly knocked back by the sheer volume of my room-mate's snoring. It was deafening. How the hell anybody in the room next door was managing to sleep was totally beyond me. How I was going to sleep was the more immediate problem, and I couldn't for the life of me see how it would be possible with Martin letting passing ships know of his whereabouts in the bed next to me, barely two feet away. I felt like I had been invited to an exclusive horn-testing session of the *QE2*'s finest.

I immediately considered the possibility of sleeping on the bathroom floor. No good, too small. I should mention at this point that the area we were staying in for the duration of this course was situated right alongside Ibiza's only airport in Playa den Bossa. Planes regularly roar overhead, either taking off or landing. Compared to Martin's snoring, however, this noise was tame. The only consoling thought I had was that by the end of two weeks of this row I would eventually collapse exhausted from the lack of sleep. Mind you, I would probably also be deaf.

Sometimes when you cough or shout or find some way to distract snorers, it disturbs their sleep pattern and they will move to a new position and so clear their airwaves for a while, thereby providing a short respite of silence. I had learned this skill when I was a child. My father would fall asleep in front of the TV after a hard day at work, and he too had a real problem with loud snoring. A clap of the hands or a loud cough would disturb him and bring a little peace. It didn't wake him, just stirred him enough. I had honed this trick to a fine art as a child. You had to be careful not to rouse the snorer completely from his slumber, for if you did wake him, and he thought the noise had come from the TV, he would just walk over and turn it off without any explanation and then return to his chair and resume sleeping and snoring. A fine balancing act indeed. Worse still, if my father thought it was his oldest son – me –

taking the piss, he would belt me on the way past, just for good measure. So the stakes were high. As they were now.

As I lay there in my bed listening to Martin howling, I decided to test my skills on him. I coughed loudly. There was a moment's silence. Was this success? A few grunt-like sounds and … all he did was change key from a deeper E flat to a louder A minor.

I tried again. And again. Martin simply changed tune and slumbered on regardless. It was intolerable. I put my fingers in my ears, but my hands got pins and needles. I put my head under the blankets, even under the pillow, but I had to resurface for fear of suffocating. I sang to myself; I stuffed toilet roll in my ears, all to no avail. Martin continued to snore more and more loudly. In the end I had no option but to wake him. I pushed him awake. 'What?' he said.

'You're snoring,' I replied.

He turned around. Hooray, I had won. There was silence. I curled up into my favourite sleeping position and waited for Dr Sleep to welcome me into the house of dreams. Then Martin started again. Louder and louder. I woke him again as politely as I could two or three more times. Eventually I was shouting, 'Shut the fuck up!' I finally got to sleep about 6.30am. At 7am the alarm went off. Martin was up first, bright-eyed and bushy-tailed. He pushed me awake and introduced himself.

'Morning, mate, I'm Martin. Sorry about not coming for a drink with you last night, I was in a session with me mates all day in Manchester before I left. I was a bit tired. Might have one with you tonight, though. Cor, you look a bit tired, mate. Did you have a late night, then? By the way, I think I snore a bit, hope it doesn't keep you awake.' Then he disappeared into the bathroom to freshen up. *Yes*, I thought, *I can confirm the snoring bit.*

Over the next couple of weeks sleeping became a real problem for me. I devised new positions for Martin to lie in, in order to try to prevent the racket recurring. Fair enough he tried them all willingly. I think we had some success when he lay on his stomach with his legs tucked underneath his body. Unfortunately, this meant he didn't sleep, but at least he didn't snore either. Eventually I moved my mattress next to the balcony door. It didn't stop him snoring, but it did reduce the volume. I really liked Martin once we had got through this difficulty. We eventually became good friends. That said, I know that I couldn't have stayed in this room for more than two weeks with him. I think I would have died of exhaustion. Or he would have died of strangulation.

A couple of years before this excursion into the world of tour operating, I had tried my hand with another company, and they had taken us all off for a training course in Majorca. It was great fun, but I hadn't taken the experience too seriously. I had looked at the letter saying, 'Training course … Majorca' and thought, *Great, a holiday*. I'd gone away to that course in a very relaxed mood. I remember packing lots of pairs of shorts and T-shirts. On arrival at the course venue, I was horrified to learn that ninety per cent of our time would be spent in an office environment, where you would be expected to wear 'office dress'. Which, of course, meant shirt and tie. I spent most of my free time in the week washing and re-washing my one shirt and tie. Over and over again.

I decided before I set off with this new company that I wouldn't make the same mistake again. So, plenty of smart office clothes were packed this time. On day one I dressed in my smart shirt, new trousers and sensible tie. Sod's law meant that I was the only one who dressed that way. One of our first tasks was to answer a practical quiz that took us all out and about to parts of the island away from Playa den Bossa all the way to Ibiza town. A distance of about five miles. This would all be done walking in groups that had been organised that morning. The groups consisted of a couple of experienced reps and a collection of 'greenies', people like me. We set off to walk to Ibiza and answer the questions along the way. The theory was that the experienced members should have a good idea of the answers and help the newcomers along the way.

Good theory, I suppose, but not so good if your experienced rep, Cerise, is pursuing the affections of another rep in the group, Motorbike Mark. They only had eyes for each other. It soon became clear that Cerise knew all the answers. Periodically she would fill in a few of the questions and then hand them back to us newcomers who were all following her eagerly down the street. We would then copy what she had given us and wait for more. Our collective fear as the new kids on the block was that if we got all the questions wrong we would all be sent home for failing. This, it turned out, was highly unlikely, as I don't believe that our papers were even looked at once they had been handed in. They all came back with the same comment, 'A good effort, well done,' written on them.

The day itself had been very hot and tiring. A heavy pair

of brown Marks & Spencer corduroy trousers probably work very well in the winter months in England; they keep you very warm. On a mildly hot spring day in Ibiza, walking ten miles in the same trousers is, to put it mildly, very hot and sticky, and very uncomfortable. I had been a little self-conscious about wearing shorts for the first couple of weeks in Ibiza, because my legs were lily white. This turned out to be no problem at all. All the dye from my cords transferred on to my legs after the first three miles. Try as I might, this dye proved impossible to remove, without taking a layer of skin with it. Some of our group might have learned a lot from that first day in Ibiza, but I learned nothing, except how to walk to and from Ibiza town in a pair of heavy cords that have been made twice as heavy by being laden down with a liberal helping of sweat.

Rather unfortunately, I had also chosen that first day to give my new hobnailed boots their first airing. This too, for obvious reasons in retrospect, was a big mistake. They stood up rather well to their first test, but reaped a terrible revenge on me. From that day on, they stank beyond all comprehension. One whiff of them could paralyse your nostrils. As they were the only sensible pair of brown leather footwear I had, and that was the company uniform, they just got worse as the season got hotter and drier. I had to lock them away at night, or leave them outside my apartment. Needless to say I reverted to wearing a cooler pair of trousers for the remainder of the course.

The agenda for the two-week course looked quite busy in theory, but some of the times allotted for different sessions proved to be wildly inaccurate. As a result, there were times when our trainers didn't know what to do with us. This left us all with a lot of free time to kill, which proved to be no problem to anybody. I had brought a lot of spending money with me to see me through the first month, and it didn't take that much effort to plug into holiday mode quite quickly. I took many long and leisurely lunches with my new friends and got drunk. I also took every opportunity to do the same in the evenings.

Martin and I got on very well outside the bedroom, and we would have lunch with Liz and a girl called Beth whom I had met in Gatwick airport on the way out. We would spend our time either bitching about other members of the staff or recounting our past. You learn quite quickly who you like and don't like, and who you want to spend time with, or not as the case may be. We passed many hours discussing our futures, where we would like to work on the island and how we would like to fare in our first six months in the job. We all preferred different areas of the island, but the powers that be, i.e. our trainers, were not going to tell any of us where we were heading just yet. At that time we had no comprehension of how big the island was or how we were going to get around; it was all so new.

Towards the end of the first two weeks, with D-day – the arrival of our first guests of the summer – coming closer, we found ourselves on a coach that took us all for a grand tour of the whole island. The guide was one of our trainers, a guy called Charlie, who had worked on the island for a couple of years. We were all asked to pay particular attention to what we would see, for after this little excursion we would be asked to fill in a piece of paper as to our preference for where we would like to work. We were told that our requests would be looked at sympathetically, but that no promises would be made. To me this was all a blur, as one idyllic location after another passed us by through the coach window. At the end of the day I couldn't put any particular preference down on paper, so I just left it blank. From what I had learned while on my previous training course in London, I felt that it was a good bet that I would be going to San Antonio to work with the youth programme. I only knew two things for certain from that tour: I didn't want to work in Portinatx and I definitely didn't want to end up in San Miguel, at the northern end of the island. I remember Charlie joking about how remote these two places were as we breezed past them and how we all laughed about them being at the end of the world. Somebody would have to go to these places. Whoever they were, they had my sympathy – they would need it.

The day arrived when our summer destinations were to be revealed to us. We all waited nervously in the reception of the hotel to be called in by our bosses and told our fate. The meetings seemed to be lasting an average of ten minutes apiece. This was to be a crucial time for all us novice reps. Some had threatened that if they didn't get what they wanted they would be heading home. There was quite a bit of tension in the room as we all waited. I didn't see anybody cry, but plenty emerged from the room smiling.

Eventually it was my turn. I was called into the room by Fanny, the lady who was to be my boss for the season, my senior rep. Fanny was a cuddly kind of person. She was about five feet tall, with a kindly smiling face and a hefty frame – she was about fifteen stone – topped off with a neat blonde bob that gave her a motherly appearance. Not at all like the kind of person you would expect to be in charge of one of Europe's leading hedonistic pleasure paradises. She sat down in a comfortable chair in front of me and went through various pleasantries about the last couple of weeks, asking me whether I had enjoyed the course and whether I was ready for the season ahead. I made all the right noises, but couldn't help feeling that I was being built up for some bad news. Finally it came.

'I want you in my team,' Fanny told me.

'I'm flattered,' I replied. 'Where?'

'The El Greco. Portinatx.'

My face dropped. I felt like I had just been told that my passport had been confiscated.

'You don't look very pleased,' Fanny observed.

'Oh I am, don't worry, it just needs time to sink in.'

I was numb. I had been dreaming of spending wild nights in San Antonio, fighting off the bikini-clad lovelies. Instead I was headed for Portinatx, which according to the reps who had worked here the year before was the second closest thing to a graveyard on the island. Still, at least it wasn't San Miguel. I would have to make a point and find the person who was off there, to see how depressed they looked.

I wasn't alone. Apparently there would be a big team in Portinatx. My first problem was that none of my friends would be there. Martin, Beth and Liz had all plumped for more fashionable destinations. My second problem was that I couldn't pronounce the place. The 'natx' bit was a real tongue-twister. Most people seemed to plump for a version that came out as 'Portinatch', so that would do for me. I was Portinatx bound and that seemed to be that.

The vast majority of the reps seemed quite happy with their destinations as we gathered together for a drink that evening. There was a feeling of relief that we would soon all be on our way to our destinations and that our guests would shortly be arriving for the season ahead.

In hindsight, I believe that I had made a mistake a few days earlier when I had performed a welcome party speech at a training session in front of all our bosses, as we all had to do. I had wheeled out my mad version of the hillbilly hoe-down that I had perfected on several previous occasions. Fanny had been present at that meeting, and she later told me that on the strength of that performance she had earmarked me for her team. Still, I suppose it was a compliment. I made conversation with my team-mates in the area, and with people who had experience of working there, and soon I had reconciled myself to six months in Portinatx. It wouldn't be that bad after all. It could be the happening place for the coming summer and it had to beat hanging around at home. And whatever happened, it would be a great experience. I was determined about that.

There was, however, a twist in the tail. I had phoned home with details of my new address in Portinatx and had packed my bags ready for the journey, when Fanny called in to the hotel for a meeting with me. There had been a change of plan. I wasn't now going to Portinatx. My hotel wasn't opening for the summer. I was quietly relieved. The company had decided that my talents would be better used in a sports complex. So they were going to send me to San Miguel. SAN MIGUEL! At this point I considered resigning. They had to be taking the piss. It felt like being imprisoned by the Iraqis, and then escaping to be caught by the Iranians. I remember sharing the news with my friends. Their eyes seemed to cloud over and lose focus. The idea of San Miguel for six months filled me with dread. Oh well, such is life. Fanny softened the blow by telling me that I would have to help out with bar crawls in San Antonio once a week and that the girl who had worked in San Miguel the year before had asked to go back. Surely, then, it couldn't be that bad, could it? Anna, my new colleague, had not yet arrived in Ibiza, but I looked forward to meeting her.

We had one more act to perform before we left for our resorts. Throughout the two weeks we had been sampling the different trips that we would be selling once we got to our hotels. Every rep has to be able to sell. It's a part of the job, and a very important one at that – no sales equals no commission. I think it's great to be able to sample these days and nights out, and it was still a great novelty to me to get all your drinks for free and your food as well – what could be better?

I wasn't the only one who thought this way. When you looked around at the end of some of these evenings, I reckon some of the reps would have had trouble remembering their own names, such was the amount of alcohol consumed. Those long, boozy nights also provided a good opportunity for us to get to know each other.

This, of course, is a ritual that the people who own these excursion venues have to go through every year. Goodness knows what they must be thinking when loads of fresh-faced new recruits descend upon them, full of enthusiasm and lots of nosy questions. It must be great entertainment for the locals. They all really push the boat out, because they know that if the reps have a good time then they are more likely to sell their excursion than someone else's. The best-selling trip in a resort from year to year can depend upon how good the owners are at making their day with the reps successful. With that in mind, the whole team are treated like VIPs when they arrive at the venues. We had done all of these trips, bar one. That was to be the 'Country Feast'. It promised to be a good evening, not least because it would be our last opportunity to socialise as a group.

The mood was very upbeat as we boarded the coaches for the little country farmhouse in the middle of the island for the evening. The farmhouse was owned by a couple from New Zealand, who treated us to an evening with Maori entertainment and food.

It was a great night and proved to be very popular through-out that season, so judging from that alone it must be a great success with holidaymakers. The food is cooked under the ground in a hungi oven and served to everyone after an explanation from the Kiwi owner, a very nice gentleman called Art. As far as I can remember, a Maori does a little dance and the entertainment begins – and ends, for that matter – with an Irish two-piece band called Sean and John. They are very good, but as far from the theme of New Zealand as you can get. Why anyone would come all the way to Ibiza to spend an evening in New Zealand while being entertained by an Irish duo is beyond me. Oh well. Suffice to say, it's a great night out and, if you are ever in Ibiza, go along and see it, it's really quite fun. (There I go, selling it again. Old habits die hard.)

Anyway, off we trundled to the Country Feast, all one hundred of us, for a romantic last evening together until who knew when. Our guide for the evening was a little Spanish fella called Diego. Martin and I had met Diego a few days earlier. We had come back to our hotel after a day's training to find Diego standing at the bar in a very unkempt old uniform that looked as though the owner had slept in it. He had a brandy in one hand and a cigarette in the other and looked completely at ease with the world. The company rules state that you can't smoke, drink or swear in uniform. We thought that perhaps Diego had been placed there as a plant by the company to see how easily we would be distracted. He took one look at us and gestured us over.

'Come on, fellas, have a drink,' he said.

'Oh it's OK,' we answered nervously, looking around anxiously.

'Please yourselves,' he replied.

'We thought you weren't allowed to drink in uniform,' we enquired.

Diego looked at us, startled. 'You can't drink in uniform, you can't smoke in uniform, you can't do fuck all in uniform. Bollocks,' he sneered and laughed heartily before swigging back his brandy, and then ordered another one. He invited us to join him again. We assured him we were all right and quickly scurried away, thinking we had had a lucky escape. Basically, Diego didn't give a toss. But I can assure you that he was one of the best guides that company had. He made every evening or day he guided great fun. He had a good way of painting a picture of the venue before you got there that made it sound like the best place on earth. 'This is gonna be the experience of a lifetime for you all this evening. You are going to sample a unique food experience the like of which is reserved for only the chosen few, and you have all been chosen tonight. You have all been personally invited, by Rose and Art, the only New Zealand couple here in the Balearics, who have prepared this special treat for us. The entertainment is the cream on a very exclusive cake, and it all takes place in their home.' We could hardly wait to get there.

On arrival, the tables were bedecked with wine – free, of course – and if you wanted beer, all you had to do was ask. Martin and I polished off four bottles of vino between us and the evening just flowed by. The excursion coincided with a bit of an episode for me, one that could have resulted in an amorous evening with one of my colleagues if I had let it get that far. Living on the same floor of the hotel as us was a girl called Flo, who was also in her first year as a rep. Flo, to put it gently, was fat. Very fat. She had the most penetrating blue eyes that stared right at you and said, 'Let's have fun.' Now, I was pleasant to her, but nothing more; I didn't want to encourage her at all. During our training course she had made a few suggestions to Martin and I about coming to her room for a massage – both of us – but we always turned her down, thinking she was only joking.

Well, that night Flo was sitting on a table near us at the Country Feast. She kept looking over and smiling at me all night long. At first I smiled back just to be polite, but, as the frequency of her stares and winks grew, I became more and more uncomfortable. I foolishly voiced my concerns to Martin, who really didn't help the situation by smiling back at Flo and winking at her, while nudging me. My concerns grew to something near to panic when Flo followed me on an excursion to the bar. She leaned towards me on the bar and whispered into my ear.

'Cy, you look all tense and stiff. Why don't you let me give you a nice slow massage? I can move that stiffness to another part of your body.' She giggled and slapped me on the bottom.

'It's OK, Flo,' I replied with a nervous little giggle. 'I'm not that tense really, I just need a good night's sleep before we move tomorrow.' And with that I beat a hasty retreat back to my table.

The final hour of the Country Feast was a bit of a night-mare. I tried to persuade Martin to accompany my every move, and to make sure he sat by my side on the coach back to Playa den Bossa. I ended up sprinting from the coach to our hotel, with Flo in hot pursuit shouting, 'Come here, you little tiger!'

On the return journey, Diego made the evening complete by singing all the way home. It was a great evening apart from Flo's pursuit of me, and certainly a good way to finish off our first two weeks on the island. God save me from fat women.

The next morning we were all packed and ready to leave the hotel to go to our respective resorts. You get very attached to each other during these courses and, instead of it feeling like the beginning of something exciting, it felt very much like the end. The truth was – though we couldn't quite feel it at that time – that this was the first day of a great adventure. In another couple of days our guests would be arriving. That was when the fun would really begin. After all the training and re-training, that would be the acid test. Now things were going to get really exciting.

SAN MIGUEL – IT'S NO SAN ANTONIO ...

TO MANY PEOPLE, the word Ibiza means complete hedonism: parties, raves, drugs, sex and wild, wild nights that never end. Throw in lots of sex with crazed women, or men, depending what your taste is, and that is pretty much the standard view of the island held by most people under the age of thirty. The reason for this misconception is, of course, San Antonio. San Antonio, as most people are aware, is Ibiza's wild party capital, which really has heaploads of the above in abundance. The media love to do their bit to enforce this view of Ibiza. You don't tend to see too many DVDs for sale that portray the gentle side of the beautiful island, its breathtaking views of the Med, its calming waters, its balmy afternoons with the sun gently falling into the sea, its magical atmosphere simply made for lovers. No, you are more likely to encounter DVDs or CDs of Ibiza uncut, unleashed, unbridled, undressed, untamed or unfurled –

unruly interpretations of this little jewel in the Balearic crown. It is portrayed as being simply the wildest place on earth, and for many it lives up to this reputation. Back in my early days as a rep, I wanted to be part of this wild side, this magnificent concoction of madness.

So, as you can imagine, my heart was heavy as I made my way to the quietest part of the island, miles from the action. No, more than that: I was pissed off, well and truly pissed off. It took me a few weeks to realise that the widely held view of Ibiza as a party venue and nothing else was just a little inaccurate. To judge Ibiza by what goes on solely in San An would be the equivalent of watching film of the Brixton riots in the early Eighties and then, from that brief glance at one of England's inner cities, deciding that the whole place was the same. It would be unfair and inaccurate. Ibiza is beautiful. But it took me, the original philistine, a few months to appreciate that. I wanted to be in San An, and here I was on my way to the end of the world. What shitty luck. I resigned myself to my fate and decided to give it my best shot, for a couple of weeks at least. If I got to feeling really depressed, I could always return to the world of sandpaper.

*   *   *

To be successful in this job, or at least to get the customer satisfaction results that the company craved to keep us ahead of the game, you had to make the guests like you. It wasn't the answer to everything, but it sure helped. If they liked you, they bought from you and so you earned commission. If they liked you, they smiled at you and talked to you; it made your life much more pleasant. If they liked you, they gave you good marks on the questionnaires. And, I suppose, you had a much better chance of shagging them as well.

All guests were asked to fill in questionnaires at the end of their holidays. Questionnaires that asked how good you were, how nice their hotel was and how attentive you were to their needs. Many guests never realised how important these forms were, but the reps waited with baited breath to get their monthly results from these things. So it helped if the guests liked you. When the guests started to like you, they asked you questions, and these questions came up again and again. *So what's it really like to do your job? What have you done with the weather?* was another favourite. *What do you do in the winter? Can you speak the language? Do you miss your home and family? Do you get fed up with all the sunshine?* The list went on and on, and you tended to have stock answers that you could rattle off. The trick was to sound like you had never heard these questions before, and that the people asking you were the first ever to do so. It could be tiresome, but when these questions started to come up, you knew you were on to a good thing. The relationship was starting.

The problem is that, over six months, they came up again and again. If it rained, you heard, *'What have you done with the weather?'* at least fifty times a day. I know of one rep who told a guest to fuck off when asked this question for the umpteenth time in a day. The guest looked at him aghast, and said, 'I don't believe you just said that to me.' The rep looked back at the guest and replied, 'Neither will my boss. Now fuck off before I get really angry.' True story this one – the rep was leaving the next day, and he really didn't care any more, but what a way to go.

I think that a lot of our guests would love to have done the job that we do, but never had the courage to give it all up and take a chance. I believe that reps live the life that some can only dream about, and I remember that when I was on holiday with the lads years before and the first seeds of curiosity were being sown in my head about this job, I too was wondering what it was really like. Now, after all the training and travelling, I was about to find out.

From the moment I was informed that I would be going to San Miguel to work, I had misgivings about the place. The experienced reps didn't really have a good word to say about it. It was the furthest away from the action in San Antonio that you could get, and most of the reps wanted to work as near to that place as possible, so the mere thought of working in San Miguel sent fear into their hearts. When you worked in these groups and were relying on them for information, you tended to listen to what they said, and so I too dreaded the thought of working in this place so far away. I had resigned myself to making the most of it, though, and as our bus trundled along the road that cuts through the middle of the island towards San Miguel, I tried to put all thoughts of being isolated and remote far from my mind.

The town of San Miguel is first visible by its church, which you can see from miles away. The steeple rises into the sky from a cluster of buildings around the base that seem to be pulling it back down to earth. When we eventually arrived in the town, there was little sign of life.

What had been an empty, barren road suddenly became punctuated by a few ramshackle houses. Then, some fifty yards on, there were a few units that could have been shops, but were boarded up. One café seemed open, judging by the presence of a few old men who glanced up from nursing tiny cups as we rolled by. It really did seem very quiet. No sign of a disco or a lively bar, nothing remotely British at all. I know this would be heaven to the dedicated seeker of all things Spanish but, as I viewed these streets for the first time, I felt depressed. There were six of us on this journey to San Miguel and judging from the silence I think that all my fellow travellers felt the same.

All of us were heading here for the first time. We were going to meet Anna, the one living person who wanted to come back for a second year to the resort, when we arrived. Just when you thought that it couldn't get any worse than this, surely, we slowed down and took a sharp right-hand turn down a dirt track. The coach slowed almost to walking pace as the driver negotiated the steep decline that led us down to Puerto San Miguel. The Port of San Miguel. Our home for the next six months. The track seemed to get a lot narrower and more treacherous as we headed down to the port. I felt like I was going to the end of the world, on the Costa del miles away, as we descended further. The thought occurred to me that if I felt like this, what were the guests going to feel like when they rolled down this same hill on the way to their two-week dream holiday? Eventually, after what seemed like an eternity descending into the abyss, the road became tarmac again, and opened out into a breathtaking vista of a small bay surrounded by high cliffs and crowned by a beautiful golden sandy beach. It really was quite pleasing to the eye. The treacherous journey down here did nothing to prepare you for this sight.

The three hotels that made the resort were almost carved into the rocks around the bay, and quite spoiled a magnificent view. The coach stopped outside the Hotel San Miguel, the biggest one of the three and the one nearest the beach, and Anna was there to greet us. This was her home; she loved this place. Anna was in her mid-thirties, about five foot five inches tall, with straight, shoulder-length blonde hair. She was quite pretty, but her features were hard. Her cheekbones seemed as if they had been chiselled out of the very mountains of the place she had made her home for the last two years. She did not smile once during our greeting and smoked continuously.

It soon became clear why Anna had chosen to come back here for another season. She was going out with the man who owned the water-ski school, and he was her reason for being here. She welcomed us ... I hesitate to say warmly, but we got a handshake at least. The coach pulled away and we were left with our cases outside the Hotel San Miguel, feeling a little forlorn and cast adrift. Guests would not be arriving for at least another three days, and so the resort was deathly quiet. It seemed that we were the only ones here, at the end of the earth. Our apartment would not be ready for a couple of days and so as a temporary measure we were to be billeted in one of the hotels in the resort.

A twist of fate had seen these rooms allocated in the Hotel

Galleon. The Galleon was right at the top of the mountain. I shuddered at the memory of hauling my suitcases around for the last couple of weeks, and looked upwards to the heavens towards the hotel. Mercifully there was a lift – albeit a service lift that smelled badly of dirty sheets and musty towels, but it was a small price to pay for the relief from lugging my cases. I dragged the offending hulks into the lift and pressed the button for the Galleon. The ascent was slow and the smell almost overpowering.

Eventually I reached the summit and the door opened. There before me were two giants. One male and one female. 'Hello!' they bellowed in unison.

'Hi, I'm Cy, the new rep,' I squeaked in reply. I hadn't quite got used to saying that yet and now, for the first time out loud to strangers, it sounded very unreal. They smiled back at me with rows of perfect gleaming white teeth.

'We know, and we know where you are staying. We are the entertainers; we will help you with your cases.'

With that, they each picked up one of my cases as if they weighed no more than feathers, and disappeared off down the corridor that lay before me.

I was shocked at the forwardness of these two monsters, but pleasantly surprised and delighted with the help in moving my dreadfully heavy load. I scampered after them, following them along a corridor that seemed to go on forever to some ridiculously numbered room – something like 45678. How many bloody rooms were in this hotel, I wondered. The couple reached the room and deposited my cases outside the door. I quickly checked my luggage and confirmed that it was indeed still abnormally heavy, and I had not been mistaken all along.

The pair stood before me, smiling. I must have looked puzzled and amazed at the same time. They registered my confusion and decided to introduce themselves. The girl was called Saskia. She was, and still is, the biggest human being I have ever seen in my life. She was close to seven feet tall and built like a shot-putter. Given her height, I was not surprised to learn that she was a former member of the Dutch national basketball team. In spite of her intimidating appearance, she was a lovely person, and we became good friends during the season. On top of her head, which seemed high enough to entertain snow, she had a wild mane of curly ginger hair. You couldn't help but notice Saskia; she stood out in a crowd, mainly because she was like a lighthouse in a sea of humans, but her hair was even louder than she was. She explained that she had come to work as an entertainer in Ibiza so she could improve her Spanish. She would be one of the workers in the resort and was anxious that we should all work together.

Her attitude was shared by her companion, Mark. He was also Dutch and, like Saskia, he spoke perfect English. So good, in fact, that if you had asked me to put money on where they came from before I actually found out, I would have said America. Mark had come to Ibiza for the summer to work in the wind-surfing school and to improve his English. *Improve*, I thought, bloody hell, he spoke the language better than I did. Mark was around six feet five inches tall. He had a lovely natural head of blond hair and he was a stunningly good-looking man. His skin was a beautiful olive colour; he was built like an Olympic athlete and he had a cheeky smile and a confidence that bordered on arrogance. I hated him immediately. Mind you, if I was six feet five inches tall, incredibly handsome and spoke every European language that was worth speaking – fluently – I might display a little arrogance too.

The dynamic Dutch duo bade me a warm welcome to the resort of San Miguel and invited me to a get-together to meet the rest of the team in the bar later that evening, so we could get to know each other. After the pleasant surprise of not having to haul my cases to this room, the bar seemed like an excellent idea. I agreed and let myself into my room, feeling quite happy that I had already made my first friends here in my new workplace. So far, I had resisted completely unpacking my suitcases, but as I was now very close to starting the season, I thought I really should get everything out and take stock. I had a couple of hours to kill before going to the bar to meet my colleagues, so I decided the time was right to try to bring some order to my life.

I emptied the cases. For the life of me, to this day I cannot think why they were so heavy. I looked at the contents lying on the bed and on the floor, and there really was nothing to wear. I couldn't make out what made up all the weight. I do, though, have to own up to having made some pretty surreal decisions when I was deciding what to bring with me for that six-month trip. I had the following list of useless items in my possession. Six pullovers, woolly. (What on earth I imagined I was going to do with six woolly jumpers in the Mediterranean summer climate, I cannot imagine.) One pair of hobnailed boots, two spanners and over two hundred business cards from my last job ... The list goes on, but modesty forbids me revealing more to you. Suffice to say that, in future, I resolved to take advice on packing, before getting someone else to do it for me!

I tidied my room as best I could, leaving a pile of the useless items in the corner, so I would see them every time I entered the room and embarrass myself into throwing them away eventually. Once this was done, I scampered off down to the bar to meet my new colleagues. There were to be six reps living in the area with me, all women, and we would all be living in the same house, once it was ready (I think it was being aired for the summer). For most red-blooded males that would be heaven, and I was no different. I thought I had landed on my feet.

Of the six, four of the girls were children's reps. There was Anna and Rhona, both of whom would be working in the Hotel Galleon at the top of the resort. Both of them were very young, and this was their first time away from home; they were shy, but happy-go-lucky. Then there was Sheila. She was another children's rep, had been with the company for years and reminded me of Mrs Baylock, the dreadful housekeeper in the film *The Omen*, the one that was sent to guard the Anti-Christ as he grew up in his father's home and who had a Rottweiller dog. Sheila never had a Rottweiller for company, though she was followed around by a stray cat for a few months. The children's rep that would be looking after the youngsters in our hotel, the Hotel San Miguel, was a short, fat Scottish girl aged about eighteen. She had red skin, covered in freckles, and a mop of the reddest hair I had ever seen. She might have been a nice girl. I can't really say. The thing is, she had the broadest Scottish accent I had ever heard. I simply could not understand a word she said. She might have been saying all manner of lovely things to us all, but I never knew.

The two reps were Jill and Tracey. Jill was a wily old campaigner who had been with the company for a couple of years. She had long ago lost her enthusiasm, and it had been replaced by ample helpings of cynicism. If ever you needed a reminder of just where your feet should be, Jill was always there to remind you to get your head out of your arse and look at your heels, planted firmly on the ground. Finally, there was Tracey. She was young and attractive, and she was residing firmly under the wing of Jill, who was, it seemed, anti-men – or, more accurately, anti-me.

So there we were, all gathered in the bar of the Hotel Galleon, ready to meet our entertainers, the boys and girls who would be providing entertainment for our guests when they arrived. The games of bingo, darts, snooker and rifle-shooting, and at night the cabaret shows. We had already met the two Dutch dynamos, Mark and Saskia, and there was one more to go: Kira. Kira was from Denmark. She was, and probably still is, stunningly beautiful and I fell in love with her about two seconds after I met her. I wanted to marry her there and then – so did every other male who set eyes on her during the season – but she wasn't into pale, skinny men from England with no language skills. She was about five feet five inches tall, with lovely natural curly blonde hair and a beautiful, kind face that lit up every time she smiled, which was about every two seconds. I made great friends with Kira, which was just as well, because she spent an awful lot of time working in our hotel during the season. She was a winner before she opened her mouth; everybody loved her. With this team, and Anna our long-serving colleague to complete the line-up, how could we fail?

Anna was to be my direct colleague, meaning that we would be working side by side in the hotel for the next six months. We had to get on. I soon discovered that she planned to run the ski school as well as carry out her repping duties. Unless I was very much mistaken, that meant that I would not be getting her undivided attention. Oh well, I had to forget all those fancy ideas of being taken under the wing of a more experienced member of staff – that is, unless I wanted to learn to water-ski. Anna had the most glorious of suntans. She was a beautiful golden brown and beside me, her pale and pasty colleague, she looked even better. In the photograph that we arranged to be taken for our information books, together we looked like an advert for the United Colours of Benetton. I was probably the palest-skinned rep ever to set foot in Spain, apart from Sarah our children's rep, that is. I put it down to my Irish heritage. It takes me a good six months of intense sunshine to even go pink; along the way, I just burn.

Anna made it quite clear from the beginning that she had very little time at all to spare for me. She treated me with contempt, as if I was the reason she could not dedicate all her time to the water-ski profit-making machine. There were others in our team in the resort, but Anna and I were to be working more closely together than anyone else. This was a bit unfortunate considering her dislike for me, but that was the way it was going to be. Our duties coincided at the same time in the hotel every day, unless she had to take a water-ski class. And we put together our own time-off and guiding rota. When I say guiding, I mean taking coaches to excursion venues in other parts of the island. I was lucky enough to get the youth guide every week, and that meant that once a week I had to gather up all the young people in our resort and take them down to San Antonio, the heart of the party area of the island, about an hour's drive away. I looked on this as my saving grace, my weekly escape from the confines of San Miguel.

Our first guests arrived along with the first of the summer rains. Good timing, really. It pissed down day and night for the first three days of their holidays. As San Miguel is only a six-month holiday resort, not every bar opens its doors for the first day of season. They kind of yawn first, and then start to clean their bars and shops; normally the resort will not be fully functional until about mid-June. When you only have one alternative bar to the hotels in the resort, and that is closed during the first two weeks of the season, this can present a slight frustration to the guests, who begin to feel imprisoned in the area. As our first customers expressed their frustration at the lack of activity, I could only sympathise with them. The rain made it difficult to use any of the great facilities outdoors, such as the tennis courts or the football pitch or the rifle-shooting range, or even for the guests to use the free mountain bikes that were on offer.

During that first week, I thought the rain would never stop. In desperation we organised dart-throwing contests and pool competitions. The attendance levels at these events was fantastic. I am sure that if the rain had kept up we could have sold the rights to cable television, such was the excitement of a double top. Our duty times were never meant to be more than six hours a day, but I found myself staying anything up to twelve hours every day. There really was nothing else to do except stay with your guests. At least this secured us the friendship of the first lot of arrivals; we developed a kind of siege mentality, trapped in the Port of San Miguel. I felt just a little cut off from what I thought was happening up in San An – and whatever it was, I still wanted to be a part of it if at all possible.

Eventually my time came. I was called upon by the youth team to go up to San An and help out with the first bar crawl. This proved to be a wild occasion and ended up with six of our guests in hospital with various injuries, after getting involved in a fight in the middle of the town. It was great fun and kind of whetted my appetite for a weekly jaunt to the fun area of the island. Alas, though, it was only a distraction. The real work for me was going to be in San Miguel. There were no wild nightclubs or the like in this area, but we still had a lot of hard work to contend with.

When I try to remember our guests from that first year, I can only think of the dickheads. I am not sure if other industries are like the tourist industry in this respect, but when reps sat around and gossiped about the people they worked with – i.e. the general public – we only ever really talked about the troublesome ones. We never sat around for hours and discussed the nice people we looked after. There were hundreds, no, thousands of nice people who came on holiday with us, not only one year, but every year. But the dickheads were as plentiful as ever, and it's those we remembered.

One that springs to mind was a gentleman by the name of John. What a character he was. John came on holiday with his wife and from the moment he arrived he started complaining. He claimed that he had chosen to come to San Miguel purely for the standard of the tennis. I should keep you in the picture and explain that Club San Miguel is very pleasant but it's no Wimbledon or Flushing Meadows. It has two tennis courts: one is in a very poor state of repair – i.e. the astro turf is ripped and worn – the other is a little better, and it has floodlights if you want to play after dark. Both nets sag like an aged stripper's bra, and they can look quite sad. I can't see Tim Henman looking at this venue as a training camp for the winter. Unsurprisingly perhaps, when John saw the courts he began to complain. He then started to moan about the standard of entertainment, which he said was 'juvenile'. He also griped that the rooms were tiny and uncomfortable, and he hated the food.

All in all, it looked a pretty hopeless situation but, bursting with a new recruit's enthusiasm, I decided not to be outdone by John. I have played a bit of tennis in my time – especially if Wimbledon was on the telly at home, me and my mates would get out our old racquets, climb the school fence and play until it got dark. It didn't put me in John's league, but it gave me the idea for a plan. I suggested that he might try coaching – coaching me. This seemed like a good idea, and so every morning I rose from my bed at 7am for a coaching session. This involved him standing stone-still at one end of the court with a bucketful of balls, which he proceeded to hit to all corners of the court, with me chasing after them, a racquet in my hand. Occasionally I would make contact with a ball and, depending on how pissed off he was, he might shout, 'Well done.' This would last for an hour every morning, with me sweating profusely and then collapsing in the bar and buying him a drink to thank him for the session. The same performance would then be repeated at 3pm in the heat of the sun, with me sweating even more.

John wore a permanent scowl. I don't think it left his face for the whole two-week duration of his holiday. We even changed the situation of his room to just above the tennis court, so his wife could sit and watch John send me scampering around the court twice daily. Occasionally she would shout the odd word of encouragement to John, telling him to hit the ball harder because I was slowing down. What a bloody performance. I don't think it made my tennis any better, but I certainly got a lot fitter and I began to lose weight. It also had the effect of making me chase anything yellow that flew past my line of vision quickly. For weeks I could be walking along, talking to a friend, and then suddenly set off in hot pursuit of a vividly coloured passing butterfly.

John, though, was not content with mere coaching. He wanted a partner – his wife was apparently far too submissive to give him a game. Then I had a brainwave. It turned out that Mark, our Dutch god and part-time wind-surfing instructor, who was predictably brilliant at everything, was willing to take John on. John had apparently been causing havoc at the wind-surfing school by complaining about the facilities there as well, so Mark saw this as an opportunity to get some revenge. John insisted that Mark play him in the evening, i.e. only after Mark had finished work. With Mark exhausted and John fresh from a mid-afternoon coaching session, the game began. It was a ferocious game that went on over three separate nights. John eventually scowled his way to victory. Still he remained unhappy with everything and everyone.

We held a weekly tennis tournament for all-comers and, against our better judgement, we let John enter. Predictably, he won. I decided to present him with the prize for winning the tournament and gathered all the entertainers, even managing to get Anna to come away from her water-skiing activities one evening so we could have a grand prize-giving ceremony to try to cheer up John and his miserable wife. We would present him with a free trip on the glass-bottom boat and a free bottle of champagne. The music was played and the ceremony began. 'The finest tennis player ever seen in San Miguel, and a good bloke [yuk] to boot, put your hands together for … John!' We waited for John to come and collect his prize. And we waited some more. No John. He had chosen to snub us. Eventually he came to our duty desk the next morning to collect his prize. He opened the envelope and looked at the contents. We waited for a smile or maybe even a thank you. He scowled at us and said, 'Pity it's not a flight home.' At this point I had to agree with him. The good thing about these kind of people is that you only have them for a couple of weeks, and then they are gone. When the day came for John and his wife to depart we all turned out to wave them off. I think we all wanted to say good riddance and give an appropriate hand sign that would involve a swift upward thrust of the middle finger of the left hand and would have ideally connected with John's left nostril. However, we are professionals and we contented ourselves with a smile and a wave. 'Goodbye, John, keep in touch.' As I said before, most of the people are nice and you are happy to help them enjoy their holidays, but do you get the odd dickhead. At least they make for good gossip.

Now, one of the reasons I came to this place was to bonk as many girls as I could, and I was certainly looking forward to a few ladies falling at my feet. After all, I had been told by some of the youth reps that your uniform, and particularly your badge, was a key to more than meets the eye. As well as being your mark of identification, it was widely known that a uniform was – to put it bluntly – a fanny magnet. But after a month in San Miguel with one night a week at the bar crawl in San An, which usually ended up in a hospital or a police station, I was beginning to wonder whether my uniform had lost its magnetism. I hadn't even had a sniff of a chance. I was beginning to think I was hopelessly unattractive after all and that my sister, who had told me this as I left our house to go to a disco years earlier ('You won't pull anything, you ugly bastard'), was right after all. Fanny had come down to check on us at least once a week and she had a chat with me and asked if I got out much. The long hours at work were obviously taking their toll – either that or my muscular right wrist must have alerted her to my predicament. She said I should meet up with some of the people I had been friendly with at the training course a few weeks earlier, and I thought why not, why not indeed? I called up Beth, one of the girls I had shared lunch with many times during our training course. She was a sweet girl and I liked her, so I thought what the hell. I made a date and took her to dinner in Ibiza town.

I put on my best brown trousers, my hobnailed boots and a beige shirt, and set off to town to meet my date. I had a vague memory of how she looked from the training course, but it was fading fast. I wasn't prepared for the way she looked when she walked into the bar we had arranged to meet at, ten minutes late. Beth was tall, about five-nine, which made her the same height as me (so I have to say tall). She had brown shoulder-length hair and lovely unblemished skin that was just beginning to tan slightly; she was slim and dressed in a stylish but sensible blue summer dress that made her look stunning and sexy. In a nutshell, she was beautiful and, I thought, way out of my league. We sat in the restaurant and tried to get to know each other. Beth, it turned out, had a boyfriend in America. I had no chance – that was made quite clear very early on, but I thought I wouldn't let it put me off.

I liked Beth a lot, and I ended up having a wonderful evening with her. It came to an end all too soon and we found ourselves heading out of Ibiza town in the little hire car I had managed to procure for the evening. I was driving as slowly as I could out of the town when Beth's spirit of adventure came to the fore, and she suggested we take a detour on to a rocky little cliff top that gave us a truly romantic view of the old town by night, with all its shimmering lights climbing out of the water up to the cathedral at the top of the Dalt Villa. That's when I decided to make a move. As we sat there in the moonlight inside the car, I reached over, took Beth's hand and gazed into her eyes. I touched her face, and ran my finger along her nose and slowly down to her lips, and I kissed her. It was a magical moment. *This is what I came here for*, I thought to myself, *now things are starting to look up.*

Beth decided that she wanted to leave the car and walk to the edge of the cliff to get a closer view of the surroundings. She gestured for me to join her for a romantic stroll in the moonlight. There was, however, no way I could leave the car, owing to the fact that I had a stonking great hard-on that refused to subside. I wasn't about to allow my overactive manhood make a grand entrance at this stage. I made polite excuses and had to content myself with talking to her from the car window. Kind of ruined the moment really. Shouting from the window was not as romantic as whispering in the car. When she returned to the vehicle, she unwittingly let in another passenger who would get a lot closer to her than me that night. A very lively mosquito proceeded to bite her no less than thirteen times. We returned to Beth's home with her scratching and trying to swat the offending fly. As romantic evenings go, it was pretty memorable. It didn't quite end the way I would have liked it to, but at least now I had hope for the future.

*   *   *

Sometimes your guiding duties took you away for a whole day. One such trip was a day out with the guests to the water park, known as the Aguamar. It was a fun day out that lets us visit the park and try out all the slides and generally have great fun. For the reps it was the easiest day out there was. You took your guests there and then simply killed time until they were ready to come home. On the coach on the way you warned them about the dangers of the sun and how it could burn them if they were not careful. Reps are great at giving this advice, but they are not always so adept at heeding it. I decided that on one particular day I would kill my time sunbathing in the park. It seemed such a good idea at the time. Five hours later, I had changed colour from a very pale white to an angry deep red. I was unable to sit down due to the searing pain in the back of my legs from my frying skin. My head felt as though my brain was far too big for the encasing skull. Very painful and very embarrassing. Needless to say I wasn't keen to repeat my role as a walking demonstration of why the guests should heed our sun-care advice.

Anna and I learned to tolerate each other during our time working together in San Miguel. As long as I didn't moan about the fact that she was hardly ever at work, due to her commitments at the water-ski school, then we got along fine. She was, though, very good at doing the paperwork and reckoning up the money we had taken for excursion sales at the end of the week, and there were times when she used her experience to get us out of some sticky situations. We didn't like each other; the relationship was all about tolerance. There were occasions, though, when we had to make sure that we worked closely and seamlessly.

One such occasion came towards the end of the season. We had gone away to the capital of the island for a team meeting. As we left the resort, it started to rain. While we were at the meeting it continued to rain. It continued for the next few hours and proceeded to flood large parts of the island. When we returned to San Miguel some four hours later, it was pouring down. This in itself didn't bother me at all. I thought nothing of it. Indeed it was quite welcome, as we had seen very little rain at all for months. I went back to my room and, as I had a couple of hours before I was due to start work, I decided to have a siesta. I drew the curtains and dozed off for a nap. I awoke later that afternoon to the sound of raindrops. I stretched and opened the curtains to let the light in. As I looked towards the hotel at the bottom of the hill, I thought I must have still been dreaming. The hotel appeared to be in the sea. I blinked. It was not a dream. Cars were floating around the hotel towards the open water beyond the building, jostling for position like a surreal marine traffic jam. Metal fish swimming to the open seas.

I dressed as quickly as I could, and made my way towards the hotel. By the time I reached reception I was thigh deep in water. Confusion and panic greeted me. Understandably, guests were fretting about the consequences of what was happening. The entire ground floor was under three feet of water; the pool had disappeared, and it was still raining hard. The guests were demanding answers to impossible questions: 'What shall we do?' And making impossible demands: 'Get us out now!' 'We want transfers to higher ground now!' I ushered as many guests as I could to the first floor. Some were happy with this, but others were not, as they thought that if the water level rose, they would be trapped. I couldn't quite work out this logic, as if they stayed on the ground floor, they would drown. Oh well. I thought I'd phone the office and try to get some reinforcements. This proved to be impossible, as the phones were out of order – this was only a few short years ago, but mobiles were not a part of our everyday life at that point, and so, without a land-line, we were stuffed.

I knew things were quite bad because, although the lights were still working, they were in fact all leaking. It was bizarre, all these lighted cascades. Quite pretty as well, though. Normally when it rained, one of the lights leaked, but never all of them together. The manager had the bright idea of ordering all his staff to fetch every available blanket in the building and push them up to the doors, in an attempt to prevent any more water entering the hotel. Predictably, this proved to be a useless exercise and the blankets were later seen floating around reception in mute defiance.

After about an hour of rushing around and trying to help people who were very scared, I realised I hadn't seen Anna for some time. At least an hour, in fact. I hoped she hadn't done anything too ambitious in trying to save the guests, and managed to fall in and get washed away. I made my way to the roof of the hotel so I could get a good view of the surroundings, and see if I could spot her. The rain was still raging. Cars and other objects were still floating all around the hotel. It all looked very dramatic and dangerous, to say the least. Alongside the building the water was flowing so fast, white-water rafting would not have been out of the question. A person could quite easily have been washed away. I called Anna's name. No answer. I called again. All right, we didn't get on so well but I really didn't want her to become fish food. I called her again, this time a little more panic in my tone. A shrill, angry cry rang out from behind me.

'What the bloody hell are you doing up here?' It was Anna, and she seemed to be all right. 'Get downstairs now, the manager wants you!'

'You're all right then,' I muttered meekly.

'Of course I'm all right. Get downstairs now.'

Lucky escape for the fish, really. They would probably have been sick anyhow.

Downstairs, confusion reigned all around. Guests were wandering around clutching their belongings and their children, and demanding action immediately. I was helpless. The rain was still pouring down; the phones were out, and it had become clear that the roads in and out of San Miguel were also blocked or washed away. The manager, Miguel, wanted all the guests to make their way to the first floor, where he was planning to serve them dinner. Not everyone was convinced this was such a good idea. Then he announced that he would be giving away free drinks as well. I was nearly killed in the rush. His reasoning was to get all the people out of the way so he could try to block the flow of water into the ground floor. The problem on the first floor was that there were only two staff in the restaurant; normally there were ten, so this was not an ideal situation. I immediately rolled up my trousers and waded in, serving the guests their free drinks in my bare feet. I worked solidly for about four hours, serving all and sundry, until every guest, British and German alike, had been fed and watered.

I didn't even notice that the rain had stopped and the water had begun to subside. Not one of our own British guests thanked me or any of the other staff. They just kept whingeing about the rain and demanding more free drinks. One German couple who had stayed in the restaurant throughout this time came up to me at the end, thanked me for my efforts, and gave me 500 pesetas 'to buy new shoes'. How nice. I was back downstairs at 10 o'clock in the evening, where I met all of our guests in the hotel, who were now demanding to be moved immediately. I explained to them all that this was impossible, as all the roads were blocked and the phones were down, but that the hotel would do anything they could to make them comfortable for the time being. They were angry and unreasonable, and later all wrote to the company and accused me of doing nothing to help them. (Wherever you all are now, I hope it is raining on you.)

The clear-up operation had begun. It was all hands on deck as every available receptacle was used to bale out reception. It took a good two hours before the water was completely cleared. The entertainers worked tirelessly, as did the maintenance man operating an antiquated water pump, and the German guests also slaved away to clear the water. Not one

Brit lifted a finger to help out, but when the manager opened the bar at the end of the ordeal to give everyone a free drink for helping out, the Brits were first in the queue. How predictable.

The next day the sun was shining, and within hours there was no sign that it had rained at all. The road was repaired and the phone lines were restored. We moved most of our guests, who saw fit to complain to the company about the weather. They joined together in a group they called the 'San Miguel Survivors' and even had T-shirts printed to honour this brainwave. Dickheads.

It felt sometimes as though we were skating on thin ice. You never really knew what you could do to help out in these situations until they confronted you. The term 'thin ice' is quite apt for Ibiza really, as the pavements that adorned the resorts up and down the island could all have been mistaken for ice. They were made of the shiniest tiles, which were as slippery as hell. Goodness knows what the people who designed these pavements were thinking about. I am sure that Torvill and Dean had a hand in it somewhere. Many people found themselves on the seat of their pants as they tried to walk up a hill in the resort. In spite of our protestations, new streets that were then under construction were being made in exactly the same way. One word of advice: if you don't want to end up on your arse, wear rubber-soled shoes when you go out walking on this island.

Ibiza was a great season, and I thoroughly enjoyed it all. I went there to work just as the dance and drug culture was taking hold of parts of the island and really grabbing the imagination of Europe's youth. I managed to avoid any kind of addiction to any illegal substances that were on offer. I found instead that I had become addicted to the lifestyle. The island had left me on a high. My appetite was now well and truly whetted. I had only joined for six months to have a laugh really, but now I found myself thinking, Where shall I go next?

SKIING

SKIING IS A fabulous pastime that the British holidaymaker has only just discovered relatively recently. Anyone who has ever made for the slopes in Europe – and witnessed the effortless way our European cousins negotiate the trickiest of mountains or the arrogance of the Germans who always seem to manoeuvre their way to the front of every lift queue – will surely testify to this fact. We are very much the beginners in this most enjoyable of activities.

As I sat down to write about my memories of working in the Austrian Alps as a ski rep, I began to wonder why we seemed to lag behind our neighbours in Europe when it comes to going on holiday. It's not just skiing, I remember working in the Balearic Islands for many months and seeing countless numbers of Brits roasting their way to casualty without even a drop of suntan lotion in sight, whilst the nearby Germans, Italians and French, not to mention the Spanish, positively revelled in the conditions. Or, why the

Brits always seemed to be so easy to spot at airports in their inappropriate heavy coats, jumpers and cardigans, making their way to the sunshine carrying cumbersome bags full of food, looking like they are about to trek to the Holy Grail – not spending ten days in the sunshine.

In light of this knowledge, you won't be surprised to find out that nearly all the casualties that litter the paths besides the moving 'T' bar chair lifts and button lifts are mostly British tourists given away by the profanities they utter as they struggle to their feet. It therefore won't be a surprise to also learn that you'd be more likely to meet Lord Lucan riding Shergar than find a British ski instructor in the Alps. It should, however, logically follow that ski classes are full of Brits anxious to learn how to master this fantastic pastime, but this isn't always the case, though. Girls, British girls that is, do tend to enrol in the ski classes for the duration of the ski holiday. After all, what could be more appealing than following a hunky foreign man, dressed in tight red pants, around the mountains for a week while regularly falling at his feet submissively? We men, though, take quite a different view about it. Generally speaking, we love the idea of skiing, it seems, but we do not like the idea of being humiliated by 'Johnny Foreigner' teaching us about this simple sport. After all, you just push off and glide, don't you?

I can't even begin to wonder why generally the British find it difficult to get into holiday mode. I've heard the retort, 'It takes me about a week to start relaxing and then, just as I've started to relax, I start thinking about going back to work,' so many times that I have come to regard it as a sad reflection of the British psyche. We simply feel guilty about relaxing. It could be something to do with our working mentality, or it could even be something to do with the fact that we all live together on our little island. It might even be something completely different, like we are just bloody different and proud of it. I will leave that particular conundrum for someone more learned to solve. For the purpose of this collection of stories from the mountains, I just couldn't help wondering why it is that we spend so much time and money going skiing, and yet collectively we are so crap at it and can't relax into it?

I don't mean to be dismissive of the rare British ski talent that we do have, far from it. When you stop to consider that our most famous British skiers, brothers Martin and Graham Bell, were outshone by a certain unlucky Scottish gentleman, the great Alain Baxter, whose downfall was to pop out for a Vicks inhaler to clear his congested nose, and as a consequence miss out on a silver medal, it's a bloody farce. The brothers were famous in the Eighties and Nineties, and that is a long time ago now. The Bells, sadly, flew the flag at the bottom reaches of international ski competitions. From my recollections, though, they were outstandingly talented, very unusual and bloody good skiers, but they never spent much time on the winner's podiums. All in all, that is a sad reflection on British skiing.

I also seem to remember, albeit vaguely, a man called Conrad Bartelski from ski Sunday as well; I think he might have competed for a while. (Sorry Conrad if I have missed any honours you may have won.) The fact that we've had only a handful of decent competitive skiers is indicative of our extreme lack of talent when it comes to this fantastic sport. Eddie the Eagle's exploits only reinforce this view. Why, I wonder, is that so?

The obvious and perhaps the most glaring answer is that we don't live in a country that has mountains with ski facilities and snow. This probably serves to handicap us a little. Whilst our neighbours in Europe can practice almost daily in the winter months, learning how to negotiate ski queues and race down slopes, we as a nation just get better at keeping umbrellas the right way out during the rainy and windy conditions that lash the UK for most of the year. Some may beg to differ. Scotland has some of the best ski slopes in the world, such as Glencoe, The Nevis range, Glenshee, Cairngorn and The Lecht. Sadly, though, they are rarely frequented by UK skiers.

There are umpteen artificial ski slopes around the country; I can count 15 that I have visited, not to mention the brilliant snow domes in Milton Keynes and *fashionable* Tamworth, just off the M42. I know, I know, they are no substitute for real mountains, but they can be used and they will improve the keen skier. These facilities, though, are generally vastly underused.

Still, every year nearly a million of us trek off to the Alps to do our thing on the ski slopes. There is a growing trend amongst people who love the idea of skiing, so much so that they save up all year for the privilege and treat their ski holiday as their main break away. Some say that skiing has had its heyday and will begin to decline in popularity, but I think not. It's a great holiday that is healthy and fun and all we need is a bit of encouragement. I was once told that skiing is the most fun you can ever have with all your clothes on. Maybe I've had a sad life but I tend to agree.

I was lucky enough to discover skiing at school. In the very British tradition, I was crap at it, and I still am. Even so, I wouldn't have dreamed of going to ski school to learn how to do it properly. Despite my lack of skill on the slopes, I was lucky enough to land a job as a ski rep and I got the chance to practice being bad – a lot! Now, I guess I am pretty accomplished at crap skiing.

I've had a lot of fun with the Brits on the ski slopes and shared many different experiences with them over the years. From past encounters on the slopes, I believe there are four distinct groups that the typical British holidaymaker can be categorised in.

The first category consists of the older, more experienced skier, who first skied as early as the 1960s, or early 1970s. They look like they have stepped off the set of a black and white movie and their ski jackets (usually dark green) are far too tight to be comfortable. They have their own set of skis and poles purchased in the 1970s and will not be swayed by any of the new fangled inventions, such as new bindings. They are usually a member of some high-faluting ski club from the UK and set in their ways, which means that they can't be taught anything about the art of skiing from any one else, especially not a foreign youth in his fancy modern gear. (Or a bloody nuisance rep, who they may refer to as a courier, or even a reptile from time to time.)

Category two is the expert, fashionable skier. They have typically been skiing once a year, for two weeks at a time for the last couple of years, and as such have learned to snowplough efficiently. When you ask them how many times they have skied they will normally say for two years. This is when a week equals a year. They have invested in some of the finest designer ski gear around and have the latest and most expensive equipment. They certainly look the part and know all the right words: piste, powder and parallel makes up a big part of their vocabulary. Unfortunately, humility, help and ski school do not.

In the third category, there is the novice or first time skier who can be found in borrowed gear or, worse still, a bargain buy from eBay. They wear a mishmash of ill-fitted skiwear that, try as they might, just doesn't look quite right (a bit like the idea of Ed Milliband leading the government; it's just a little bit surreal). They can occasionally be seen practicing in the morning ski classes, which is followed up with an afternoon off in some bar or chalet, wincing at the sight of the blisters caused by the poorly fitted clobber they borrowed from their mates. They've heard all the usual stories from their friends about how skiing is such a wonderful and healthy holiday, but after a morning of monumental effort and extreme pain, they really can't see what all the fuss is about, and vow never to ski again.

There is one other category I haven't mentioned and that is the good British skier. They are rare and largely not interested in ski reps, but they are there and they can be spotted whizzing past everyone. I, like many others, envy their grace and style.

My time on the slopes was chiefly spent with the first three categories, and as I have said before, I had a ball with them all. Whether it was taking them hurtling across Europe on a snow train, skiing them blindly to within inches of tragedy at the top of a mountain in a blizzard, or consoling them after an accident; I have great memories of those amazing times. And, I can confirm that skiing is definitely a sport where you can have the most fun ever – and still keep all of your clothes on!

If I may, I will make one more observation about Brits who go on ski holidays. We may not be gifted in the skiing department, but the rest of Europe can't hold a candle to our abilities when it comes to après-ski. For those of you not familiar with après-ski, it is the posh French phrase for getting pissed in a bar after skiing and generally having a great time. In this category, we positively excel over our European colleagues. And this is where I will begin.

Getting pissed. A wonderful pastime for tired British skiers fresh off the slopes from a hard days snow ploughing. Many go straight to the nearest bar at the bottom of the nursery slopes. These bars can earn a small fortune and are worth a lot of money, so to keep the partygoers happy they ply them with Schnapps, Glühwein and cheap snacks; the night can whizz by. Before you know it, it's close to midnight, the ski boots have become weightless and the ski jacket is cast aside. Pub bands roar out the classics, 'Alice, Alice, who the fuck is Alice?', and the punters love it.

It may surprise you to know that although the Brits are the kings of the après-ski festivities, we have some stiff competition vying for the title of best pissheads. The Dutch also love a party and can be heard shouting down the Brits with their rendition of 'Alish, Alish, who the fuck is Alish?' in many of the Tyrolean après-ski bars. The Brits and the Dutch also share a mutual dislike for the Germans, so it can be a match made in heaven.

Getting pissed and skiing, though, are not always the best companions. A heavy nights drinking does not always help when an early start is the order of the day, especially if you are in ski school. That may explain why there are so few Brits and Dutch to be found in ski lessons.

I remember on one occasion when a guest – fresh from a very heavy night partying until the early hours of the morning – had pretty much gone straight onto the ski slopes the next day. The enormity of the previous nights boozing caught up with him at around 11am and the mixture of drunkenness and high altitude suddenly struck him. The result: he fell and managed to fracture his cheekbone as he hit the floor. He was in severe pain and still very drunk. The emergency services were called and a helicopter quickly turned up to take him off the mountain. Upon finding him spewing up what smelled like pure alcohol, and shitting himself inside his all-in-one ski suit, they refused to take him onboard the helicopter and quickly took off. The patient instead had to wait to be transported by strecher off the mountain by the rescue service. They strapped him onto a stretcher and whisked him down to the medical centre. It must have been a cold and sobering descent for him...

To be truthful, I always felt terribly out of place in the ski resorts I had worked in. I never quite felt like I belonged. I was a crap skier and had never really hankered for this life as a youngster; it just seemed like a cool thing to do when I was in the Med during the summer. It seemed to be the perfect antidote to the blazing hot days in the sun, but on arrival I couldn't help thinking that my journey to the slopes had been far from straightforward.

A SLOW BULLET
TO THE ALPS

THE YEAR 1992 was a good one for Spain, but it was also a great year for me. I'd worked in Ibiza and had the time of my life. It couldn't get any better, could it? Oh yes it could. Life was about to transport me to the heavens – well not quite the heavens, but certainly a little nearer. I was headed for the mountains. Skiing, here I come...

This was also the year that the Olympic Games came to Barcelona; a tremendous and grandiose event that was to take the world's interest in sport to a new level. In that same year, I had hoped to represent my country in the Olympic Games. That was my life long plan. I had boxed from the age of 11 and had represented my club, then my county, and eventually I had been called upon to train with my country. I had made the squad and my dream was on course. Sadly, like so many other potential Olympians, my plan had floundered when some eight years before the Barcelona Olympics, I discovered the delights of girls and drinking.

The return was more immediate and so my ambitions fell by the wayside. However, 1992 was still going to be a great year for me. This was the year I truly discovered the joys of skiing. Tame in comparison to the Olympics, I know, but it was a great point in my little life.

I remember watching the start of the Olympics in Barcelona and thinking, but for a few beers and a knee-jerker in the back of our local pub's skittle alley some years before, I could have been there. I remember hearing about the alleged irregularities that were uncovered by the press at about the same time, which shed doubt on the fairness of the bidding process and where the Olympics were to be held. I scoffed and thought that it was better not to be part of the tainted event. A small and hypocritical consolation though it was.

A similar kind of dishonesty, albeit not on such a grandiose level, was being exercised in a small Spanish island in the Med. Ibiza to be exact. As I pondered my application, in the hope of securing a position as ski rep in one of the busy Austrian Tyrolean resorts, I plied my colleague with drink. He a veteran ski rep of some two years told me of all the resorts he had skied in, before securing his prized position in the ski team. I soaked up all the information given to me, along with copious amounts of San Miguel, before retiring to my room to fill out my application form with all the new information.

I can't quite remember how they celebrated in Barcelona once the Olympics had been secured, but it couldn't have been as joyous as my own celebrations when I received my winter 1992/93 placement in the final days of September 1992. I was appointed as the ski rep for Soll in the Austrian Alps. It could have been in Space for all I knew, but it mattered not, it just meant that I had won the prized position of ski rep for the winter, something that is normally only reserved for longstanding loyal members of the company, or expert skiers who could represent the company with panache and style. I was neither of those two things. Ok, I had skied for one week on a school trip back in 1980s, but I guess that might not bring me up to the standard required, but hey, I was a fast learner, and once you are there it's half the battle won.

I raised my glass to my friends who had all received their winter placements during the course of the day. Many of them weren't happy with their winter destinations, mainly because they were heading for resorts that were considered less attractive than Austria. Most of them were bound for the resort affectionately known as 'fly and die', which also went by the name Benidorm. Most had applied to ski resorts, and they were more qualified than I was, but I'd been a little more creative on my form to secure a position on the slopes. They weren't to know that, though, and I decided it was best for all if they didn't find out about my creative skills just yet. Austria here I come, I thought. I sank another beer and then went home to look it up on the map. I was going to a place many called heaven on earth.

Apparently, the Olympic Games in Barcelona were a great success. Once they had secured the prized event – by whatever means, fair or foul – they made the most of it and prepared thoroughly. They probably had a few years to digest the enormity of their achievement and grasped the nettle like a fleeing robber clutching his swag with the alarm ringing in his ears. I had something like six weeks, and although I did my best to prepare thoroughly with a three week break in Tenerife, and a good deal of time boasting to pretty much anyone who would listen about my future winter plans, I was just a little worried as the day for departure edged closer.

When rail travel began to revolutionise way of life at the turn of the nineteenth century – linking the whole of the UK together by knitting little parallel lines between dark satanic mills and their surrounding communities – I'm sure no one ever imagined that years later these same train tracks would serve the needs of bargain hunting tourists desperate to find a cheap way to the ski slopes of Europe. Yet, fast-forward a few years and an alternative escape route had been imagined up by the great minds of the seemingly ever-expanding tourist industry in the UK. Sadly, for those innovators it never really took off. Somebody, though, had to be the guinea pig. By a cruel twist of fate, I became a part of the first venture into the Alps by train. When I received the good news that I was to be working in the Austrian Tyrol for the winter of 1992/93, I didn't imagine in my wildest dreams my dream placement would involve rail transport.

Some three months later, I found myself wondering what the hell had gone wrong. I was patrolling the corridors of a speeding train as it meandered its way through the French countryside at 100 mph towards its destination in the

Austrian Alps. On board the train there were over 100 moaning, travelsick British tourists who had chosen this form of transport to the slopes, as opposed to paying the extra £10 to fly in a fraction of the time.

The train affectionately became known as the 'Vomit Comet', and I was the custodian of the comet for the time being. It was my duty to accompany the would-be ski demons all the way to the Alps on the 18-hour train journey to their Austrian hotels. I was stopped at regular intervals by my fellow passengers complaining about the extortionate price of the drinks on board (mind you, £15 for a can of beer and £10 for a coke seems a little bit on the high side. But you could hardly get off and get one elsewhere).

On arrival I had to wait three hours, during which time I could take advantage of the 'perks' by skiing anywhere in the region absolutely free of charge. This was in between getting changed, seeing to any personal dietary needs, such as feeding my face, having a shower and allocating bunks for the return journey. Then, if I didn't collapse from sleep deprivation, I was free to ski to my hearts content. Once three hours had elapsed, I was back at the station to usher the returning tourists back to Calais. Needless to say, during my stewardship of the comet I did very little skiing.

This was most certainly not heaven, nor was it anything like the job I had imagined when I secured my dream placement after filling out those application forms with a pack of lies during the back end of the summer. I was unhappy at the predicament of my weekly journeys through the heart of Europe, but I had to accept my fate.

So where had it all gone wrong? Firstly, I should explain that over the years, and especially on the snow train, I'd have to listen to many people plan their ski breaks and hear them boast about tackling the off-piste black runs and storming the little mountain taverns as they refuelled for the next day. As a result, I couldn't help feel that the sport had become a touch elitist, and needed a change. This is where I would come in, I thought. Unhindered by my lack of knowledge of the ski set, or even an ability to ski in the traditional sense, I would gracefully take to the slopes with my natural athletic ability, revolutionise the ski culture, shake things up a little and consequently help the sport break out from its growing image of elitism. That was my plan: the truth and outcome was a little different.

The day had begun so beautifully. The sun had shone in the early hours of the morning but the weather was still freezing. Fresh snow had fallen during the night, and the pistes positively glistened invitingly as the new team of ski reps and guides approached the slopes for the first time that season for their competency tests. This was the first day for all. There were no paying guests; it was just a chance for the ski experts to find their legs and for the lift managers to test their machines after months of inactivity. It was a perfect day and perfect for skiers. I struggled with my unfamiliar equipment and I had forgotten just how cumbersome ski boots could be. I began to think that my plan to revolutionise the sport might need a rethink when they handed me the longest skis I had ever seen. How the hell was I going to carry them let alone get the things on, or stand on them in ridiculous diving boots and then move in them? Everybody else seemed to be managing fine and having fun. I was now beyond the point of no return as I picked up my poles and headed slowly for the lift some 20 yards away. 20 yards can seem like 20 miles when you are weighed down by what fells like half a ton of equipment and several layers of clothing, which is supposed to keep you warm but was now sending sweat cascading down my face and body. This was supposed to be a sport?

My father's advice, 'Your lies will find you out', was ringing in my ears as I hurtled down the aptly named black slope, uncontrolled and pretty much in freefall towards a very solid looking wooden hut. My heart was pounding wildly and the word 'shit' barely audible was croaking from my dried up throat. I could smell fear as the hut grew larger. I had to call upon all my previous experience from a long ago school trip but, try as I might, I just couldn't remember how to change direction. The hut was not actually part of the recognised piste, and so the people responsible for grooming this section had thoughtfully piled up all the excess snow around the unforgiving wooden erection. This was very fortunate for me, as I sped towards the shed with the grace and control of a human cannonball that had misfired. Had it not been for the piles of snow I think I may well have seriously damaged the construction, not to mention myself, beyond repair.

I sank deep into the surrounding snow in a mix of poles, skis, goggles, gloves and pride. I came to a sudden halt. Everything was still and quiet for a brief second. I did a quick check from the middle of my head to other outer regions of my numb body. Everything seemed to still be in place.

Then, from behind me, I could hear a voice.

'What the fuck was he doing? He told me he could ski.'

I knew I was still alive, and my hearing seemed to be working because I could hear a great deal of laughter and derision directed my way, as my colleagues began to dig me out. I began to regret not listening to my father's advice all those years ago. Later that night, after I'd been helped out of my ski gear and back into something that helped me to walk like a normal human, I headed to the bar. The bosses were waiting for me, I had to put up my hands and confess to them that my apparent lack of ski knowledge wasn't just me trying to find my 'ski legs' again, but was in fact just that – a lack of ski knowledge. Not a single bean: I was there under false pretences.

The leader of the ski team was a small fat man clad in a chunky jacket called Dave. He looked as though he didn't need to take anything off to reveal how solid he was underneath. You got the impression that the jacket was not as chunky as it should have been and that a lot of the padding was actually not padding at all, but all man. Quite a considerable man. Had he been in better height-weight proportion, he could well have been over 8ft tall. He had a thick black beard that just didn't know when to stop growing. It practically covered his whole face. The connection between his face hair and face fungus was hard to distinguish and he resembled a cross between a miniature

Chewbacca, the giant bear like creature from *Star Wars*, and the wolf man. The similarity ended there, though. This alien being was anything but friendly, and I got the impression he was just a little bit pissed off with me for wasting his time on the slopes. He would now have to recruit a new expert to guide the guests around the Alps.

Wolf man hauled himself in beside me just after 8.30pm, effectively blocking any chance of escape as I finished my dinner that first evening, and proceeded to read me the riot act in a succession of grunts and spits that would have made Roy Hattersley leap for cover. He remarked that my familiarity with the sport of skiing could only be likened to how a member of the Masai-Mara tribe from Africa might have shown a similar understanding of the London underground system on his first visit to the capital.

'You haven't got a fucking clue, have you,' he spat. It was an observation, albeit a fairly aggressive one, rather than a question.

I had to nod in agreement. I thought it better not to tell him about my thoughts on how the ski fraternity had become elitist over the years. I didn't think he would agree with my views at that moment in time.

To my horror he pulled out the application form I had filled in some time ago with a list of destinations I had previously skied in. It read like an expert skier's guide – Banff, La Plagne, La Grave, Kitzbühel, St. Anton, to name just a few of the destinations I claimed to have honed my ski skills in.

Wolf man reeled them off one by one before me like a

lawyer for the prosecution. I was condemned without any defence. He finished his performance by barking, 'I can't decide whether to send you home tomorrow or make you wait a week. You'll have to meet me in the morning and I'll let you know then.'

He got up and left me at the table to ponder my future and regret my creative instincts, which had carried me here from Ibiza. I sat at my table and looked out of the window at the Austrian countryside shimmering like a scene from a Christmas card. It seemed so ideal and homely, yet I now felt about as welcome as a plane spotter at a Greek airport. I'd been found out and the adventure felt like it was over before it had begun.

Next morning I met wolf man for breakfast. He informed me he was heading back to the UK for a ski exhibition and had managed to book me a flight back to the UK so he would drop me off at the airport on his way.

As I loaded my kit into his car I felt sad that I would be leaving all this beauty behind. I had resigned myself to the fact that I would probably never get the opportunity to work in this place again. I began to think that perhaps Benidorm would not have been so bad after all.

I watched my colleagues as they left the hotel from the side entrance that lead to the slopes, kitted out in their sleek ski wear ready to take on the mountains for another day. Jealousy is not quite as deadly a sin as envy I believe, but I had to opt for the latter of the two evils, as I watched them effortlessly make for the lifts, laughing happily as they slid off. My feelings of envy quickly subsided to self-pity, as I climbed in beside wolf man for the heavy journey home with my only other companion, disgrace.

Wolf man decided not to waste the opportunity and gave me a good rollicking as we made the hour-long journey to the airport along the Austrian autobahns. I tried to switch off as he droned on, but his bad breath, no doubt a consequence of being up all night howling at the moon and eating shit, kept me quite alert.

'We think you're a cheeky bastard Flood. You can't tell lies like that on an application form for a prized job like this. Christ knows what could have happened if we hadn't checked you out and then let you loose with our customers. You might have killed someone, or worse, ruined the reputation of the company.'

He thought for a while and searched for more verbal ammunition to make me feel good.

After a short silence he settled for, 'You are a twat.' I ignored this. 'Do you hear me?' He persisted and stared at me as we weaved dangerously across the carriageway. 'Yes,' I replied. Better a twat than a dead twat I thought. I did in fact know I had been a twat for want of a better word, and I really didn't need reminding of the unfortunate turn of events.

Silence ensued again for a few minutes before wolf man burst into almost uncontrolled laughter. 'I just can't believe what a bloody cheek you have,' he howled. 'Fortunately for you, neither can anyone else at head office. You are a wanker and a twat, but we like you. We've decided to give you a second chance.'

My heart leapt. Was I hearing correctly? Had the altitude helped slip me into a dream world, I wondered.

'Well, do you want to work in the ski programme?' he demanded. I looked across at him and nodded. I couldn't believe what I was hearing. In my mind I was already on my way to Benidorm, if I didn't get the sack first for falsifying documents.

'You mean I can still work in the ski team?' I said in my best wimp-like humble voice.

'Yes, we like you, and although you are a lying bastard, we are going to let you be part of the team. We have a special job for you, one that requires the kind of skills you've got. Apart from lying that is.'

My heart leapt again. Somebody had recognised what I had always known: I was a special person.

'We want you to work on the snow train,' he announced.

'The snow train?' I replied, thinking to myself what the hell is that?

'Yes, the snow train,' smiled wolf man slightly deviously.

I resisted the urge to say, 'What the fuck is the snow train?' and settled for 'Great, I can't wait!'

'Good,' said wolf man. 'You are still going back to the UK for a training course and then you will be bringing the first lot of passengers out here on the train for the first week of the season. Oh, and by the way, when you arrive with the guests, you will get a chance to learn to ski properly, and if you do well then you can join us here in the resort next year.'

'Great,' I enthused.

I was confused. I didn't really know what to think at this

point. I desperately wanted the chance to work in the ski team, but I had no idea about how this snow train business worked. I pictured happy locomotives trundling through the picturesque Austrian countryside with hordes of contented tourists waving from the windows as we pulled up to the slopes. These pleasant thoughts occupied my mind as I boarded the plane back to the UK.

The reality was just a little different, but would turn out to be my passport to the slopes. Albeit by a fortunate turn of events, well fortunate for me that is, but not for all.

I managed only two weeks of hell on the snow train before a love sick rep dropped out of the programme in the Alps. I was 'Johnny on the spot' and found myself first inline to take her place. Suffice to say, I didn't need to be asked twice.

ADOLF HITLER
RUINED MY HOLIDAY

'ADOLF HITLER HAS ruined my holiday.' This was not a line I'd expected to be confronted with from an irate tourist on a winter sports package tour in 1992. A time traveller didn't say it, and it wasn't a training exercise, it was a genuine complaint from a fully paid-up guest on one of our package holidays. If the first line seemed a bit surreal, the second had me reaching for the phone book to look up the number of a psychiatrist in the area.

'Your hotelier has just threatened me with a shotgun. What are you going to do about it?' What indeed, I thought.

When I arrived in Austria in December 1992 for my first winter season skiing with the elite reps, and the British tourists in their winter guise, I had no idea that this would be one of the worst Austrian winters for many years. There was absolutely no snow for weeks. It was rain, rain, sunshine and then more rain. When you think of the worst winters in the UK you conjure up images of snow falling down in abundance, the gridlocked motorways, closed schools and dire warnings telling you not to make any kind of journey unless you want to die.

In Austria, the opposite was true. There was no snow. From the beginning of December to the end of January, no snow at all. Mercifully, it was cold, very cold. The people who groom pistes for skiing are true artists and they really earn their money when the snow doesn't fall. They go out and collect it from anywhere, even if it means taking it from a mountain and bringing it to a valley, which is exactly what the men who groomed Soll in the winter of 1992/3 did throughout those snow-deprived months. It's imperative that these men keep the resort open. The livelihood of all the workers in the resort, including the hotel owners and the restaurant staff depend upon it. Fortunately, for the resort, the cold helped to preserve what little snow we did have once the piste groomers have found some.

The worst nightmare for any resort in the winter ski programme, or the tour company for that matter, is to consider closure due to lack of snow. They will do all they can to preserve what little bits of snow they can find. They will use snow cannons to produce artificial snow, they will push snow towards the runs from the side of the mountain, they will transport snow in from other resorts – anything but closure, for that would be financial disaster. Every person wants to arrive in their chosen ski resort and be treated to a scene that looks like a beautiful Christmas card with snow in abundance covering the mountains and clinging to the roofs as far as the eyes can see. In the year of 1992, Soll looked more like a summer postcard with a blot of Typex on the lower nursery slopes.

Technically, because of the little bit of snow that was jealously guarded at the bottom of our mountain, we had snow and we stayed open, so bookings could not be cancelled and claimed back on insurance. Profits of the tour companies also had to be protected. Life was tough as the guests queued up to complain about the crap conditions, and predictably the reps were blamed for it all.

Holiday companies gamble. It's a fact. All the seats for the season are sold months in advance. Brochures are filled with pretty pictures of snowy mountains packed with happy tourists skiing to their hearts content. You would never know that there might be a risk of the weather letting them down and not delivering the bounty on time. It does happen, though, and when it does it can turn out to be a bit inconvenient to say the least.

The year 1992 was also one of the years the major British holiday companies were locked in a price war. We sold seats on flights and didn't even have enough beds in the resorts for the arriving guests to sleep in once they reached us. We sold them cheap and worried about the consequences once the planes were on the way. This was a recipe for disaster or, if not disaster, severe discontent.

As soon as the planes were in the sky, we reps were dispatched to find somewhere for the guests to stay. We had a small budget and instructions not to fail. Find beds, anywhere, just find beds. We did find beds but they were not good beds, and predictably they caused problems for the fee-paying guests.

Some 47 years after the death of Adolf Hitler, it seemed that some Austrians still saw fit to honour his memory by placing his picture on their wall in their homes. Such people, I am sure, were never meant to provide homes in the mountains for travelling British skiers. That, though, is exactly what happened as we scurried around the resort in a desperate attempt to find beds for the guests arriving in droves. We had no time to vet the accommodation for our new arrivals; all we needed to know was that they would provide a bed for the guests for the pittance we paid them as a fee. In truth, most of the accommodation we secured for the deals was crap. We might have got away with it if it had snowed, but it didn't, and the guests noticed big time how crap the accommodation was. They especially noticed if the resort secretary of the Adolf Hitler Appreciation Society owned the accommodation, and even more so if you decide to retreat to your room after pointing out the offending portrait.

On the face of it, the pension block house in question looked like a pretty good place to spend a week on the slopes. It was situated half way up the mountain in easy reach of the slopes and it was very small. It had the potential to be very cosy with only three bedrooms in total. I gave it the once over and on the surface it looked clean and tidy, so I thought, yeah, go for it. I paid the man the money and told him to expect his first arrivals the following Sunday. If only I had looked at the photos on the walls...

The guests, in this case a group of four – two girls and two boys – duly arrived at the resort on the Sunday afternoon in January. They made their way to their accommodation and settled in. Seeing the lack of snow around them, and filled with our promises that snow was on the way, they settled themselves into the resort and did what many decent British tourists would do in such conditions, they had a drink, and another and another. Sometime during the evening, they began to look more closely at their accommodation and, as they scrutinised the decor on the walls of their appointed guesthouse, they came across the picture of Adolf smiling back at them. Hardly believing their eyes, a scene that wouldn't have looked out of place on the set of *Fawlty Towers* began to unfold. A certain amount of shouting and goose-stepping began to take place before the owner of the guesthouse came to investigate.

Witnessing the scene, he flipped and demanded the would-be skiers leave immediately. They didn't take him seriously and retreated to their rooms. He then went to fetch his hunting rifle and returned to repeat his demand one more time. This time they could see that he wasn't joking, gathered their belongings and fled to our office where luck would have it we weren't available. They tracked us down in the pub next door and began to accuse us of being, amongst other things, Nazi sympathisers. This was indeed a first for me, and although I was quite shocked, I found it all rather amusing. Four irate British tourists carting their suitcases into the local bar screaming abuse about one of the neighbours made for a quite a scene. Try as I might I just couldn't get them to see the funny side.

We managed to get them re-housed in another guest-house some way from the slopes, and we did check the walls first this time, fortunately, there were no surprises in store. Our guests, not content with our efforts to re-house them, went to the national newspapers on their return home and after another altercation with the UK press hounds, the block house was never used as accommodation for skiers again. Good job really.

*   *   *

Generally, the ski fraternity have more money than they do summer guests, or sense for that matter. They know what they want and they know they are going to have to pay for it. Skiing is not – and never has been – cheap. The guests in Kitzbühel, which really was the top end of the scale in the Tyrolean, mostly resented the presence of a rep being there altogether. I remember one particular woman clad in a beautiful fur coat arrived in the resort and mistook the rep, me, for a porter. 'Take my case to my room, you bloody reptile will you,' she barked, as she got off the coach. Suffice to say I didn't carry the case. She was most indignant.

In spite of the skiers having plenty of money to spend on a skiing holiday, many of the groups of lads who come away together still can't resist the temptation to shit in their rooms, either in their beds or on the floor. I found myself on numerous occasions explaining to the lads that they would have to pay for the damages they had inflicted on their accommodation before they left the hotel. Hotel owners confiscated many a passport and held it to ransom before letting various groups go home.

I remember one such meeting with a group of lads. One of them had shat in his bed and had left it for the hotel cleaners to clear up before going off to enjoy a days skiing. Upon their return, I was waiting for them in the bar. They, of course, pleaded innocence. 'Maybe the cleaner shat in the room?' one of them protested. Eventually someone had to admit guilt. The lad concerned had been caught short in the night and shat in his bed. I said to him, 'Did you just lie in it all night long?' He replied, 'Course not I moved onto the floor. What do you think I am, some sort of animal? I wasn't going to lie in it, was I?' There really was no reply.

Life on the slopes can be very different but it was also great fun.

The great thing about this amazing job is that it is diverse, one day you are on the slopes looking out at snow-capped mountains, sipping a warm Glühwein, and the next you are on your way to the sun and back to Greece.

THE CHARM
OF GREECE

PEOPLE WILL TELL you all kinds of weird and wonderful tales about Greece. Stories of fog on a hot summer's day in Athens or about the well-meaning, laid-back attitude on the Greek islands, the heat of summer, 130 degrees in the shade, with people dropping like flies from heat exhaustion while forest fires rage all around. Or the Greek hospitality and charm that can make up for shortfalls brought about by that relaxed way of life. All, no doubt, have some element of truth about them and are all coloured with the rosy glow of memories in the sunshine. Greece is a wonderful place for both travellers and workers alike and I was curious enough about it to go and find out for myself. I figured that six months on a Greek island, preferably a small one, ought to do the trick.

Working for a big tour operator can have its advantages. For a start, they travel to thousands of places all over the world. You are never more than just a number when you are a rep, so you can never have the luxury of choosing exactly where you work but, as luck would have it, Kos was to be my new destination and that seemed like as good a place as any to live and sample the joys of Greece. The danger with taking up a position in a new destination is that you never can tell where you will end up living and working. You can keep your fingers crossed and hope, but you never know where you are going until you get to the island and receive your directions to your new home.

Let me explain a bit about Kos. It's not a really large island on the face of things, only forty-five kilometres end to end. Very accessible, with fairly good roads, and ruggedly beautiful with a majestic mountain range crowning the centre of the island like a jagged spine that runs into the sea along the edges. The beaches are good, but not spectacularly so, and there were four main tourist destinations:

1. Kos town. Busy and the nearest thing to cosmopolitan that the island had to offer. Lots of shops and bars, restaurants both Greek and multi-national. A varied nightlife and, best of all, steeped in historical monuments. The Odeon, the Gymnasium, Hippocrates' plane tree, the Asklepion, the list is endless. Secretly I loved these places. I think I must have been a Greek god in an earlier incarnation. If so, the only physical resemblance I retain to my former life is that my skin looks like the marble statues that adorn the Greek monuments – alabaster white, and it stays that way, no matter what exposure it gets to the sun. Kos town was my sort of resort.

2. Tingaki. This place was just on the edge of Kos town;

quiet and remote and twenty minutes from the centre of town and it really could be quite charming. Steeped in history itself, it lay within easy reach of other monuments so that it could be included in almost any day-long historical tour of the great monuments of this island. It sported a working salt lake, a fact that was not lost on five million of the island's mosquitoes that also live in Tingaki, feeding on tourists' blood. The beautiful villages of Pyli and Zia are nearby and easily accessible. As a bonus, it had a very 'Greek' feel to it and it could sometimes feel as though the ugly side of the international tourist market had passed it by with its worst excesses, making it uniquely appealing.

3. Kefalos. This was the most 'Greek' area of the island. The village of Kefalos was a rare thing to come across in this day and age. Rather than invite thousands of tourists into their village to overrun it and no doubt eventually take over their quiet community, the people of Kefalos had been very clever. The resort of Kefalos has been built down the road from the main town. This is a perfect arrangement for the locals. All the tourists are trapped in a few hotels down the hill that lay close to the sea. Meanwhile, village life prospered up the hill overlooking the scenes of tourist life. Excellent idea. It's like building a toilet with its own sewer well away from your house. Sometimes, if the wind is in the wrong direction, you might get a bad smell, but you never have to step in shit. As a result, Kefalos remained the one truly Greek resort on the island. It was a rare beauty.

4. Lastly, there was Kardamena. Walk down the main street in Kardamena and you could be in many places in the

world. Benidorm, San Antonio, Blackpool, Weston-super-Mare on a rare sunny day, even Skegness or Scarborough. Anywhere, really, but Greece. 'Maxine's Hair Salon Design' stood proudly alongside an English breakfast bar proudly proclaiming its UK patronage. It was the first of many such bars. Copies of the *Sun* and the *Daily Mirror* punctuated the lewd souvenir shops selling hideous postcards of close-up photos of penises sporting miniature sunglasses and strategically placed cigarettes, the latest thing in novelty post. How the hell anybody could send a picture of a weirdly decorated member, owner unknown, to their next-door neighbours – or, worse still, their relatives – to tell them that their holiday was fantastic was well beyond me. The great British public has no sense of decorum. It seems that vulgarity is the new thing in kitsch postal fashion.

Kardamena was the destination in Kos for Union Jack vests, pot bellies, stretchmarks, limited vocabulary and parochial football shirts, the ninety-minute TV gladiators' badge of allegiance. On arriving on Kos, my first impressions were that Kardamena could be a sad place.

Where would you want to work on this island that is so diverse and has such a range of things to offer? Kos, with its melting-pot audience in search of history, thrills and bargains? Certainly.

Tingaki, with its aloofness and charm? Possibly.

Kefalos, with its truly unique Greek way of life? Yes, that too.

Or Kardamena with its new-found identity as Little England? No thanks.

Off the boat in Kos we were met by our new resort manager.

'Ah, you must be Cy, pleased to meet you. You are going to Kardamena.'

Pleased to meet you, too. It was going to be a fun season.

*　　　*　　　*

Kos was one of those resorts that are open for business for British tourists for just six months of the year, and so for the cold winter months it could be a lonely and very quiet place. We arrived in April, approximately three weeks before the first planeload of British tourists. My first impression of this tiny little Greek paradise was that it was deathly quiet. We had spent the night before holed up on the nearby island of Rhodes and had just taken a four-hour ferry ride across the mercifully calm Aegean sea to be deposited on the silent and deserted main port of Kos town. A few fishing boats lay abandoned around us, and the obligatory harbour master doubled up his role as customs and excise officer and welcomed us on the island as we disembarked from the tub that had carried us to the concrete jetty. Our first steps on to the Greek playground of Kos. Home for the next six months.

After our first brief exchanges with our new resort manager we were given directions to our new home in Kardamena. An open-top jeep was waiting to take us on the half-hour journey to our destination. Our driver for the occasion was a girl called Sharon, who had arrived a couple of days before us and was to be our companion for the next six months. Sharon was a 23-year-old ex-travel agent in her first year in this job. She was about five foot five with short, dark hair, slightly chubby with big rubbery lips and the broadest of Yorkshire accents. She seemed quite bubbly, happy and full of enthusiasm. And wow, could she talk. Hind legs and donkeys spring to mind when I think of Sharon and that was just for starters. She said more in that half-hour journey to Kardamena than I think I had said to my girlfriend in a two-week holiday. I switched off on the way out of Kos town, so I never really took in anything beyond the first fifteen years of her childhood and her impressions and thoughts of ancient Greece. I do, however, remember arriving in Kardamena with my ears ringing and longing just to get out of earshot. It sounded as though perhaps someone had frightened Sharon and she was talking herself up to us to get herself some credibility as the new girl in the job. We were brand new to the island of Kos and didn't really care about any rep politics within the resorts, so most of her incessant talking fell on deaf ears.

So there I was in Kardamena, for me probably the most undesirable of the resorts to work in. But every cloud has a silver lining. The good news for me was that I would be sharing accommodation. This is not normally something that would get me excited, as other people's bodily noises tend to irritate me to the point of distraction, almost like nailing my ears to the side of my head with rusty nails. But this time I was going to be sharing with my long-suffering girlfriend, Beth. All right, she farts and burps in her sleep as well, but I can forgive her; when I wake in the night and see her face, my annoyance at having my sleep interrupted immediately subsides, because she's lovely. I was happy, but was she? When the news began to sink in that we would be cohabiting I watched her face for any signs of discontent, but there were none. She was either very pleased or a very good master at hiding her feelings. Whatever, we moved in together into our new home exhausted from our journey and ready to face the next six months in this little corner of the world.

*　　*　　*

Our accommodation for the season was a roomy second-floor apartment in a block of three floors. Situated right in the middle of what would be the busy resort area just off the beach; it was unremarkable and bland, but functional. Once the season had got under way it would become loud, to say the least, and in the midst of the busy part of town. Turn right out of the main reception door on the ground floor and walk to the end of the alleyway that runs down to the main shopping area of the resort, and you could almost lose your eye on one of the hooks protruding from the leather shop on the corner. These hooks were designed to hold bags, belts or other enticing touristy goods to lure more travellers into the shop, but if business is ever brisk then the hooks, which are white metal, could be empty. If this is the case, then they are perfectly positioned to cause the maximum amount of damage. They were just about eye height, with a little hook on the end, and they blended in nicely with the whitewashed buildings all around. Several times I've been just a nose-width away from sporting one of these hooks from my right eye, but luckily I've always managed to avoid a blinding collision. Turning left outside the door, you were confronted by a large expanse of waste ground that doubled as a car park in high season, and this was surrounded by apartment blocks similar to ours on all sides. The sea was nowhere in view, even though it was very close by. Through the abundance of accommodation a little street threaded its way through to the main square of Kardamena, which was the focal point of the resort. It was not much of a square, really. When you think of the beautiful squares in the middle of cities and towns all over the world, such as those in Prague, Paris, Barcelona and New York to name just a few, then Kardamena didn't really have a lot to shout about. It was about the size of half a football pitch with a pole-like contraption in the middle, and surrounded by a few bars and shops. Nothing more than that really, but it was the square, and the centre, and one look at it told you that during the height of the summer season this would be a very busy and noisy place to be, the place that all the youth would flock to. Its bars advertised cheap beer and loud music and it had all the appropriate elements, with a few seats scattered around the central pole-like erection, and a stone's throw from the beach. By mid-season it had not failed to live up to my expectations.

As I said, Beth and I were on the second of three floors. Below us were two more reps, our colleagues in the same team. First of all there was Natasha. She was in her second year in the job and her second year in the resort of Kardamena. A lovely girl who was a positive mine of information, what she didn't know about the times of buses and ferries, and Lord knows what else, really wasn't worth knowing. At first my cynical mind wouldn't let me trust Natasha. I figured that nobody who knew that much about a resort and was willing to pass it on could really be that nice. But I was wrong. I am arrogant enough to think that I am a pretty good judge of character, after my years of studying in the great university of life, and I scoffed at Natasha's information-volunteering sessions as pure bullshit. Lucky for me I had the good sense to keep my forthright opinions to myself. Nothing worse than playing your hand early in a new resort only to confirm your status as a complete dick. It tends to cast the die, on the whole. Natasha really was a lovely girl and an invaluable source of information. She stands five feet six inches tall, with a very full head of blonde hair that kind of reflects her personality. It's like champagne popping when she pulls out her scrunchy, bubbly, full, promising and wickedly disorganised in a sexy way. As soon as she puts the scrunchy back in, the order returns. We made friends and I was allowed to call her Nat – a trivial but significant step.

Nat's flatmate was called Julie. She had worked for the previous two years in Ibiza, so I did know a little about her; in fact, we had even spent a short amount of time working in the same team the year before. Just to backtrack a little, I had met Julie in the departure lounge of Manchester airport on the way out to Rhodes on the first leg of my journey to Kardamena. When she told me that her destination for the summer was to be Kardamena as well, my heart sank.

Julie in Ibiza was, not to put too fine a point on it, lazy. No, I'll go further, she was lazy with a capital F: fucking lazy, and in this job, when you work closely with people and rely on them for support, you just cannot be doing with lazy people in the team. When I first discovered that Julie was in the same team, I went into a deep depression. Once again, though, I was wrong. Julie never tried to deny her less-than-industrious past, but she put it all down to love. Apparently, she had been hopelessly smitten by a Spanish bar owner who had done his best to make her life difficult, and this in turn distracted her from her daily toil. The mere sight of Vicente – the beloved in question – sent Julie plummeting into a state of quivering moistness that would cause her to slip out of the nearest door and directly into the waiting arms of the said Vicente. However, here in Kardamena there was no Vicente to distract her from her duties and, to our amazement, Julie became a model rep. There were no more moistness attacks, and she became known as a loveable little Geordie with a knowing, cheeky grin. So there it was, Nat and Jude on the bottom floor and Beth and I in the middle. Our landlady lived on the top floor. Her name was Dyonisia.

Dyonisia – what a lovely lady. I'd say she was about five feet tall – or short, whatever way you look at it – with a permanently fixed smile, a grey helmet hairstyle and always attired in an unflattering full-length black dress that did right up to her neck and sported long sleeves. The attire suggested that she was a widow, constantly in mourning. Whatever her personal circumstances were, Dyonisia never let it affect her relationship with us – she was never anything less than kind and considerate to one and all. I had one encounter with her when I discovered I had forgotten my key to the apartment and went upstairs to Dyonisia's flat to borrow a spare one. She opened the door and seemed delighted to see me, particularly as I entertained her by my attempts, using the best hand signals I could muster (you guessed it, I didn't speak any Greek and she spoke very little English), to explain that I had lost my key and was hoping she'd have a spare. She motioned for me to follow her into the kitchen, where she was preparing a special dish for her pet cat. At least, it seemed that way to me, because the cat was perched on her kitchen worktop, helping himself to the culinary delicacy on hand. Dionysia, as I have said before, is a very small frail figure and, you would think, a slow, charming old lady. Well, she moved with the speed of a world flyweight champion when she saw the offending feline. Now, cats themselves are generally thought to be no slouches when it comes to self-preservation and speed of foot, and don't normally get caught with a sucker blow, but this one was not up to the challenge. He simply did not see that right hook coming. Dyonisia caught him on the side of the head, a truly solid blow that made him jump instinctively to the floor, where he set himself up nicely to meet the trajectory of Dyonisia's foot, which caught him squarely on the rump and sent him squealing careering towards the open window, out on to the roof and to safety. It seems that Dyonisia did not own a cat after all.

Mission accomplished, she reached for the 'cat food' and offered it to me. I was busy trying to explain to her that we didn't own a cat either when Dyonisia cut me off:

'I have big boy too. You eat, you be big too, you be strong.'

She smiled up at me and I realised with horror that she

wanted me to eat the food that the cat had been so interested in a moment before.

Now, after seeing the type of punishment she had dished out to the cat, I wasn't about to risk an onslaught myself. I used my fork to shovel a morsel into my mouth. This was met with smiling approval from Dyonisia, who was watching me closely for any signs of dissent. She ushered me towards a chair. I pleaded that I had to rush to get changed and get back to work. Even though the plate was very small, the snack seemed vast, what with my stomach protesting that it was not for me.

Reluctantly, she let me leave but insisted that I take the food with me to finish off in my own home – in order to get big and strong. Needless to say, I beat a hasty retreat to my apartment below and made a guilty rendezvous with the bin. This was the first time I sampled any of Dyonisia's culinary delights. And the last.

To complete the run-down of our team in Kos, I must tell you about Deidre. Deidre was our boss. She had met us off the boat upon our arrival on the island and in all the confusion I hadn't really got a chance to get a good look at her and make my usual prejudicial appraisal. The next day, though, that was put right. Deidre called a team meeting in the office, which we all attended. On average all the bosses I have worked for during my time with various tour operators have averaged out at around twenty to twenty-five stones in weight. After my second year in Ibiza I seriously wondered whether being obese was a requirement for the job of boss. Maybe it was the stress that made these people overeat. Or maybe big is powerful. Anyway, true to form Deidre did not disappoint when all twenty stones of her trundled into the office, like a smiling Nellie with the circus far behind, to introduce herself. Deidre was, and still is I suppose, jolly in her personality. Jolly bad at man management, jolly nosy, jolly unreliable, jolly greedy, jolly fat, jolly hard to find when you need her, but a jolly nice person to boot. She was great fun to go out with, because she told you about all the private and confidential information she had access to as a senior member of the organisation, but it made me think about how much she told other people about me. Obviously, everything she knew, so the answer was to tell her as little as possible, then you could rest more easily. I'm afraid her constant gossiping lost Deidre the respect of all the team eventually, but we still had some good times along the way.

Beth and I found a local stable where we could go riding every week. Deidre, on hearing about this, reminisced to us about her exploits on riding some of the finest horses in the world on a previous posting in the Far East. She begged us to take her with us on one of our visits to the stables. After a while we gave in, and off we all trundled for a jolly afternoon riding through the beautiful Greek countryside. Whatever Deidre had ridden in Egypt, and I have no doubt that she had done a fair bit of riding in her time, it was definitely not horses. Right from the outset it was a complete embarrassment for poor old Deidre. Try as she might she just could not persuade her shapeless bulk up on to the weary horse's back. The horse took one look at her and, to his credit, decided not to co-operate. Eventually the stable owner, Janis, had to be commandeered to help Deidre aboard. I could see from the look on his face that he had been dreading this prospect. There was no gentle or polite way of getting Deidre up on to the beast's back. He just had to stand behind her, lever her upwards and then push her massive bottom over his head. I felt sorry for Janis, as Deidre rose miraculously over his head. At one point I thought she would fall back and crush him, but eventually she was mounted, and we were off.

Surprisingly, the horse did not bow under the weight, and just about managed a slow stroll around the set course. Deidre giggled and clucked and screamed the whole way round. The horse was completely disinterested in the whole journey apart from the odd blink or extremely unpleasant and loud fart. Deidre positively loved the experience and became a regular horsey multi-gym user every week. Needless to say, I did my best not to accompany these sessions for fear of splitting my sides with laughter.

There was one more member of our team: Mia. Mia was a career rep; she had worked abroad for many years and was a positive mine of information like Julie. She had no ambition to move up the ladder at all, and I found that a little strange. We didn't have an awful lot to do with each other, but there was never any love lost between us. During a course of a season abroad, feelings can fluctuate quite a lot but I can honestly say that my feelings for Mia remained consistent throughout the season. I didn't like her then, and I don't like her now, but she probably feels the same way about me, so there.

Anyway, likes and dislikes aside we were a good team – the

most envied on the island, in fact – and the mixture of experience and natural chemistry seemed to work. We were to have a very successful time together.

With the team assembled and bristling with start-of-season enthusiasm, off we went to check out our new resort, eager for action and keen to see the hotels we would be working in. Kardamena was quite a small resort, probably only about three miles from end to end and about a half a mile wide. The beginning of the resort started about four miles from the airport on the south-west of the island and ran right up to the far end at the foot of the Dikeos mountains, the range that ran the length of the island of Kos, like a twisted spine. Width-wise it stretched half a mile away from the sea. In spite of its size, Kos is a dramatically beautiful island, with breathtaking views from the majestic mountains and pleasant green valleys. You can see why Hippocrates, the founder of modern medicine, decided to stay. Mind you, I am sure if he had seen some of the hotels and some of the inhabitants that stay in them during the summer these days, he might have changed his mind.

In fact, I thought that there was only one particularly ugly place on the island, and that, as you'll no doubt have guessed by now, was Kardamena. The place was like a malignant cancer. More hotels took their first steps into existence to meet the needs of the planeloads of eager visitors. In the small space that was Kardamena, there were over 200 different accommodations, ranging from seedy little hovels to mediocre small hotels, and a few grand fine hotels. All of them were full to bursting in the midsummer months of

June, July and August, but in the second week of April, soon after our arrival, there was hardly a soul to be seen in the resort. At such a time it has been deserted even by the locals, and it is no wonder when you saw the half-built embryonic edifices that would one day be the new hotels, and the sprawling, colourless concrete bars and dwellings spewing into the sea. It was quite simply hideously ugly. Anyway, it was still home for the next few months and we had to make the most of it, so off we went to check out our surroundings and look at the hotels that would be our places of work. First stop, The Sunny View.

The Sunny View's proprietor is a little old Greek man called Yiorgos. Like most of the Greek apartment owners on the island, Yiorgos speaks excellent English – he has to, it's his livelihood. As we drove towards the complex it was a beautiful and bright sunny April day. The complex was a little out of the way, i.e. a mile from the town of Kardamena along a narrow tree-lined road that could potentially become a dark lonely alley after nightfall, but we didn't let this spoil our impressions for the time being. Yiorgos gave us a pleasant welcoming greeting as we entered his hotel. He is tall, beautifully tanned from years of sunshine with dark hair greying at the temples, and he was dressed in a casual white shirt and blue trousers. His handsome demeanour made him look as though he had just stepped from the set of *Zorba the Greek*.

He invited us both to have a drink and Beth and I indulged in our first beer of the day – after all, 10am is not too early in Greece. Yiorgos then gestured us towards the complex, which is a small block of apartments about twenty yards away from the bar we were drinking in, and to get to it we had to pass his guests' swimming pool.

In the brochure this pool had been described as 'Olympic size'. As I surveyed the small square hole in the ground surrounded by stacked sun beds, I began to wonder just what kind of 'Olympics' the author of the brochure had in mind. Frog Olympics maybe, or perhaps this was just the children's pool area? No, I guessed not. 'See my beautiful pool,' exclaimed Yiorgos proudly. 'I have sun beds for everyone, and there are no Germans allowed.' I surveyed the small hole in the ground that was 'the pool'; to add insult to injury, it was a deep, murky green colour. I'd love to tell you how deep it was, but I couldn't see past the murky slime that adorned the surface. Yiorgos registered my concern, gestured dismissively with his hand and explained, 'Don't worry, is a little green now, I waiting for a chemistal from Athens, and it will be very clean for guests.' He smiled reassuringly. I was doing my mental arithmetic: here we were in mid-April, and he had two days to clean the pool, i.e. transform a murky pond into a crystal-clear Olympic pool before the guests arrived. Hmmm. But you can't really argue with a confident Greek hotel owner. They are so persuasive and charming, and most of the time you never win anyway, so it's just not worth the effort.

Yiorgos led me into one of his tiny, but tidy apartments overlooking the dirty green hole. It was in the process of being cleaned by one of those little Greek cleaning ladies who smile all the time and permanently brandish a cleaning brush in their hands. I often wondered where these ladies come from, or where they go at night, because you never see them on the streets. They are always attired in the uniform of the cleaning lady – a blue apron over a puffy white dress. They are always smiling and knocking on doors. They are always very short and never speak English. I reckon they must be mass-produced on some cleaning lady farm in the Med somewhere. In all my time abroad I never had a conversation with a cleaning lady, never exchanged any communication save for a smile as they passed me in hotel corridors and I have never met anybody who has had any more than that. I'll have to investigate that one day. Anyway, back to the story.

Yiorgos banished the cleaning lady with a threatening gesture and a Greek insult. He watched her as she left the room, in case she malfunctioned and showed any sign of dissent. Then he stepped into the toilet and I politely turned away. 'No, come, I want you to see,' he proclaimed from within, in a broad, echoing voice. I stood perplexed as Yiorgos gestured, smiling from inside the tiny room.

What could he possibly mean? Could his willy be deformed in some way? Perhaps he had some other amazing sight on his genitalia that he wished to share with me, or he had multi-coloured piles. 'Come, I want to show,' he echoed again. *Oh well, I am a man of the world.* I shrugged my shoulders, took a deep breath and followed him in. I looked into his eyes; he smiled at me, moved closer to the pristine throne, and brought his hand down in a sweeping movement far too exaggeratedly for comfort in such a confined space …

And flushed the toilet. 'See,' he shouted triumphantly. It wasn't blindingly obvious what exactly he meant. I looked towards his nether regions for a clue. His trousers were still done up; his willy was still in his pants. What could he be referring to? 'Flush toilets,' he proudly exclaimed. He beamed at me. I looked back and tried not to look too perplexed. 'Yes, they certainly do work,' I chipped in. When a leading hotelier's pride and joy is his flush toilet, you begin to wonder what you have let yourself in for. He flushed it again to show that the first time had been no fluke. I nodded, made my excuses and retired for a confab with my colleagues. It was sure going to be a long, hard season.

COLDITZ AND POLYVOTIS

I FOUND ACCOMMODATION standards in Greece to be very different to those of some of the other places I had worked. One thing that I remember is that it takes a long time to get used to putting your used toilet roll in the bin beside the toilet, and to some people this arrangement was positively Stone Age. Just remember to be very careful and check your bins if you ever have a Greek friend over for dinner; I am sure old habits die hard. Regular travellers to Greece became used to this system and just get on with it, but week after week during the summer I met my new arrivals in the hotel and was immediately greeted by a torrent of complaints about how they couldn't understand why they shouldn't put their toilet roll directly into the loo. The brochures did make a half-hearted attempt to warn people what to expect, but most people never read the bloody things. Then there was the problem of how you actually word the warning.

'You wipe your arse with the toilet paper that may be

provided and put it in the bin beside you, which may or may not have a lid, depending on how hygienically minded your apartment owner is.' Yes it was a tough one, and for some people it was just too much to take, so they flushed the paper down the loo anyway and be damned. Which was fine, until the toilet became blocked. Oh fiddle!

Cockroaches too were a constant problem; they loved the hot climate and the Greek kitchens that were, for the most part, only half-heartedly cleaned. One day cockroaches will evolve and realise how terrified they make humans. Several times during my Greek season I was called to deal with marauding roaches in our neighbours Nat and Julie's apartment downstairs. Looking back I can easily imagine that these invading roaches were as big as clenched fists; in reality, they were probably no bigger than a thumbnail. I would chase the terrified insects out into the street or pound them under a shoe or a brush until they exhibited no sign of life at all. I always had to appear brave and unconcerned and pretend to wonder why the girls were so terrified by this ugly beast that was so small, but if the cockroach was ever to change direction and challenge my right to step on him, I wouldn't have stayed around to argue, I can assure you. In spite of my attempts to leave our kitchen dirty, to test the theory that roaches do not like unclean places to live and dine, Beth would not take part in my experiment, and so in my spare time I could be regularly found washing and drying dishes, or mopping the floor for visiting cockroaches to inspect.

Summer had begun and out came the Brits, ninety per cent of them unprepared for the dodgy plumbing and devious vermin that awaited their arrival in the little Greek paradises. Beautiful scenery could be found, beautiful beaches even, but pitfalls abounded around every corner. During my Greek spell I came across many accommodations that could only be reached after driving along pothole-infested roads, and then climbing steep flights of stairs to steamy non-air-conditioned rooms, in which cockroaches waited.

I remember one evening I dropped two young girls off at their new apartment from the airport. As I switched on the light in their kitchen I was confronted by a large, shiny black cockroach sitting on top of the gleaming cooker. I'm sure it was smiling at me. If it could have spoken, and it looked like it was attempting to, it would have said, 'Hi, I'm Spiro the resident roach, welcome to Kos.' The girls, obviously horrified at the sight, screamed. Spiro, obviously startled by their unfriendly reaction, darted off the worktop towards the bedroom. I had no option and I had to act fast or he would be gone. I stamped on him and tried to grind him underfoot. I could feel him squirming and trying to push my foot up through my shoe.

I forced my foot to stay put as he struggled beneath me. It took four good hard stomps before Spiro would play dead and I could kick him out of the front door into the night. Believe me when I tell you I was petrified. 'Was that a cockroach?' one of the girls enquired. ''Cause I am not staying in an apartment with cockroaches in it.'

I must have become quite good at lying by that stage in my career as a rep, or at least not showing any emotion, not even fear. ''Course it's not a cockroach,' I replied. 'We don't have them here in Greece,' I lied and, to my amazement, they believed me. Oh well, it brings a new meaning to the line 'Trust me, I'm a rep.'

I left them to think it over, and took Spiro with me. Or I intended to anyway. But after I'd kicked his lifeless body along the corridor, he promptly got up and ran away. Resilient things, these roaches.

I found myself wondering what brought people back to Greece year after year and I reckoned it must be the Greek hospitality. The Greek people are simply so kind. Most Greeks tolerate the sometimes rowdy behaviour of European tourists without uttering a word in protest. On occasions the Brits have proved themselves to be a little more drunken than some of their European colleagues when on holiday, but the Germans and the Scandinavians can hold their own, believe me. I remember one time in the hotel I was working in a German gentleman was berating the staff at the reception desk because of the state of his room. This large, tanned, perfect specimen of manhood (as they annoyingly so often tend to be) was shouting in English at the smiling receptionist, who was unable to help the distressed but angry German, because it was mid-August and the hotel was completely full. The German, realising that his impressive command of the English language was getting him nowhere apart from gaining him a large but appreciative audience from his curious fellow occupants, gave one final insult to the hapless receptionist: 'You peasant, if it wasn't for me you would still be working in the fields.'

I cringed at this remark, and once the dust had settled I

spoke to the receptionist. He really wasn't bothered about the insult, but told me that the gentleman concerned might have trouble retrieving his suitcase once he arrived back in Germany. It turned out that the receptionist had a friend in the airport and he was busy arranging a suitable destination for the German's luggage once he boarded his flight back home. Needless to say, the proposed destination would not be the one the angry tourist was bound for. It's always worth remembering this the next time you upset an hotelier abroad: they do have friends in the industry.

In spite of my initial, negative impression of Kos, scratch the surface and you could find a beautiful side to this island. Behind some of the notorious and rowdy drinking dens and nightclubs of Kardamena you could still find little old Greek ladies clad in the traditional black dresses going about their daily business, just inches from the vomit and empty beer bottles that were the aftermath of the previous night's revelries. The place was simply so full of charm. Fishing boats that provided a lifeline for so many moored up on the picturesque quay at the end of every day, and the captains tended to their nets, while the returning pleasure boats sneaked in alongside them, disgorging their exhausted and sunburned cargos. Life seemed to carry on regardless under the sometimes patronising but always curious gaze of the tourists released from their closeted lifestyles back home for two weeks of sunshine and discovery. For my money, this was Greece's fourth invasion of recent times. The Germans had a go during the war, then the Italians, followed by the brief liberation by the Brits, and now the tourists are here.

That Greek life should not only just continue on the islands, but also even prosper under such a deluge of visitors, says much for the resilience of these people.

The weather was obviously one factor that tempted people to the Greek islands year after year. British summertime is so often a rainy season punctuated by the odd hour or two of sunshine. Those hours can become days, but such days are random and intermittent. It makes planning a holiday rather difficult, so Greece made for a pleasant alternative. Kos became abnormally hot from June to the end of September. May to mid-June was beautiful springlike weather, with maybe a smattering of rain, which dried almost as quickly as it fell. June, July, August and September had beautiful clear blue skies and radiant, boiling sunshine. For some, it could all get a little too much. To survive you needed to drink pints of water every now and then in order not to dehydrate. The average Brit in Kardamena never drank very much water at home, so why should they drink it abroad? You told people until you were blue in the face, but still ended up spending a lot of time taking shrivelled Brits to local doctors, and in the worst cases hospitals, to remind them of who they are and why they are there. But still, it seemed, they never learnt. All this need for liquid refreshment made water a very valuable commodity. Some supermarkets could survive on water sales alone.

In spite of the lack of rainfall in the summer the island appeared to be very green and fertile. This is largely due to the underground springs and good – in fact, brilliant –

irrigation system that some of the islanders employ. The hotel where I worked was particularly enterprising when it came to keeping their gardens green and rosy. The manager decided to dispose of the hotel's considerable sewage by spraying it directly on to the gardens. Brilliant idea. He installed a sprinkler system all around the hotel that intermittently sprayed shit and piss over different parts of the grounds, all day and all night. This was not lost on about 80 million of the island's resident mosquitoes, who couldn't believe their luck. After breeding in the murky, smelly pools created by the spray, they then went off to dine on any number of the foreign delicacies especially imported for the occasion. For the mosquitoes it was heaven. For the guests it was hell. I remember one evening after a particularly busy session tending to the moaning masses that occupied my hotel, I decided to escape the premises by leaving, as I frequently did, from a ground-floor window. This meant I had about a fifty-yard dash towards my car across the lawns. Imagine my horror when halfway across the lawn I hear the familiar noise of the sprinkler system bursting into life. I had been taking verbal shit all evening, now it was time for the real thing. There was nothing I could do except run faster. Ugh!

You needed a car if you worked in my hotel. It was quite a long way from the resort centre, about three miles in all, so that made transport necessary in itself, but it also made it quite useful for making hasty getaways when the need arose, as the angry guests ganged up. It was the biggest hotel on the island and easily the most troublesome place to work. When it was full it held just over two thousand people, and four hundred of them were mine. There were mostly two nationalities: British and German.

The German guests' main complaint was that the hotel catered mainly for the British, and they made their feelings on this point known to anyone who would listen. The British firmly believed that the hotel catered mainly for the Germans and complained loudly to me about the fact. Some days could be sheer hell. Because the hotel itself was so far from the main town of Kardamena and so, in a sense, was isolated, there was a courtesy bus that ran to the village four times daily. It was a great idea, but with over two thousand people to cater for it was woefully inadequate. Let me assure you that the Germans did not take to the idea of British orderly queuing systems too kindly. Napoleon said we were a nation of shopkeepers. Not so. Based on my knowledge of the Brits, we are a nation of queue builders. Take a look around you when you go out. If there's not a queue when we walk into a shop, we will organise one. Post offices have now helped us along with this and put up little guide ropes to help us.

Anyway back to the bus. The Brits in the hotel would first study the timetable of the courtesy bus and, about half an hour before its intended departure time, would begin to form an orderly, very British queue. Nice straight lines would stretch back and forth by the bus stop. Anxious pale-skinned Brits, clad in their uncomfortable and unfamiliar attire of shorts and gaudy T-shirts, would be waiting anxiously, with their baby buggies, blow-up life rings and floating plastic crocodiles, skinny white hairy legs, ice-cream-wielding children, bags packed with buckets and spades and wet wipes, nappies, rolls from the breakfast buffet, warm bottles of lemonade and copies of yesterday's *Sun* and *Daily Mirror*.

And then the bus would arrive. Tanned and muscled, young and old, Germans would appear from everywhere, pushing the overladen Brits out of the way and using their children as steps and levers to haul themselves on to the rapidly filling bus. All hell would then break loose. Fighting, swearing, punching, kicking, finger-waving, threats in a variety of accents and languages, as well as some unhelpful comments concerning the Second World War were commonplace. The poor little Greek driver would be helpless. When he had packed as many bodies on to the bus as was possible, he pulled away towards the village with his half-gloating, half-fuming human cargo. Then the Brits who hadn't been able to get on the bus would come looking for me. I could do nothing, except for warning them what to expect when they arrived.

At times it almost got out of hand and nearly turned into an international incident. More than once the little driver refused to leave until the fighting had stopped. On several occasions the manager had to come out of the hotel and board the bus to remind people that they were civilised and to behave accordingly. Who would believe it, the Greeks as international peace brokers!

If you didn't make it on to the bus, you could always get a taxi. The taxi system, however, was nothing short of a joke. There were seven licensed vehicles for the whole of

Kardamena, which had roughly about six thousand visitors at any one time in the summer. The mayor was not going to upset the seven taxi owners by granting any more licences. So, predictably, the system struggled to cope. If it weren't so frustrating, it would have been laughable watching people waiting up to three hours for a ten-minute journey to town. The situation at the hotel could not only put you off Greece for a lifetime, but also foreign travel in general. During the month of July, I had many guests who decided that the taxis and courtesy bus were a dead loss, and decided to walk to town along the beach. I should explain that it was theoretically possible to walk along the roads, but that was really taking a risk, as the road was more like a winding path, with no road markings, no lighting and no pavements, with lots of little turns that hid you until a car was almost right on top of you. Not such a good idea, really. The walk along the beach, though, could be quite pleasant, albeit a little long and sandy. Unfortunately, halfway to town, the guests would be stopped at gunpoint by the Greek army, who had chosen that month for manoeuvres and exercises. They sent them back from whence they had come. These exercises went on for the two months of peak season, and there really was no way past. Some wag, no doubt while they were waiting for a taxi, painted the name 'Colditz' over the gate of the hotel – and, may I say, not without good cause.

The brochure had described the hotel as a 'good destination for all, families and couples'. So why the rush to get out? Why not stay around and enjoy the entertainment? Why not indeed. I'm afraid I got a little bit cynical thinking this one over. The fact that this hotel, unless you were lucky enough to get a taxi, or avoid the guns of the practising Greek army, was virtually inaccessible, was not lost on the owners of the complex. They had a captive audience and they knew it.

The price of drinks was double that of the ones in the village. The bar staff were ignorant and sullen to a man, and the entertainment was laughably crap. The three-strong entertainment team had all the credentials needed to be a successful entertainment team in a large international hotel with over two thousand guests. They spoke English, German, Greek, Spanish and French, and no doubt a host of other languages as well. They were keen (for a while) and enthusiastic (for a shorter while), and full of good ideas. All the necessary qualities. Except they couldn't entertain anybody to save their lives. They did try, but they were absolutely awful. The cabaret nights were a shambles. They used to do things like glove puppet shows. Good idea, but for two thousand people minus a few busloads, it was a total non-starter. People could be seen huddled into corners late at night forming tunnelling committees, such was the desperation once the 'entertainment' had come to a close at night. Mind you, if I was entertaining without pay for a while – as it turned out this crew had been doing for a couple of months – I might consider a glove puppet production as well.

There was a supermarket conveniently placed on the site as well and, in the true tradition of the hotel, this was extortionately overpriced. They sold things such as pegs, playing cards and picture frames. They only had bread and milk in limited supply twice a week, and all the drinks on sale when closely inspected were on average six to eight months out of date. Just to put the icing on the cake, the water and electricity would occasionally fail without warning. Many people overlooked these shortcomings and put it all down to the 'charm of Greece'. I think not. I complained bitterly to the beleaguered manager, who really could do nothing, as the people who owned the complex needed to invest to make improvements, and it seemed they were unwilling to do so. At times it was a fun place to work, and once I even met a bloke who had been the year before and came back to see it again, so it wasn't all bad. It just seemed that way sometimes.

Some days when I jumped aboard my trusty old Second World War jeep, which this company had supplied me with to get to and from work, I just felt like driving past the hotel and on into the sea. Common sense prevailed and I stuck it out and tried to laugh at it all for the rest of the season. There was, however, one saving grace. The former head barman of the hotel had realised long ago the futility of trying to persuade unpaid staff to work diligently in the pursuit of excellent customer service, and so had left the hotel to set up his own venture. He opened a tiny bar less than half a mile away from the lumbering monstrosity of the hotel. It was like an oasis, though it was a cancer for the big hotel: once the disillusioned guests got wind of this little outpost, they fled in numbers to its sanctuary.

The owner was a man full of character. His name was

Manoli, and he liked to be known simply as 'the Captain'. He wasn't English; he wasn't Greek or Spanish or German; he was a true European. The Captain was a short, stocky man with a weather-beaten face. He was always dressed in a pair of dark trousers and a white shirt tucked into his trousers that did little to hide his considerable paunch. All this was topped off with his sailor's peaked white cap; he certainly looked like a captain. Manoli spoke with real authority about any subject you cared to mention. He knew his history and would often enthral his listeners with tales of the rise of civilisation – never boring, simply friendly and interesting.

I swear he used to hear my jeep coming towards the bar as I screamed delightedly away from the big hotel, for as I neared the bar I could see him putting the finishing touches to a beautiful ice cold beer. Beer has never tasted that sweet, before or since. He listened as I reeled off my litany of frustration about the big hotel. It was a story he knew only too well, as he had experienced the same frustrations himself when he had worked there as head barman. Manoli became my part-time soul mate. He told me that he had left the hotel for the same reasons I hid in his bar. He hated the money-grabbing attitude of the owner, who was completely mercenary about taking all he could get during the summer months and damn the consequences. He enjoyed his new role in his little bar; his own boss to do as he pleased. He was always pleased to welcome members of the management team from the big hotel, who would come to spy on his set-up and see why he was able to poach people from their empire. Unlike the staff in the big hotel, the Captain smiled and welcomed all his customers, and served them with a little courtesy and at a fair price. As a result, they always came back and sometimes they brought their friends. It was a splendid irony: without the hotel he would have gone out of business, and they knew it, and more importantly so did he. They tried to buy him out, but he wasn't selling, at any price. They cut off his telephone supply, and so he re-routed it; they cut off his electricity supply, and he got round that as well. He was just too bloody clever for them. The Captain had something more than just the qualities of a well-positioned leech. He was always very friendly to anyone who came to drink or just browse; everyone was welcome at the Captain's bar.

Manoli always worked alone, apart from two elderly farmers – a husband and wife – who came to help only when they felt like it, a curious arrangement but one that personified the relaxed friendly atmosphere of the bar. I remember once asking him if he ever got lonely. 'No,' he replied, 'I have Annabelle.' I wondered who Annabelle was. He looked at me and then pointed her out to me. She was certainly beautiful. She looked back at me with her deep brown eyes, which complemented her olive-coloured complexion. She had a beautifully full mane of well-tended hair and long, sleek legs. Four of them. Annabelle and Manoli were very happy. Man and donkey living in perfect harmony. I can still see Manoli's smiling face as I screech into the space in the front of his bar. He puts my fresh cold beer on top of the bar and then slaps the palm of his hand on the table and shouts, 'Takka, takka … Annabelle, he is here again.' The donkey heehaws in greeting. I collapse into a chair and Manoli sits opposite me, ready to listen to my woes. I hope he survives for many a year with his two fingers stuck up in the air towards the big hotel, saying, 'Look at me, this is the way to do it …'

One saving grace of the big hotel was that it boasted its own private beach and it really was beautiful, sporting a breathtaking view out into the fabulous Aegean sea, which glimmered invitingly. Out on the horizon you could see the nearby island of Nissyros. It never failed to look beautiful and mysterious from a distance, but once you took the trouble to make it across to the island by courtesy of one of the many pleasure boats that left daily to travel to the island, it surpassed all expectations. Nissyros was truly a Greek island paradise, with its own hidden surprise, and I was lucky enough to go there once a week, every week.

The hidden surprise? Nissyros featured the remnants of an old volcano called Polyvotis smack bang in the middle of it. The place itself was shaped like an inverted cone. From the port of Mandrakis (it has not been lost on me that most Greek ports are called Mandrakis), the hills rise in every direction to a peak high on the horizon. A road wove its way around the rising mountains, steep and high, sometimes at seemingly impossible and dramatic angles.

It was a breathtaking journey up the mountain, and you held your breath as you reached the summit. You might be forgiven for thinking the journey was exciting enough and that it could be the highlight of this day out, until you swept over the top and were confronted by an amazing sight. There before you lay probably the steepest drop you'll ever see, leading into a green and fertile valley that looked like the land that time forgot. The road was twice as steep as the one you had just climbed and wove its way down to what, at first, looked like a distant pancake. The nearer to the bottom you got, the more the smell of sulphur filled your nostrils, and your neck strained as you tried to get a look at the growing pancake that steamed away before you through the greenery. You were entering a dormant volcano. It was quite simply stunning and from the moment I set eyes on this island at the start of the season I was hooked.

The company took a trip across there every week and it was part of a rep's job to guide this trip. The journey across the stretch of water to Nissyros could be treacherous, and the slightest swell could force those with no sea legs to part company with their breakfast. This served to make this particular guiding chore quite unpopular among the team, so I gladly took up the duties every week. I did gain from this experience in the sharing of work, because it meant that I got off an airport shift back in Kos that might begin at four in the morning, so I reckoned I got a good deal on this exchange. Seasickness or not, I always felt I had the better end of the arrangement.

This little island had about one thousand inhabitants in all, and most of these people made their living either from tourism or from harvesting pumice on a nearby island. The tourist industry on Nissyros depended very much on

Polyvotis, so the islanders organised regular trips from the port to the volcano through the precarious mountain passes and on into the amazing volcano itself. I don't know if it is still taking place, as in these safety-conscious days, I am not convinced that holiday companies could live with the idea of sending their charges into a live volcano and exposing them to such pungent levels of sulphur dioxide. The rickety coaches also left a lot to be desired and I wouldn't like to bet on their continued operation, but this really was all part of the charm of Greece. The island had about four little villages, and seemed happily untouched by the stresses and strains of the modern day. It was said that most youngsters try to leave the island to find their future and you could understand why: you could not live on charm alone. Some, however, remain. I reckoned you could tell who the locals were. They looked at you with dark, brooding eyes that broke into a welcoming but mysterious smile when you acknowledged them. Some unkind reps in the team suggested that the mysteriousness was down to inbreeding, but I am far too polite to suggest that. Though I did wonder …

Because tourism was such an important business for the island, whenever a new boat came into the port carrying another batch of curious tourists in its bows – tourists who were carrying pocketfuls of holiday money that they were just itching to part with – the restaurateurs came out of their empty establishments and stared jealously at the cargo, making sure that no greedy tour guide pointed them away from their hostelry. So there I was in early May with my first packed busload of British tourists curious and excited to see the awaiting volcano. I was the guide and all these people were my responsibility. To them, I was the expert on Nissyros. In fact, I had only been there once before and, not to put too fine a point on it, I was shitting myself. I was, though, more than ready and determined to help them to enjoy the day. As we sat on the bus waiting for the journey up the mountain to begin, we fell under the watching eyes of encircling restaurant owners, like greedy cats watching the arrival of a new fish tank full of lively juicy specimens.

We began the steady but steep climb to the top of the mountain, one eye on the view and one ear on the grinding and protesting gearbox as the ageing coach dragged us up the hill.

We reached the top and then began our descent. This had to be one of the best journeys in the world. As you dropped down into the spectacular volcano, the passengers could not fail to be impressed, and the sighs of excitement followed by stunned silence confirmed this feeling. Every nerve-jangling turn in the road took you nearer to the volcano known as Polyvotis. You left the coach at the lip of the volcano itself and were greeted by giant nameless insects buzzing curiously around your head, all of which simply added to the mystery of this unique sight. The whole thing was quite awesome.

I gathered my guests around and gave them my practised spiel. It rolled off the tongue. I regaled them with tales of the filming of James Bond's *Moonraker* here, mixed in with tales of battling Greek gods; their videos whirred and the cameras clicked. I was centre stage and I loved it. I was building them up to the climax: the walk into the crater itself. I warned them about the rickety twisting path and a rumour about an imminent eruption went in for good measure. The nervous laughter convinced me that the stage was set and the punters were ready for the descent. We began our journey down. Your one concern at this point is to get the party into and out of the crater as quickly and as safely as possible, and back in time for lunch. I gave them twenty minutes maximum in the hole and then started them back up. After fifteen minutes or so, most had begun the journey up unprompted. I was feeling pretty pleased with myself; it had been a success. I was smiling inwardly and looking forward to lunch back down in the port and the relaxing journey home.

I began to make my way out of the stifling crater up the steep climb back towards the coach. Then, from behind me came a blood-curdling scream. My heart leaped into my mouth as I forced myself to look back down the slope. I half-expected the volcano to have started to erupt, such was the ferocity of the scream. Mercifully it hadn't, but things were nearly that bad. One of the guests, walking backwards as he had been taking photos, had stepped into one of the steaming geezers. He quickly stepped out again (most people would, given its temperature of around 200 degrees) but not before he had burned his right leg from toe to knee. By the time I reached him, his leg was a steamy red bloody mess. People were panicking and his girlfriend was screaming. All he could think of was his new trainers. Somebody shouted,

'Call an ambulance!' That really was a good idea, I had to agree, but even Greek ambulances don't normally drive into volcanoes. People had started to bring water down from the top of the crater to cool the poor guy's leg. I quickly realised that the only way out of this was going to be to carry him out of the volcano.

I was lucky enough to have the services of two willing volunteer guests to help me with the load. The poor fellow was in agony; as the shock began to wear off he started to realise the potential horror of what he had done. His girlfriend too was starting to get very panicky, and I was considering smacking her in the mouth to render her unconscious until a thoughtful lady led her away and tried to comfort her.

It took us a whole forty-five minutes to get him to the top. Of course, lunch would be ruined by now ... I then had to persuade a reluctant miserable old git to give up his front seat so I could sit the injured fellow at the front. With the patient loaded on we set off for a breathless journey back up and down to the port of Mandrakis. I was relieved to find that on arrival the bus organiser had managed to radio ahead and so the woman at the office had her car ready to whisk the patient off to a doctor. Three bars later we found the island's doctor. He finished his drink and then climbed into his car and we followed him to his surgery. This was, in fact, a multi-purpose surgery: it was also the dentist's, the joiner's and the painters' workshop. A couch was cleared and the patient, by now delirious with pain, was stretched out on it.

The doctor went about the gory business of clearing away burned skin and clearing up the mess. One by one the dentist, his patient, the joiner and his apprentice, followed by the painter with all his brushes, filed in to wince at the poor man's discomfort.

All in all it was quite an amazing and terrifying experience for a first time in the volcano with guests. Come to think of it, the whole trip was fraught with danger, but mercifully it was my one and only mishap on the island of Nissyros for the whole season. It's best to get these things out of the way early if they have to happen. From that point onwards though, whenever I went to Nissyros I was always a little nervous of what might happen. Shrieks of joy from the volcano could quite easily become heart-stopping memory joggers. The patient, by the way, was a fellow called Dan. I reckon he was about twenty-one at the time, an out-of-work photographer, and as it happened a bloody nice chap. He was eternally grateful for my help in extricating him from the clutches of Polyvotis and taking him to a medic. His leg turned out to be not as bad as it had first looked and I believe that in time it healed nicely. I will always remember him as the man who fell into a volcano and lived to tell the tale. He took bloody good photos as well. Good luck, Dan, wherever you are.

*   *   *

One by one the weeks rolled by on this Greek island and the days seemed to merge into one. There was no difference between a weekday and a weekend; the only thing that differentiated one day from the next in a rep's life was an airport day, a welcome party day or a cabaret day. The workload was quite tough, and a day off was a treasured luxury to recharge your batteries. After working in Spain for a couple of years, Greece could be quite a culture shock for a rep at first. There was a belief that you either worked in Spain or Greece, you never changed from one to the other; standards – and guests for that matter – were quite different. Spanish holidaymakers would never dream of putting the toilet paper in the bin, after all. At first I found myself missing the world of Spain – it just seemed that they have known tourism for a lot longer and are a little more ready for the annual invasion of the Brits. I did get used to Greece, though, and all thoughts of Spain soon disappeared. You get used to the late nights and early mornings at the airport, the cockroaches and the rats, the primitive roads and the positively antique hospital with its do-it-yourself attitude to medicine (and this in the birthplace of Hippocrates). If you are going to get ill anywhere in the world I suggest you steer well clear of Kos. If you have no family to clean you and change your sheets, they don't get changed, full stop. Anything that gets any more serious than cleaning cuts and bruises or boil lancing should be shipped immediately to Athens at the first opportunity.

All this to contend with, and that's before any guests got hold of you. It was not surprising, then, that many who come to work as a rep in Greece didn't actually stick it out for the duration of the season. I found our whole system of accounting pretty primitive in Greece as well. In Spain I was used to selling trips to my guests and then they would toddle off and be guided by professional guides. In Greece there was no such luxury as professional guides – this was all done by our good self. The workload could seem daunting, but it was no good moaning about it, you just had to get on and do it. I must admit I spent my first weeks in the resort being in a state of shock about the amount of hard slog facing me.

I was just learning to come to terms with all this when our resort manager informed us that she would like to do a cabaret night on the island for the first time, in order to boost company profits. True to form, we would have to organise the venue, rehearse a show from scratch, arrange a sound system, sort some music out, arrange drinks, make and design costumes, choreograph some dances, publicise and sell the show, work out the profit on all sales for the agent, the company and ourselves, and, of course, separate this from our normal weekly accounts, and then perform in it on a weekly basis.

'When?' we asked.

'In your spare time, of course,' replied our very under-standing and very humane boss. Of course. 'You've got three weeks. Go for it.'

And go for it we did. I had always enjoyed taking part in cabarets wherever I had worked previously and fancied myself as a bit of an actor, so I took charge. The end result, once we got there, was great. It was fun to take part in and the customers really enjoyed it. I like to kid myself and think that it could never be bettered, but I am sure the teams that have followed us have surpassed our efforts. Anyway, I'll content myself by saying that it was the best cabaret that this company put its name to that year on the island of Kos! It felt like a triumph, but it was a long, hard road to get there. The whole thing began to take shape on a cold May evening up in the hills of Zia at an open-air venue that we had decided to use for the event. Springtime in Greece is marked in the day by pleasant sunshine that changes very quickly at night to fairly cold temperatures. We were huddled together in the venue after another long day at work, most of us inappropriately dressed for the climate. As we sat there freezing our nuts off and totally devoid of any enthusiasm for the extra workload, it was difficult to see how this chilly gathering could be transformed into a screaming cacophony of appreciative human zeal in the coming months.

The plan was for the venue owners to demonstrate to us all how good their venue could be by feeding and watering us all, and then demonstrating their resident band and sound system. That was the plan. The food was cold and very late and barely edible. The band, it turned out, had never met before and the sound system simply refused to work. Everybody was completely devoid of ideas. The guitarist of the band stood on a little platform that was supposed to be the stage; he seemed to have been tuning his instrument for over an hour. He looked across at us all huddled together, our arms tucked inside our short-sleeved T-shirts, gave us all a nod of acknowledge-ment, then turned his back on us all and proceeded to struggle through a few bars of rock and roll. I think this was supposed to stir us into action. Nothing happened. Being a former musician myself, I felt for him and I made my way over to the stage to talk to him and sympathise with him over his plight. Like most men in Greece he was called Janis and spoke no English. His mouth was hidden behind a thick droopy moustache that, together with his sad brown eyes, made him look permanently depressed. Frankly, if I had played the guitar as badly as him I would have been permanently depressed too. There were two more in the band also called Janis, and all equally sullen. I christened them the Flying Zimbinis. Their depression was infectious.

Our exasperated resort manager appeared and ordered us all to retreat to a nearby anteroom to see whether the slight change in temperature could conjure up any enthusiasm. Having had the misfortune to have been involved in some pretty awful tour operator cabarets in previous years (dressing as a chicken pursuing a randy worm springs to mind), I was determined that we should all try our best to come up with something that would not shame us all. There was no way out of it; we were going to have to do this show whether we liked it or not.

I stood up, made a quick declaration of intent and volunteered myself for a couple of well-worn old favourite sketches, and so rehearsals began. Some of you reading this may have been to reps' cabarets before, some of you may not, but whatever your view, I can assure you all they are bloody hard work to put together. The rehearsal time is the hardest part. You either get together last thing at night at about 10pm after work and rehearse until well gone midnight when you are desperately tired, or you get a meeting organised for midday and dance around in the searing heat. Either way, everybody to a man was pissed off. We must have rehearsed for twenty hours all told to put the show together. We had dances, comedy sketches, recitals and skits and even managed a bit of West End musical for good measure.

The day before our first show, when we were all expecting a full house, our resort manager came along to see our first dress rehearsal. It was crap. She applauded politely. I stayed silent, though I have to say that inside I was confident it would be a success. I decided very early on that I wanted to compere the show. There were two other candidates who wanted to do the job and I politely gave in when they expressed their enthusiasm to do the job as well, but I knew I would eventually have my way when they realised how difficult it would be to fill all the gaps in. I was in my element. I like to talk and I love an audience. I had a compere companion who filled in when I needed to get changed or wanted a drink. Her name was Elizabeth. She was a pretty little girl with a superior, pompous manner that at times bordered on offensive. This came across wonderfully well to our audiences, and I was almost ecstatic when I realised how bad she was, because she made me look better than I was. Elizabeth used to wear short little black dresses that showed off her legs. She had a short little body that was quite attractive, and an attractive face framed with shoulder-length dark hair, but she also had the most amazingly stumpy little pair of legs I have ever seen. When she walked on stage she looked like she had two small children clinging on to the backs of her legs. The sight of

Elizabeth's legs inspired me to reveal my own highly offensive pins in a *Dad's Army* sketch, such was my glee at having her as my assistant.

And what of the audience? Well, free wine and chicken and chips ensured we got a full house of three hundred people week in and week out. Predictably, quite a lot of them found the cabaret a good opportunity to exercise their rights as British tourists and have a moan. They moaned about the seating: the chairs were uncomfortable, too hard, too soft, wrongly positioned, the wrong height for the tables and too wobbly. Then the food: it was too hot, too cold, not enough, too much, too boring, too Greek, too English, too German, served too quickly, served too slowly. And then they got to the free wine. It was too red, too white, too cheap, too strong or too weak. The great British public might be shy and timid at home in the UK, but put them abroad and they moan about everything. Unfortunately, as I've mentioned before, you only tend to remember the dickheads and the moaners. The truth is that the vast majority never say a word. Whatever, we really tried our best and, though the facilities were not the best we could have hoped for, the show itself was excellent. To my knowledge, in all the weeks that we put the show on, about twenty weeks in all, only one family complained that the show was crap. We gave them their money back and politely told them to fuck off.

Kos had many amazing sights and sounds, but none more amazing than the Kos have-transport-will-travel sex machines. I'm talking moody smirk; I'm talking cool in 100 degrees; I'm talking smile and take it easy; I'm talking 'Reps, who are they?' 'Tourism, what's that?'; I'm talking 'Twenty-four-hour shifts, so what!'; I'm talking 'Fifty-five lives in my hands, but who cares 'cause I'm cool.' I'm talking married, with hairy chest, shirts with no top buttons, white socks, forty cigarettes a day, mean, cool, angry when provoked. Real one hundred per cent testosterone, the personification of Greek manhood: the coach driver.

Not quite the same as the UK equivalent. In Greece, the coach driver was a different animal; a legend. They were all married with constantly pregnant wives; it seemed that a hairy chest was a requirement for the job, coupled with a fuck-off devil-may-care attitude and an endless supply of white socks and slip-ons. Every one of those drivers, no matter how old or ugly, or how much their breath smelled from the intake of cheap strong cigarettes, managed to persuade a female rep into bed at least once a season. Apart from anything else, I couldn't imagine anything worse than smoking the strongest and cheapest cigarettes in tropical heat – it made you stink – but it seemed to work in the coach driver charm school. Any female rep who failed to be propositioned by a coach driver at least once a season was either fiercely protected by overzealous workmates or hopelessly ugly. Or both.

I often wondered what coach drivers and reps actually talked about when they went out together. Greek is very difficult to learn, and in my experience there were very few reps who can actually conjured up more than a general greeting in the language. Likewise, it would be rare indeed to find a coach driver with anything more than 'Hello' in his

English vocabulary. It brought a whole new meaning to the term 'pillow talk'.

All our drivers on the island of Kos were, without exception, excellent at their job. They had to be to avoid the suicidal manoeuvrings of confused, moped-wielding tourists as they meandered their way around the island. Sadly, some of the drivers back then loved to race as well – particularly during our cabaret night or the even more well-attended Greek night extravaganza. Inevitably at the end of these gatherings, packed coaches taking drunken tourists back to their hotels after the festivities would be heading in the same direction; and always, without exception, coach drivers love to race each other. Once they had split off en route to their respective resorts, the drivers liked to test their prowess – and that of their coaches – to the maximum. Several spins around the same roundabout would ensue to see how far they could lean their machines before faltering. A common sight at the end of a cabaret or a Greek night would be a white-knuckled rep clinging on for dear life at the front of a speeding coach, beside the coach driver from hell who would be leering into the night. The guests in the rear would be oblivious or too pissed to care. Perhaps this is what impressed the girls. I'll have to try it out and let you know.

Airport days prompted a gathering of the bus driver clans. A Greek conspiracy meant that all the tour operators' flights to Kos landed at approximately the same time on the same day every week. The kindest word I can find to describe this day was mayhem. Absolute mayhem, in fact. Let me explain. Kos airport was, back in 1994, a very small airport. If you

143

imagine Gatwick airport, and think of the small newsagent's office just to the right of Arrivals, well this roughly equated to the size of the Arrivals hall in Kos airport. Now, imagine that little shop with five planeloads of guests milling around looking for their luggage and you had Kos on arrival day. Just for good measure, throw in a couple of fan heaters on full blast and then you have the full atmosphere.

In this cauldron the smell of sweat clung in the air, as people gathered around the two conveyor belts ready to claim their luggage. One lesson we could learn from Greek baggage handlers is stress management. They had, say, five 767s on the ground awaiting to be off-loaded. They were also aware that all the arriving guests were waiting in the stuffy arrivals hall, suffocating in the intolerable heat. One would think that the thing to do would be to spring into action, hauling bags off as quickly as possible in order to reduce waiting times for the travellers who had come to visit their homeland. Wrong. They discussed strategy, had a fag – usually a smelly one – and pointed at the planes accusingly.

If by some chance a small Cessna-type aircraft should appear out of the sky with a Greek pilot at the controls, everything changed. The handlers rushed to the tiny plane and offloaded the Greek travellers' belongings as quickly as possible. Meanwhile, the foreign tourists waited and slowly suffocated. Two conveyor belts at the tiny airport's International Arrivals hall were woefully inadequate. But there was worse to come: only one of them worked. As long as I was in Kos I never saw belt B move an inch. It was a bit of an irony that most people seemed to be drawn towards this belt, because it was nearest to the door, and fresh air. Still, if you have ever waited your turn for your luggage to arrive in any airport in the world with anxious fellow travellers ramming trolleys into the back of your legs, you will know how frustrating this wait can be. Kos airport had alleviated this problem by only having eight trolleys. Two of these trolleys were broken. I am not exaggerating when I tell you that you could wait up to three hours for your cases to appear.

Anyway, while all this was taking place, the bus drivers from all companies gathered together for a bus-driverly chat and an exchange of smelly fags. They usually took up residence in front of the Arrivals hall and stood in a circle, laughing raucously under a cloud of smelly cigarette smoke and leering at any passing female. They were obviously comparing roundabout lap times and drinking capacities. This gathering was sacred and was only reluctantly interrupted when angry guests in their confusion tried to board the coaches by way of the driver's door (a common mistake). This brought the drivers running angrily to their trusty steeds. For the driver's seat was a sanctuary upon which no other bottom must perch apart from, maybe, that of his heir. Should you ever find yourself in a similar position to this or any of the other situations described in the preceding pages, then bite your lip, and remember: this is all part of the charm of Greece.

THE JOYS OF LANZAROTE

I GRIPPED THE arm rests and prepared myself for landing. The seatbelt sign had been on now for a couple of minutes, and the cabin staff had finished their preparations and strapped themselves in ready for touch-down. I was remembering a conversation I had had recently with an aircraft technician friend, who had told me that the most vulnerable time for any flight was always take-off and landing. Funny how these conversations always come back into your mind at the most inopportune of times. The cabin had gone quite silent as the nerves kicked in, coupled with the excitement of landing, or maybe all the rest of the passengers knew my mate the aircraft technician as well. Suddenly, and without warning, the sound of the engines changed and the plane lurched sharply upwards into a steep climb. There was an audible collective gasp as we picked up speed. From behind me I heard a scream and a few worried people strained to look out of the windows as we roared upwards and away from our intended destination. I felt giddy with the feeling that my body had just raced away from my stomach at 100 miles an hour. In the circumstances this was the least of my worries, as terror began to take hold and I feared the worst.

I looked forward and saw one of the cabin crew sitting facing me. Sometimes you can look at these people and they have that look of seen-it-all-before nonchalance, or they just carry on talking to each other, oblivious of the fear amongst the passengers, but the scared look in this crew member's eyes did nothing to dispel my own fright or fill me with confidence. By now, many of my fellow passengers aboard this 757 had also begun to fear the worst. Some had started to cry audibly and there was much muttering of either discontent or fear from all around. It seemed like ages – though it can only have been seconds – but the passengers were becoming louder and louder, bordering on panic until the sound of the captain's soothing, apologetic tones filled the cabin.

'Sorry about that, folks, just experienced a bit of crosswind. Nothing to worry about. We will have you all safely on the ground in a couple of minutes. Meanwhile, please keep your seatbelts fastened and your seats in the upright position. Thank you.'

For one awful minute I thought he was going to tell us to enjoy the rest of the flight, but he spared us that one. His reassurance was very welcome and, although some were convinced that there was really nothing to worry about, the suspicious smell that filled my nostrils told me that perhaps some had already been worrying unduly. We did a quick circuit of the island once again, and within twenty minutes we were safely on the ground.

As I walked down the stairs to the tarmac in Lanzarote I considered doing a quick impression of the Pope and kissing the ground. Then I thought that perhaps he only kisses the ground after a poor landing. I considered this for a moment, and then made a mental note never to fly with Italian airline Alitalia. I decided against any show of affection for the tarmac and started to consider my return journey in six months' time to England. I wondered how long it would take me to get back via ferry and car.

Here I was in my new destination, with a new company, at the start of another summer in April 1995, ready for another season serving the great British tourist, who at this moment was searching out a rep to blame for the terrifying landing we had all just experienced. I knew very little about this island, except what I had read in the guide books I had managed to get hold of when I had found out that I would be working here just a couple of weeks earlier. The line that stuck in my mind was one in a guide book that said, 'The best view of the island's capital Arrecife is from the window of an aeroplane as you fly away from the island.' This did nothing to arouse any enthusiasm in me for this new destination, but whatever I found here, it had to beat the alternative of gripping the seat of an aircraft in mortal fear as you plummet towards the earth.

Lanzarote is in the Canary Islands, which lie just off the coast of Africa. It's the fourth largest of seven islands. Suffice to say it's big enough. Sometimes during my stay it seemed to be too big. Too big by far.

The island is volcanic. To truly understand what that means you have to go and see for yourself, but to try to put it into a nutshell, it is brown and barren, with the odd smattering of very hardy green vines, which serve to give us the local wine, El Grifo. It's a good wine. Lanzarote has a few hills in the south of the island that add to the sumptuous brown landscape by sometimes changing colour to black when the sun shines at the right angle. The beaches too are either brown or black, and they can sometimes go a deep shade of brown or dark black when the sun hits them in a certain way. It's all very exciting stuff. To philistines like me, it was all very uninspiring, so much so that sometimes I felt almost retarded as I was unable to see beauty in these landscapes. Many people, however, did find this place exciting and appealing, and made their homes there or returned on holiday year after year. I wouldn't want to anger these lovers of Lanzarote. Suffice to say that it grows on some people but it didn't grow on me.

As I said previously, the guide books gave the island's capital a very poor review, so I decided to go and see it for myself. After a good look around I concluded that the capital, Arrecife, was sad. When I was there it was in dire need of a face-lift. By day it was hard to find a café or bar that was anything like welcoming, busy or even open.

The streets were largely devoid of life. It was as if the locals were afraid to venture out for fear of being seen. Grey streets led on to more grey streets choked with traffic that seemed to be driving around in circles, filling the air with exhaust fumes. It almost seemed as though Arrecife had been built for use in a movie. It was like a fictional town that had had an experimental bomb dropped on it, one of those bombs that kills people and leaves buildings intact. A scene from the 1960s show *The Avengers*, perhaps. There was a big gravestone smack bang in the middle that used to be something called 'The Grand Hotel'. It typified the apathy of the people responsible for allowing Arrecife to be so ugly. The hotel was burned out, completely gutted some time in the early Eighties. It stood alone, gutted, black and sad. Somebody's misplaced dream that begged the slumbering giant soul of its originator to wake up and banish it forever. Maybe this did happen soon. The sooner the better. Maybe when someone got round to doing something with the 'Grand Hotel', it could be the start of a face-lift to make Arrecife worthy of its title – a true capital.

Arrecife, though, was just one small part of Lanzarote, and I had been assured by many people that the rest of the island held many beautiful secrets. So with this in mind, I decided it would be a good idea to venture forth myself and discover the black jewel in the Canary crown, as I had heard it described.

Although I had made up my mind already that the capital was something close to a dump, I hoped the rest of the island would be a great improvement. Surely the thousands of people who come to this island year after year wanted more than forgotten movie sets for Sixties *Avengers* productions? We would see. To be fair, the rest of the island did get a lot better, and there were some really nice places to spend your time. Not many islands could boast a world-famous artist as a favourite son, but Lanzarote can. Cesar Manrique lived and died on the island, and he has left his mark everywhere. Lanzarote should be grateful, for his hard work has left great works of art all over the island. They intrigued many, brought thousands of curious fans to the island and they also had a great novelty value as well. The most obvious legacy of the Cesar Manrique occupation of Lanzarote is the many giant moving wind chimes that you can see adorning many of the island's road junctions and roundabouts. Sadly, poor old Cesar was killed on a road junction not far from his house – he was probably eyeing up the site for his next creation at the time. To anyone who has not yet been to Lanzarote and not seen one of these giant mid-junction Manriques, they are something similar to one of the creations you might find in one of Britain's many giant retail shopping centres up and down the country. The ones where hordes of people gather around to witness the clock strike one, or any other hour for that matter, when the mouse is released or the hammer falls on the chime, or one figure appears to meet another figure.

If you haven't got the picture by now, you will just have to go and see for yourself. I will try to explain so that you will know what you are looking for when you get there. Manriques are giant scaffolds of twisted metal that move in the wind. That in itself is quite a good idea, as there is an awful lot of wind on Lanzarote; it seems to be windy every day. When you arrive on the island you will know when you see your first Manrique. It's a bit of an irony really that poor old Cesar was killed on a junction – I wonder how many tourists have been trying to figure out one of his creations as they are driving by in their hire cars, mindless of the traffic all around them, and mashed up their vehicles in the same way.

It's worth mentioning at this point that the car revolution had definitely hit Lanzarote. It seemed that everyone there drove. The streets seemed to be choked either with cars desperately trying to make their way somewhere or other, or cars that had been parked illegally, because all the legal spaces have been used up, and so serving to block the slow-moving traffic. The type of car that everyone drove says something about the inhabitants of this place as well. For instance, in Ibiza everyone seemed to favour the Clio or a small Renault. In Greece, the Panda was still very popular. In Lanzarote, the favoured car was the giant four-wheeled-drive ego extension favoured by the macho men. Those cars were in abundance everywhere on the island, and for the life of me I couldn't think why. The car revolution hit about the same time as the road-building revolution in Lanzarote, and as a consequence the island sported an excellent system of roads, all well tarmacked and easy to negotiate. If you observed the number of super-duper four-wheel-drive vehicles per head of the population, you might have been forgiven for thinking that you were living on the moon, or some far-flung desert-like destination that was totally inaccessible.

This abundance of cars could make life hell for the

pedestrians. At first sight you would believe that the government of the island had foreseen this problem and thoughtfully installed lots of zebra crossings all over the place. But be warned: in Lanzarote, the zebra was not the same as the zebra at home. Far from stopping at zebras, the traffic seemed to speed up just to get past them. Many an unsuspecting tourist has been seen stepping out tentatively on to the alleged crossing, only to receive a very loud and prolonged hoot of the horn as the traffic continued to roar by. I came to the conclusion that these zebras were either one of two things. They were either a good place for the traffic to invite pedestrians to cross so they could see them more easily and so therefore would be easier to hit, or just a clear space for the pedestrians to see all the traffic before deciding whether or not it was safe to cross. I suspect the latter. What they definitely were not was the zebra crossings that the Brits had come to know.

It seemed that everybody on the island had a car. Apart from me. Well, I had to put that to rights, so off I went to the car hire shop to pick up my vehicle for the next six months. I was given a Ford Fiesta. Although this was very far down on the scale of cars in Lanzarote, to me it was a trusty steed, and I really needed it to get around the island. Part of my job on Lanzarote was to go and check out the excursion venues for the summer. These were the places where we took our guests for theme nights, and we might change the theme from one season to another – so for instance, an old ranch in the country might be the winter venue for a country dancing evening. The summertime might find the same venue offering a Wild West night – it just depended on what kind of clientele came to the island in each season. So off I went into the countryside in the south of the island to a remote little farmhouse to speak to the owners about the forthcoming summer Wild West evening. As the venue was way out in the country, and a little remote, I figured it was best if I drove there. My plan was to take a quick look around, say a few hellos and then come home again to the city. My journey took me right into the centre of the island. Tarmacked roads eventually became dirt tracks. I eventually arrived at a gateway at the end of a leafy driveway. The wooden gate was open and led along to a two-storey house constructed of dark wood and stone. Judging by its charm, and the surroundings of vines and flowers, the house had been here for years. At first glance, it was magical.

I walked up to the heavy wooden door and, just as I was about to knock, the owner pulled the door open and greeted me with a friendly smile. Vicente was a tall man, with a dark complexion and even darker hair. He was six feet tall and looked devilishly handsome in a very Spanish way. He was attired in the traditional uniform of the successful Spanish entrepreneur of the day. An immaculate white silk shirt, completely uncreased (the type of shirt that creases like an old chamois when I wear it), and expensive Armani jeans, rounded off with a hand-made pair of cowboy boots that on him looked anything but naff. His dark eyes were welcoming and warm. He could have almost passed for a typical Spanish matador. Vicente, though, was English. Very English. His real name was Pete and he had come over from

London a couple of years before to find work in the sunshine. He had stumbled across this old farmhouse after making friends with the owner's son, who had bought a bar in Puerto del Carmen and had given Vicente his first job. Vicente had become friendly with the bar owner's mother and was shocked when he learned that she had decided to sell her beautiful farmhouse – which had been a family home for many years – to move to Madrid, as she could no longer afford to work there. Vicente saw endless possibilities for the old house, a guest house or even an old country retreat for the stressed businessmen types from Britain. He persuaded the woman to let him have the farmhouse at a rental price for a year to see if he could make it into a successful business and, if this worked, he would buy it from her. Seemed ideal. In practice though, the retreat idea failed due to the expense, and the health and safety of the venue; it was just very old and too far out. However, it had just begun to take off as an excursion venue for British tour operators. It was far enough out in the country to allow the Brits to party into the early hours without disturbing anybody. They could be as offensive as they liked, and nobody would give a toss. Great idea. He styled the place on a Western theme and dressed as a cowboy to welcome the punters in, employed a couple of barmen and hired a horse rider for the night, played a bit of country music, served beans and sausages, and there you have it: Lanzarote's OK corral. I admired his logic. It was a bit sad to see such a lovely old farmhouse being used for something so different from its original use, but at least it was surviving – for now, anyway.

I got talking to Vicente and we had a few drinks. Before I knew where I was I had been there for three hours and was feeling a bit sozzled by the time it came for me to leave for the long drive back to my home in Puerto del Carmen. I bade my farewells to Vicente and set off into the night towards my car. I did a quick mental check, as you do when you are drunk, and concluded that I was fine to drive home. I have to add at this point that drink driving rules in Spain are the same as those in the UK. In Britain, I would never dream of getting in my car, even after one drink. Here in Lanzarote I felt indestructible. Big mistake. I set off towards town and, thinking I was doing rather well halfway home, I decided to stop for another drink in a bar just outside town. I was delighted to find a couple of friends in the place and joined them for another drink. This was my one for the road. I set off again about an hour later, and this time I decided I would use the back roads home to my house. This involved me going through Lanzarote's red light district. I figured it would be safer. As I drove slowly past the seedy little clubs, I was distracted by the array of prostitutes that seemed to decorate every street corner and bar front. Or was I just seeing double? I can't remember. I was lost in thought looking across the street at one such bar, when I took my eyes off the road for just one second too long. There was a loud bang and I was jolted painfully forward in my seat as the car juddered to a complete stop. Luckily I had the good fortune to have put on my seatbelt before I set off, so I hadn't gone through the windscreen. I can tell you this: forget about black coffee and miracle cures, the best way to sober up is to have an accident. I turned my head to look back towards where I should have been looking to see what I had hit. There, at the front of my bonnet, was a huge four-wheel-drive Land Rover. An ego extension. Right now it was a Fiesta extension. And thankfully, it was empty. I panicked. My first thought was that I had to get out of there.

I slammed the car, which had mercifully refused to stall, into reverse and set off backtracking the way I had arrived. To my horror, the jeep wouldn't let go. Shit. I thought about running away from the scene, but that idea quickly passed, because with the amount of alcohol I had consumed I wasn't sure whether I could still walk, let alone run. I decided to continue to drive backwards, thinking that eventually the jeep would have to detach itself. Fifty yards further down the road the jeep was still stubbornly attached to the front of the car. Then I had a brainwave: I decided to zigzag. Several manoeuvres of careful zigzagging later, the jeep came free.

I quickly turned into the road and sped off into the night. As I write, I still find it hard to believe that I actually did this. It seems that deranged by drink I thought I would be able to get away with it. What a tosser. Somehow that night the car and I made it home, and I retired to my bed for a drunken sleep.

The next morning I woke up without a care in the world. I was a little thirsty, sure, but none the worse for wear. I had no memory of the night before. No memory, that is, until I turned the corner out of my house and into the garage. The car was well and truly mashed. The front bonnet was twisted and broken; both headlights were smashed and the grill was completely missing, revealing the radiator and several other anonymous parts huddled around it. Last night's events came flooding back in a terrible flash.

The night before, as I had grappled with the jeep and my own little car in a forerunner to television's *Robot Wars*, in my twisted drunken logic I had dreamed that I had remained unseen by anybody else. This little wrestling match took place in my own little world. The fact is, several prostitutes and their punters, plus a few passing motorists, all bore witness to this surreal ballet. Some of them had thoughtfully taken my car registration number and reported me to the police. It would have been fitting had they been waiting in the bushes as I walked into the garage that morning. Fortunately, they were not. I had an attack of guilt and immediately phoned the car hire company who, it must be said, were expecting my call. They told me the police wanted to speak to me, that I shouldn't worry about the car and that they would come to tow it away. This was probably very sensible, as I don't think it was quite ready for another round of my driving. The police made me wait in the station for a couple of hours before they interviewed me. I was not arrested, merely cautioned, and told not to drive while drunk again. I insisted that I had not been drinking, but my pleas fell on deaf ears. My boss was not so understanding and she took the car away from me for a month. I put the whole experience down to a lesson for life. I am ashamed of my night on the tiles and I have never taken a drink and driven again. I have also stopped wrestling with jeeps.

*　　*　　*

The saying goes that 'The rain in Spain falls mainly on the plain.' The wind, however, would seem to blow mainly over Lanzarote.

The temperature in Lanzarote during the summertime could reach into the high forties. So you would think that a bit of wind blowing now and again would be quite refreshing, but when it felt like a hairdryer, full in your face, and it contained millions of grains of sand, it could be quite uncomfortable. It did, however, make it easy to dry clothes. It was just that it makes everything you dried outside look like it had been sand-blasted.

There were three main tourist resorts on the island: Playa Blanca in the South, Costa Teguise in the north and Puerto del Carmen smack bang in the middle. Of these three, Puerto, as it was fondly known, was the main tourist area and always the busiest spot on the island. It had one long sea-front road that went on for about a mile. The usual array of souvenir shops adorned the walkways along the beach. All the T-shirts and newspapers came sand-blasted from their front line positions.

Endless British bars punctuated the tacky souvenir shops, with the odd German hostelry thrown in for good measure, and one or two Irish ale houses as well. Car hire companies also adorned the side streets inviting you to join in with the endless traffic queues. Nothing really that remarkable, pretty much the same as you would find in lots of other European destinations for British holidaymakers. However, right in the middle of all these shops, bars and car hire centres was the anti-cultural centre of Lanzarote, the single most popular venue of the whole shooting match. And it's called Centro Carmen.

I'll try to describe it to you and recreate the atmosphere. By day it resembled a medieval dungeon, with open doors. It was on two storeys, underground and overground, a large, almost early Eighties tacky retail park. It had lots of bars and shops tightly packed together. On second thoughts, scrap the shops bit – there was only one, and that was a sex shop. And I can't describe it as I never plucked up enough courage to venture inside. Suffice to say that the windows were all blacked out, with a white stencilled sign saying simply 'SEX SHOP' emblazoned on to the black background. Anyway, the whole area was dark and dingy ... seedy is probably a better description, actually. Loads of cockroaches shared centre stage with discarded used condoms and spent needles with their sleeping users lying beside them. If Lanzarote was like the body of a beautiful woman, a comparison that I have heard made in the past, then Centro Carmen would bid very strongly for the position of arsehole, without much fear of competition. Shit poured out of it from about 7am onwards. Come the night-time, the lights went on and the suppositories poured in. This was the place to be if you were young, free and single in Lanzarote.

The bars pumped up the volume as they bid for the loudest pitch; outside the touts adorned the already busy streets, pushing leaflets into faces, promising free drinks and top-class entertainment. The drug pushers moved in to feed on the young and the party really began. This was hedonistic/nihilistic paradise, Lanzarote style. I frequented this place a few times during my time on the island and, although it could be a wild place, at least it stopped all the trouble pouring out along the streets. The madness was all in one place, and if you didn't like it, you shouldn't have gone. Simple.

If you ever wondered whether you were wearing well in this life, there was a sure-fire acid test to see how well you were doing. If you walked along the streets of Puerto del Carmen without getting touted, then you were past it. If you got a ticket or two thrust into your hand, then it was time to consider the anti-wrinkle cream. If you got ten or more tickets and invites to fantastic clubs, you were still as young and vibrant as you thought you were. It was a major truth test, but it gave you a quick answer. Take it from me, it could make you feel fantastic or precisely the reverse. I dare you to try it some time.

Every rep wanted to work in Puerto del Carmen, mainly because it was near to the action, and as a result of the guests thinking likewise there was a demand for accommodation here for our customers, and so most of our hotels were there. Lanzarote was not an island that was overpopular with youth, but it did get its fair share of youngsters during the summer, and predictably they brought their share of problems with them. It was a fact of life that lads tended to come on holiday in groups of anything from two to twenty-two in size. They all believed that they were going to come on holiday and get loads of shagging in, regardless of whether they were ugly or not. Somehow, they believed that once they had lain in the sunshine for a few hours and gone a bright lobster pink they become irresistibly attractive to women, and that copious amounts of cheap alcohol would give them the gift of the gab that they never had at home. They also believed that they could live with their mates for two weeks in a small Spanish apartment and still get on with them as the dirty linen piled up. The truth could sometimes come as a bit of a shock. Girls – single girls, that is – tended to come on holiday in groups, but usually just in twos. Larger groups were rare. The maths was not difficult to do but, roughly, it meant that there was not always enough of what the lads wanted to go round.

Girls didn't really come on holiday to cop off with the lads from Wigan when they could do that at home, did they? I think it was more likely that they would like to meet a dark Spanish hunk, not cop off with lads from home and suffer from horrendous hangovers that are the revenge for drinking cheap booze. Tell me I am wrong.

Worse still was watching your mate cop off, which could cause you to start to re-evaluate how much this friendship actually meant to you, and could lead to a bit of a falling out. Question: how many groups of lads, or girls for that matter, go on holiday as friends, cook their brains in the sunshine, partake in the local cheap tipple and come back as enemies? Answer: loads of them. It was a sad fact of holiday life that the falling out usually occurred in the middle of the night. Many an evening I lay cooking in my apartment, unable to sleep in the boiling temperatures, and listening to the verbal slanging matches taking place all around. Lads who were lifelong buddies at home now found themselves bound together in a tiny twin-bedded apartment with the dirty socks and smelly pants piling up all around. One of them cops off at the disco and takes his conquest back to her apartment to get to know her better.

Lad number two comes back feeling pissed off to discover his mate has taken the key and locked him out. He can't even get in to the room to engage in a spot of hand relief, and his patience is getting well and truly frayed. He sits outside the apartment for a while, feeling sorry for himself. Eventually his mate returns and greets his long-lost buddy with a manly pat on the back – the bit he couldn't reach on his own with the suntan lotion, and which is now stinging like hell. This only serves to send the anger levels even higher. By now the clock is creeping towards four in the morning.

OK, this is a dreamed-up scenario, but it wasn't far from the truth. One such balmy night, I was beginning to doze and drift off into the twilight world of Dr Sleep's waiting room, when from across the street I heard the sound of two British lads falling out. 'You fuckin' bastard! My mate! I never thought you'd do it to me!' My eyes spring open, and it sounds like the perpetrator of these sentiments is standing at the end of the bed bellowing. 'Fuckin' bastard, let's have it out now, come on, you bastard! I can't believe you'd do it to me, your best mate, fuckin' bastard!' These words were usually delivered in either a broad Cockney accent or a very gutteral Mancunian brogue. The only thing that is certain is that they are the unmistakable words of an Englishman. I lie there listening to the unfolding drama, and think to myself, *Why don't you just get on with it and beat each other up, and put the whole block out of its misery?* It can, however, go on for hours. If any other occupant should dare to try to intervene in this public row and shout over to the warring lads to 'Shut the fuck up' – as one wants to do sometimes in these situations – that person can then himself become the target of the lads' derision. The rows could sometimes go on for hours and, as the heat of summer rises, so did the instances of this curious brand of midsummer madness, which seemed only to affect the Brits.

It's worth mentioning that, in all my time in foreign climes, these scraps were only ever staged by the British public. I never heard a stand-up row in any other language in the middle of the night. I could never honestly say that Germans or Italians or the Dutch don't have similar barneys, but I can say that I never heard the word *schweinhund* bellowed out in the middle of the night. Mind you, the reason for this was probably because they were all down putting towels on sun beds at the time. At these times, your rep conscience pricks away at you and you think, *Should I get involved in this?* Reps are never trained in how to get involved in punch-ups or verbal slanging matches. Most of us believed in self-preservation, and you tried not to get involved in violent situations until they confronted you head on and you had no choice.

Such was the case one summer's evening when I walked into a hotel in Lanzarote to be seized by a very excited receptionist who begged me to go to room 225, where he believed a murder was in progress. I was almost paralysed with fear myself, but I had to go, even if it was just to discover what was actually really happening in there. If there really was a murder taking place, I didn't want to be the next victim. I asked Paco the maintenance man to accompany me to the room. He refused. I begged. He refused. I pleaded. He refused. I offered money. He still refused. I decided to go for the manager. Valuable time was ticking away, and who knew what was happening now in room 225?

I found Pedro the manager sitting in his office. I explained my problem; he summoned three of his gardeners and a barman, and off we all went to room 225. Pedro was a big man, about six feet three inches, with a rather rotund girth. His size was such that he commanded authority. And his gardeners and barman were even bigger. I was wasting away in the Spanish heat of the summer. As I was about ten stones in weight and standing a measly five feet ten inches tall, they towered above me. And still they insisted I lead the way. This I did. Like David leading Goliath and his close family friends into battle, off we went to room 225.

By the time we reached the second floor, a small crowd had begun to gather outside the room. They parted all too readily to allow me to get to the door. I had already ascertained that the people in the room were a Mr and Mrs Kahn – my guests, who had arrived the day before. I stretched to my full height and knocked once on the door. From inside I could hear a shout of 'Bitch,' followed by a loud slap, and then a scream. 'Get back you slut'. Another louder slap, followed by a sob, another scream, and a cry of 'Help!' We all winced collectively, and I knocked again. The door opened slightly. Mr Kahn poked his head through the opening, smiled at me politely and said, 'Hello, can I help you?' in a very controlled, well-spoken manner, as if he was completely unaware of the row we had just heard behind him.

'Yes, Mr Kahn,' I gulped. 'I'm Cy, your rep here in the hotel. Welcome to the island and can I talk to your wife please?' At that moment her head appeared from between his legs. Her face was bloody and bruised, and she was pleading with us to help her. She was a pitiful sight.

'Help me,' she cried, whereupon her husband cleverly back-heeled her under the chin and she disappeared in a heap out of sight. He looked at me, said, 'Excuse me, my wife is drunk, I have to go. Goodnight,' and shut the door. I looked behind me towards Pedro, his henchmen and the group of onlookers now gathered around at a safe distance who, in spite of their concern, were all reluctant to help me.

'It's been going on all day,' one of the neighbours helpfully informed me.

'You'll have to go in,' said Pedro.

I had to agree, but just how was I going to 'go in' exactly? It's at times like this when you need the SAS, but where are they when you want them?

I decided to knock again, this time with a little more force. Slap. 'Bitch, I'll kill you!' Bang. 'Ahhh …' Slap, 'What do you mean no more, I'll give you no more!' Slap. Slap. Sob. Sob.

I knocked again twice, and very loudly this time. I had to get in there. He opened the door again slightly, and I decided

I had to really go for it. I put my foot in the gap he had created and insisted, 'Mr Kahn, I really must speak with your wife, I'm worried about her.'

'No, she's all right, I will take care of her.' Mr Kahn was a big man himself – it seemed that the world was full of big men on this day – but he didn't resist my efforts as I pushed the door in on him and finally gained entry. His wife, a big woman – the world's full of them too – promptly threw herself at me and grabbed hold of my head, screaming, 'Help me, he's going to kill me!' She held on tightly to my head, squashing me between her head and breasts. I managed to release myself and coax her to sit down on one end of the bed.

All was quiet now. Mr Kahn took up a position at the other end of the bed and lit up a cigarette. He took a long drag while he inspected his bruised knuckles. Then he looked towards me and said, 'She started it.' I looked behind me at the faces peering in through the open door. The manager and his entourage, seeing that I had not been beaten to death, suddenly became very brave and strode into the room looking big and fearless. There was nothing to fear. Mr Kahn's anger and violence were all reserved for his wife; he was a coward. They argued like children while I stood between them. The manager decided he would have to separate them for the night, on the understanding that the next day we would try to get the lady a flight home to the UK, which she so desperately wanted.

She was battered, bloody and bruised, and she made a pitiful sight. I was worried for her safety and I stayed with her for most of the night in a secret room far from her violent husband. She cried bitterly and we nursed her wounds. I left vowing to come back early in the morning to arrange a flight back to the UK for her safety. The next morning I raced to the hotel ready to do the right thing. I met Mr and Mrs Kahn in the hotel reception. Arm in arm. 'Cy, we won't be needing that flight home after all. Thanks anyway.' I was flabber-gasted. Human nature is a funny old thing.

*   *   *

Sometimes when you were doing this job, and the sun was shining and everyone was enjoying themselves, and you have managed to get over the initial shock of being in a new environment, you had to pinch yourself just so you could remind yourself that this was work. I grew up thinking that work was a necessary evil, something that had to be done to put food on the table and pay the rent man. My dad toiled away on a building site most of his life, and he never ever came home and discussed with us whether his work gave him spiritual fulfilment or whether it satisfied his creative needs. We were only concerned with whether we would have enough to eat until the family allowance came on Tuesdays, by which time the Thursday wages would have been eaten. Whether you enjoyed work or not was completely immaterial, you just had to do it.

My father used to say that man was born to work, and I came to grow up with that same belief. I always felt a sense of disbelief and a little guilt as I left my apartment and walked down the hill towards the beach in the beautiful sunshine. All around me people were having their holidays and enjoying themselves. And I was the man who helped them to enjoy themselves. I got plenty of chances to enjoy the sunshine and the scenery. Girls would fall over themselves to give you their undivided attention. I was a celebrity in the resort; in most bars I went into I was given free drinks and treated like a VIP. And – this is the best bit – I was getting paid for it. I used to wake up and think, *It doesn't get any better than this*. Some days were packed with incidents, and could be very tiring, but it was a small price to pay to live and work in such an environment.

When you went home at the end of another season, your friends were in awe of you. They wanted to know what it was really like. Was it really that good? You tried not to gloat … but not that hard. So many people wanted to do this job, but could simply never pluck up the courage to take the plunge. They wanted to talk to you about it – which was fine for a while, but eventually you got bored and tried to fob them off. 'Come and see sometime for yourself, you can stay with me if you like for a week or two' was the standard phrase I generally used to close the conversation. Many said they would and you know they never would, but occasionally you got a phone call and it was your long-lost second cousin twice removed taking you up on your offer.

'Hi, Cy, it's Paul here, you remember we had that chat at Christmas two years ago?' You think, *Shit, who on earth is Paul?*

'Of course I do! How are you?'

'Good news, buddy, I'm fine. And guess what?'

I shudder. 'What? Go on surprise me.'

'Me and my mate Mike are coming out to see you next week!'

My heart sinks. 'Great, can't wait to see you. Where are you staying?'

'That's even better news … we are staying with you!'

Shit. 'Oh fantastic.'

'I knew you'd be pleased! Pick us up at the airport next Tuesday. We are going to have a great time! See you then!'

Such was the course of one conversation that I had while working in Lanzarote. Don't get me wrong, it's great to see friends and family. The thing is, they forget you are not in the resort to have a six-month holiday but to work, and inevitably where they want to stay during their annual vacation is your pad, your retreat. It's a bit like working in London and having to go out every lunchtime with people you hardly know and eat and drink with them, and then go and see them again every night for two weeks, guide them round by the hand because they don't speak the language and show them the sights as well. On top of all this you have to take them home every night and let them – and their mate, whom you do not know at all, and like even less – sleep on your settee. Believe me, it can try your patience.

Tuesday morning, as promised, Paul and his mate Mike were waiting for me at the airport. Amid the throng of arrivals in Arrecife airport I didn't recognise them at first. After a while I thought that perhaps they had missed the flight and were not coming after all. That would be really

CONFESSIONS OF A HOLIDAY REP

good. I was doing my usual airport duties and was quite caught up in the mêlée of a busy day when I felt a tap on my shoulder. And there was Paul. Pale, smiling and looking very excited. I hardly remembered him at all. He is one of these cousins you only see every now and again at the odd Christmas, a funeral or a wedding. Usually trying to shag another of your cousins or having a deep conversation with an elderly member of the family. He grabbed hold of me and gave me a big hug. It was as though we were lifelong confidants reunited after a long break. I tried to reciprocate his enthusiasm. He was positively bursting to get to the pub, then the beach and then get down to some serious shagging. He introduced me to Mike, whom I didn't remember at all, though I feigned recognition.

After the duties had finished some two hours later, Paul, Mike and I were crammed into my Panda with their three suitcases and collection of duty free goodies – the usual four hundred cigarettes, a couple of bottles of booze and a number of hold-alls – and off we went towards my apartment in Puerto del Carmen.

The boys looked a little disappointed as I showed them around my little two-roomed studio flat, and explained to them that they would have to sleep on the floor in the front room-cum-kitchen in their sleeping bags. I explained to them both that this was my home and I was not on holiday there, that I lived there and tried to keep it clean and tidy so I could relax when I was not on duty. I also explained that I probably wouldn't be able to spend every night with them, but that I would try to get some time to go and have a drink with them now and again. They nodded in complete understanding and sympathy, thanked me for letting them stay and promised that I wouldn't even know they were there. A good start. The first night I decided I would show them around Puerto del Carmen, just to get them started, so they wouldn't have to waste time searching out the best places to go.

It all went so well at first. We had a good evening, and I left them at around midnight so they could explore the clubs alone, while I returned home, and emptied my pockets of the hundred or so cards for free drinks and invites to groovy clubs that I had picked up along the way, and turned in for the night to be ready for another early start the next day.

They seemed so happy as they strode off into the moonlight in the direction of Centro Carmen. Earlier in the day I had gently tried to lay down some ground rules for their stay at my home. I kept it simple and tried to understand that they were on holiday and wanted to have a good time. I asked them to come in quietly and try not to wake me or the neighbours, as I lived in a residential area. If they did pull a member of the opposite sex, I asked them to try to go somewhere else if possible, but if there was no choice, then I pleaded with them to try to be as discreet as possible when letting them in and out. Finally I asked them not to shag any of the reps, as I really didn't want them back at my place.

I thought this would be simple enough, and they both seemed like nice, sincere fellows, so I thought that maybe it would all go quite well after all. I had quite a good feeling about it as I dropped off to sleep that night. I had given Paul my spare set of keys so they would have no trouble letting themselves back in at whatever time they arrived home. Maybe I was going to enjoy getting to know my cousin Paul again after all. Sleep came quickly and peacefully.

I awoke from sleep at the normal time, around 8.30am, and made my way to the bathroom. I got myself ready for work and made breakfast. Then I remembered the lads. Where were they? I looked around the room and there was no sign of them. *No worries,* I thought, *they must have copped off and gone home to some other bed.* I locked the apartment and went off to work as normal.

I returned home that evening to find that the apartment was still untouched. The lads had not been back all day. I tried to remember what they had been wearing the night before. I thought it had been long trousers, possibly jeans, and short-sleeved shirts. In the Lanzarote sunshine this would have been too much attire to lie on the beach in all day. By now I was getting a little worried. I couldn't remember whether Paul had a phone. Part of me was saying, *Forget them they're on holiday and they're grown men,* while another part of me was thinking, *What if something's happened to them?* As time wore on to 9pm, I was so worried that I decided to open another beer and watch the television.

About 10.30pm there was a knock on the door. I opened it to be confronted by two fully uniformed members of the Guardia Civil – the Spanish police. I always tried to remain on good terms with the law whatever country I was living in, but I guessed these guys were not here to share a beer with me and have a chat.

'Señor Flood, boss of holiday company?'

Not entirely truthful, but I nodded, not wanting to complicate things.

'Your family he in prison. Tomorrow go to court in Arrecife, 9 o'clock, you can talk to him at 8.30.'

I gabbled in Spanish to him as best I could and tried to find out what Paul had done, but the policeman would not tell me. I was shocked. In all my time in this job my dealings with the local police had been very good, and although they could sometimes be a little heavy-handed with the Brits (that is, in comparison to our own police force, who have to administer law and order with their hands tied firmly behind their backs), I had never known them to go to all the trouble of taking someone to court. It's all just too much paperwork for them. Unless, that is, it was very serious.

I left the house, and made for the police station, only to be told that I couldn't see Paul or Mike until they had been to court in the morning. I was getting really worried now, and thinking how I was going to explain this one to the family, except that I had no idea yet what it was that I would have to explain.

I was at the court by 8am. I registered my interest, explained I wanted to speak with my cousin and was directed to a chair in the main hallway and told to wait my turn. By this time I was very anxious indeed. By 10am, with no sign of any cousin yet, I was becoming frantic. I caught sight of the policeman who was at my house the night before; he nodded in recognition, but when I asked what was happening he waved me away and told me that he would talk to me soon. By 12.30 I was getting pissed off. I was going to go and confront the girl at the desk for the umpteenth time, when first Mike and then Paul appeared in the doorway of the court building, still dressed in the clothes they had put on for a night on the town two days ago, except for the fact that the shirts were now a little dirty and dishevelled. I was ushered into a side room and allowed to sit down with the two boys. They looked very sheepish and tired.

As they told their story I began to feel like a priest at the last confession of two condemned men. It turned out that after I had left them everything had gone well initially. They were having a great night out; they were chatting to the girls and they touted to some of the good nightclubs, and were generally enjoying the fare on offer. Several hours and a few more glasses of beer later, they decided to head for home. By now the relaxed holiday atmosphere was taking hold of them, and they decided they would like to go for a swim. Being sensible lads they realised that it would be dangerous to go into the sea, and they couldn't find it anyway. Then they spied a pool just a short hop over a wall on the way to my apartment. They bounded the wall, stripped off and jumped in. A good thirty minutes of frivolities followed, after which the lads decided they had now had enough and decided to get out, get dressed and resume their drunken journey home. Just before they left however, at 5.30am, they decided they needed to relieve themselves. One of them –

they weren't quite decided who at this point – thought it would be a good idea to top the pool up with a little wee wee. Another thought was, Why not go the full hog and have a jobby? At this point, two of Juan Carlos's finest had driven by, noticed the commotion in this private pool and thoughtfully shone their car headlights on to the area to help the lads get a better aim.

The boys did their business and decided to leave. The local constabulary, no doubt bored by a relatively quiet evening in the area, decided to call up their mates to witness these two young examples of British youth leaving the premises – premises that, it turned out, belonged to the chief of police – having left their calling cards behind. Realising that this would be a good opportunity to get in some much-needed truncheon-wielding practice, the police decided to apprehend the lads. You could say that a struggle ensued, but the only struggle that I can imagine was the struggle by the police to make sure that the blows landed did not hit Paul or Mike anywhere that could be seen in the court room. In short they got a bloody good hiding, and you might say deservedly so. Can't help thinking that in England they would have got community service, like cleaning pools for a week or something. Both the lads were a little tearful following a couple of days in a Spanish cell. As is so often the case after a bit of Spanish justice, they were considering a visit to the court of human rights, and all sorts of other appeals, but this quickly passed from their minds as the magistrate fined them a couple of hundred pounds each and sent them on their way. I have never seen two lads more glad to see freedom than Paul and Mike. This was their first trip to Lanzarote and probably their last.

The rest of their holiday was taken in more of a subdued mood, but they still managed to party on. There was one terribly late night when the lads returned to the apartment at around 4am, and proceeded to vomit loudly until the early hours of the next day. They also discovered that Spanish television was a little more broad-minded in its attitude to adverts than its British equivalent, and one day they sat in for the whole afternoon just to catch a glimpse of a certain sales pitch for floor cleaner.

As you can imagine, I ran out of patience with them by about the third day. They also managed to lose my spare set of keys for the apartment and they burned my saucepans while trying to do beans on toast. Apparently just as the beans reached boiling point, the TV advert for floor cleaner came on the telly, and they were distracted.

By now, they realised I was fed up with them, and so before they left they decided to clean the flat. This was a nice gesture, but predictably it all went wrong. They cleaned the windows with newspaper, which merely served to transfer the print on to the glass, and they swept the floor with a brush, which merely served to redeploy large amounts of sand to different parts of the apartment. The place looked like 'Cell Block H' when they were finished. I was quite happy to see the back of them. It's always good to see family and friends, but it's always nice to see them go as well. Come to think of it, it's just the same as being at home really.

CY FLOOD

My Lanzarote season eventually rolled to an end. They say
that things are always better when you look back at them.
That's what they say. I reserve judgement.

TEAM
TENERIFE

THE FIRST HOLIDAYMAKERS to discover the subtropical delights of the Canaries probably went to enjoy the bracing Atlantic breeze that sweeps the northern coasts of Tenerife and Gran Canaria and to walk amongst the vegetation and forests. Tourism, such as it was in the twenties and thirties was for the stout-hearted, adventurous and strong-minded only. Clad in stout gear and sturdy walking boots, the pioneers of the tourist industry, who would arrive in boats, steam ships and clippers, would never have imagined taking their clothes off in public or enjoying more than one or two glasses of the powerful local wine. I wondered what they would make of it all nowadays with the hordes of drunken youths vomiting in the street, shagging like rabbits and sleeping on the streets unable to navigate their way back to their hotels: a far cry from the idyllic past of curious travellers discovering a new world.

Until 1977, the Canary Islands main airport was the tiny

former military landing strip in Los Rodeos, tucked away in the clouds above Santa Cruz de Tenerife, the island's capital. Even in the height of summer, dangerous mists would surround the runway in minutes making take-off and landing a hit and miss affair. Los Rodeos was a bottleneck to the expansion of tourism in Tenerife. There had been plans on the drawing board for years to build a new airport in the south of the island where most of the tourists were headed, but they were continually shelved due to lack of funds. It took the world's worst air disaster to turn Tenerife into one of the most popular tourist destinations for British holidaymakers.

On the evening of 27 March 1977 a terrorist threat from a little-known independence organisation had shut down Gando airport, the neighbouring island of Gran Canaria, and as a consequence two jumbo jets, one Dutch and one American, had been diverted to Tenerife's Los Rodeos airport for the night. The next morning, with mist still hanging over the airport, the two giant aircrafts crashed into each other as one attempted to take-off and the other taxied onto the runway. Over 577 passengers and crew died in the initial and horrific crash in what has become known as the worst ever aviation disaster in history.

Following this terrible event, the Reina Sofia airport, big enough and long enough even to accommodate Concorde, was built and ready for operation in record time. Fog free and close to the main resorts of Playa de Las Americas and Los Cristianos, the modern airport, opened by the queen of Spain, provided the gateway to the sun for millions of

British holidaymakers in search of thrills and adventure on a grand scale.

I arrived in Tenerife on a wide-bodied jet, surrounded by wide-bodied people. Company employees are flown to and from their destinations on company jets along with company guests, plane loads of tourists and the occasional travelling rep. The crew members know who you are but the punters should never find out. I watched with some satisfaction as the plane filled up with tattooed blobs of lard heading for meltdown, as they tried to stuff their cooler boxes packed with sausages, bacon and other ingredients – pivotal in making the great British breakfast – into the overhead lockers. They would be the ones staying in budget accommodation I surmised, and would only be on half-board; hence they would need breakfast three times a week.

After failing to lodge his over-packed, egg-shell blue coolbox into the overhead compartment, a large sweating man flopped down in the seat beside me. He promptly fell asleep and only woke up as we passed Mount Teide, the spectacular dormant volcano which dominates Tenerife.

A roar of beery gases erupted from his inner regions as he leaned across me to stare out of the window.

'Where you staying?' he enquired.

'Well I don't know yet. I'm here to work, so I go where they put me I suppose.' I blurted out, in an unguarded moment.

'What? You're a rep? You work on the island for this company?'

'Yes,' I replied confidently.

With that he spun round like a snapped spring and bellowed down the aisle.

'Here Kylie, you remember last year we could never find a rep. Well I've got one here, captured.'

Until the plane drew up to the landing apron some 90 minutes later, I was subjected to a torrid tale of abuse, complaints about toilets, sunburn, stomach problems, drunken vomit, expensive outings and giant cockroaches. Why on earth he and his family had decided to come back to the island for more defied logic. Why I had decided to come to this paradise was also troubling me, as I disembarked the aircraft and ran for cover.

Soon after my arrival, I was invited out for a drink with some of the new team I was going to be working with. We went to a popular bar in Playa de Las Americas that was frequented by holidaymakers and 'workers' (people like me who come to the island to make a living).

At 12.30 by Las Americas standards the night was still young and the town reasonably quiet, but in a few hours it would be full of energised youth. For now, though, it was just a steady buzz of curious drinkers.

Our group decided it would be a good time to visit one of our 'money bars', one of the places that 'looked after' the teams of reps in return for us taking our guests to their bars during our twice weekly bar crawls. This particular 'money bar' was rumoured to be a great spot and we were always assured of a warm welcome. Well, that's what we thought.

As I turned into the bar, I caught sight of my friend and

colleague Mark running towards me pushing tables and chairs out of the way in a curious Olympic-like dash for the street. He had a terrified look on his face. I half smiled in recognition, a little confused by his apparent state of emergency. When I saw a man, who I later discovered was the owner of the bar, in hot pursuit wielding a baseball bat decorated with jagged nails and screaming obscenities (well, I guessed they were obscenities by the ferocity and fervour of the multilingual delivery. I might just have made out the word 'cunt', but I couldn't be sure), I guessed that there had been some kind of dispute. I stepped aside on this occasion and watched Mark disappear into the night whilst the owner quickly ran out of steam and turned around, looked at us, smiled warmly and then welcomed us to his bar.

'Welcome to Tenerife,' he bellowed, 'this will be the greatest season yet!' It was a good start at least. I was left to ponder his words, as I gazed up to the stars, checking for low flying insects.

In Tenerife, cockroaches fly low and slow. Cockroaches are a large brown African species that arrived some considerable time ago on the seven lumps of lava that make up the Canary Islands. They were among the first living things to make it across this stretch of the Atlantic that separates this idyllic archipelago from the Sahara desert. Many more travellers would follow in time.

Contrary to popular myth, cockroaches do not exclusively reside under the beds in hotel rooms. Their tastes are far more proletarian. The popular holiday resort of Playa De Las Americas on Tenerife's southernmost tip was infested with cockroaches and the ones that knew the area frequent Las Veronicas, a dilapidated eyesore made up of three interconnected blocks of bars and discos. Las Veronicas sat at the end of the T-junction that funnelled young tourists towards this mecca of tackiness and debauchery. They lay some thirty feet below, where the road turned left or right. The cockroaches lived in the crevices in the retaining wall, in the drains and in the culverts that overlooked the palm-fringed zone. During the day the cockroaches feasted on discarded fried chicken, the contents of hamburgers, pizzas and the solid bits of vomit that ended up being deposited on their domain. Such was their appetite that the unfortunate few got crushed by passing flip-flops. But come sundown, the contented cockroaches took to the air for some clever formation flying. With the street lamps to guide them they launched themselves from their vantage points towards the succulent feeding grounds of Las Veronicas. Cockroaches are not renowned for their flying prowess; their eyesight also leaves much to be desired. Hence they often failed to notice the hordes of holidaymakers that thronged these badlands.

When a cockroach hit a hairdo or lumbered into a bosom crammed into a shocking pink Lycra top, the effect was dramatic. The first indication of such a collision was a screech, followed by a total collapse of the target and the flight in all directions of the victim's companions. After a good deal of close body searching, the cockroach was normally located and despatched, but the drama was not over.

'I'm dead, I'm dead, where is it? It's gonna kill me, I've probably got fuckin' AIDS now! Do something!'

'Sharon, look, it was only a cockroach and I've squashed it. You'll be fine. Do you want to go back to the hotel?' I would reply, desperately trying to suppress a growing need to bellow with laughter.

'Get lost, Cy, you useless bloody rep, and stop fuckin' laughin' at me.'

Trying to help Sharon get back up on to her multi-coloured platforms was like trying to right a capsized giraffe. There was very little to decently hold on to and she did go up an awful long way. Her friends surrounded us like jackals, close enough to find out what was going on but still very clearly out of harm's way.

'What do you mean it was only a fuckin' cockroach? It's your fault, I want my money back,' she wailed.

'You ain't heard the last of this,' threatened Sharon's new boyfriend, whom she had met the night before.

'Well, I'm very sorry, but I must point out that if we don't hurry up and get to Bonkers, you won't get the free voddy and Red Bull slammers down your neck.'

The thought of more alcohol had the desired calming influence. Sharon was put back up the right way and on we marched – all fifty of us. I went ahead as usual, looking up at the stars and looking out for low-flying insects. Cockroaches on the bar crawls really became a regular part of the daily spectrum of this new destination – Tenerife.

I spent the best part of two years of the nineties in Tenerife, working for a tour operator that specialised in the youth market, and I found it to be a place of great extremes and excess. It could be extremely beautiful or extremely ugly and many people live life to its full there, indulging in every excess, including drugs. During my time in Tenerife, illicit substances became more and more a regular part of the lifestyle, so much so that you almost became blasé about their presence.

The fact that there were drugs around wasn't surprising; it was who was taking them that I found a little worrying. Nayim, who had become my friend during my time on the island, had told me he was a reformed character and that he'd given up the dreaded cocaine a couple of years before after blowing – or rather, inhaling – close to £100,000 on his addiction. However, Nayim, like most of the bar owners of Las Americas, lived a crazy and demanding lifestyle. Pretty much twenty-four hours of every day was taken up by cleaning their bars by day and by doing some form of accounts and working in them by night, and consequently into the early hours of the morning. He kept law and order with his own personal policeman: his baseball bat. This was used more as a deterrent than as a tool. I can only say I never saw it brandished in anger, but apparently some of my colleagues told legendary tales of being pursued by an angry Nayim, with bat in hand.

The bar owners would be directing their touts to hassle and lead the beautiful youth, with their pockets full of money, into their bars. Just to stay awake to meet these challenges takes a superhuman effort, so I guess that occasionally some form of chemical assistance was sought. Competition was fierce in this area. Bars were stacked closely together and the price of failure was high, so they fought with each other for the passing trade. A live band, attractive and scantily clad bar staff, and a seemingly endless supply of pushers selling Es and cocaine could usually guarantee a healthy patronage that kept the money flowing over the bar and into the pocket of the owners. Owners like Nayim.

Nayim was fab. On paper he was a model of Spanish entrepreneurial success. He owned two thriving bars that served as the main aperitif before the revellers moved on to the famous Tenerife all-night clubs. Clubs like Billy's, which Nayim also owned, a real honeypot for the youth on holiday. Well-known dens of vice and iniquity that the Brits loved in particular. He sent his children to private school; his wife lived in a suitably grand house in the hills away from Las Americas. He owned a beautiful new Jaguar car that he seldom drove due to the fact that he spent most of his life either working or sobering up. He dripped gold jewellery and he always wore the finest of clothes with designer labels well displayed. And he could be extremely charming.

Spain should probably be very proud of his achievements and his eye for opportunity. Spain probably *would* have been very proud of him and many of his fellow bar owners in the area, except for the fact that he, like most of his colleagues, was Lebanese. The pride of the Lebanon resided and thrived in the South of Tenerife. Nayims, Jamils and Yassers outflanked the Joses, Domingos and Pedros of this world. I'd love to tell you why, but there simply doesn't seem to be one reason you can put your finger on, apart from hard work and charm.

While Spanish bar owners stood by bitter, envious and alone in their deserted bars watching hordes of Brits heading for the Lebanese-owned havens, the Nayims and Yassers turned on the charm. They employed beautiful people in their bars and, as their touts were out working on the streets, they would take a line of cocaine, sit back and admire the fair, while counting their money.

Competition for the tourists was fierce in Las Americas. As well as the Lebanese and the Spanish vying for the custom of young Brits and Germans, close on their tails were the hopeful bar owners from the UK, Ecuadorians and all other manner of wannabes from South America and Europe. For the moment, it seemed like the Lebanese had it all sewn up. I think that, back then, Tenerife attracted about three million tourists every year. They all had money to spend and everybody who owned a shop, bar or any other moneymaking venture – and there were thousands of them – wanted that money. One particularly large shadow loomed across Tenerife, that of some of the richest men in the world, known as the Tenerife mafia. Their influence was felt everywhere, and there was no doubt at all that they had a positive influence on the island. Timeshare and several of the most popular American-style eateries were the clearest evidence of their influence. They had not yet decided to branch out into the world of small, tacky bars full of mainly British youths in search of sex, booze and drugs. Maybe that's because they had been too busy trying to fend off the attentions of the Spanish judicial system, but when they had managed to convey their message to the Spanish government – 'fuck off' – they may have found the time to turn to new business ventures.

Well, I hope I've set the scene of what life can be like in Tenerife – or, to be more precise, in Las Americas. Corruption, drugs, vice and every other evil under the sun. The perfect playground for British youth during the summertime.

I first arrived in Tenerife in December 1996. I had two years managing the youth programme there and it was an experience I'll always remember. If you had come to Tenerife any time between May and late September, there would have been a good chance that you'd have travelled to the island on a charter plane that was ninety per cent full of British youth. They were loud, abusive, overbearing, quite wealthy, drunk and extremely vulnerable to shark-like sales people. They found courage and strength in groups and usually those groups are one of single sex – with the intention of meeting the opposite sex and shagging them. The meek, shy rep, content to give the best possible customer service to the bulk of our clients, would fail miserably with these people. To be successful, you needed a team of people who could stay sober longer than their guests, not be intimidated by their brash behaviour and be strong enough to relieve them of their money in exchange for trips that usually ended up in bars, and clubs ... where they may well have gone anyway.

If we were going to be successful during my stewardship,

we'd need a team of five or six of these people. A tall order, but I got them. The fact that these six reps were at large, in my opinion, was a bit of a wonder in itself. Each and every one had different devious qualities that could be found in boundless supply in many of her majesty's prisons in the UK. (It's quite ironic to think that one of the team, who has since left that company, has become a prison officer. I didn't think that this was the side of the fence that his qualities would be most appropriate for.) Together there was a kind of secret brotherhood between them, but outwardly, they played the part of despising each other. They trusted absolutely nobody and they were all hardened drinkers. They were also determined sellers and party animals with a capital 'F' ('fucking party animals'). This was the kind of team that would milk the South dry in summer and help the company profits to soar at the same time. They were known as the Tenerife 'Death Squad'.

First there was Dom. He was an arrogant twenty-eight-year-old, six-foot-tall, hardened boozer, who seldom rested his head on a pillow before seven in the morning, unless there was a damsel waiting to be deflowered, of course. He was, at most times, thoroughly rude and abusive. He had two stock phrases: 'I'm not fuckin' doing that!' and 'Here's twenty-five coins, go and talk to someone who gives a fuck!' Translated: make a phone call.

I sometimes look back and wonder how I managed to work with him for six months. Several times I considered making enquiries about hiring a hitman to visit him, even if just for a knee-capping. It probably would have been a waste of time anyway, as I suspect Dom would have sold him some excursions instead and sent him back to me. Dom was an unbelievable salesman. He was an expert at getting groups of young lads and girls to part with their money in return for pub crawls and the like.

He would pull himself out of bed at about 10.30am, race to his hotel, start his welcome meeting at 11am and, after helping himself to a pint of cider, he would then proceed to sell his socks off. He sold like hot cakes. When it came to guiding excursions, he was a master at crowd control. He used to stand back and watch what was happening and bark a few orders at his colleagues, who all hated him, and manage to diffuse any trouble before it began.

I hated him too, but I had a sneaky admiration for his unbelievable stamina. I remember one particular occasion, I checked to see if Dom was on duty one hour after he should have started – predictably he wasn't. I challenged him about this later on in the day. He didn't deny his absence; apparently he had pulled one of his colleagues.

'Where were you this morning?' I asked.

'Well, I was up to my elbows in that bird, so I couldn't make it.'

I hated him, but you had to admire his honesty.

Then there was Mack, who at most times was Dom's best friend. I am sure that was the only reason he stayed the summer. He told so many lies, I think he started to believe them himself. When the reps sold excursions, they took money from the guests, which they then had to pay to their supervisor once a week. Such was the forgetful (to understand the true meaning of this, see 'dishonest' in the dictionary) nature of Mack, who kept losing his money with such alarming regularity that his cash had to be collected on a daily basis. In spite of my best efforts, Mack kept on failing to account for all his monies collected and, by the end of the season, he was some £5,000 in the company's debt. This resulted in the termination of his contract. I could say that it was the end of a promising career, but I would be lying ... funny how these things are catching, eh?

Then there was Tina. She was everything that has caused comedians to slate blondes for years. She was thick, dizzy and very sexy ... but she had dark hair. Well, she had a token dyed blonde fringe. And massive tits. She spent the season learning her trade from the master, Dom. Tina used her sex to sell her share of excursions. She must have endured hundreds of cries of 'Get your tits out for the lads.' I witnessed said tits out and about on several different occasions as she secured yet more money from groups of youths looking for fun. I reckon quite a few groups of girls who stayed with us that year hated Tina for her brash, up-front personality and buxom appearance. She was all hair, teeth, tits and suntan and she knew how to use it all to get her what she wanted. I know her sales were fabulous. I'm sure her sexual conquest score was equally fab as well.

Next there was Paula, the Scouser. Paula was the total opposite of Tina. Her broad accent gave away her origins immediately. Her solid, stocky frame gave one the impression that she was not to be messed with and, whereas Tina had most of the male audience drooling over her, Paula frightened the life out of her male guests. If she wanted a shag, however, she went and got it. She hounded her quarry until they were too fed up or too pissed and gave in. Paula once showed up for a meeting dressed in a cloth that was supposed to be a sexy little skirt. Dom took one look at it and quipped, 'Is that supposed to be a designer label on that skirt, Paula ... "King Edwards?"'

It took Paula about thirty seconds to realise that Dom was comparing her to a sack of potatoes. Having twigged, she replied, 'Fuck off coke head!'

Yes, there was a fondness between them all that was unrivalled.

Biggsy was the fifth member of our troupe and was a former member of the Army. He reckoned it was harder being a youth rep than being a soldier, as the night exercises were more demanding: an eight-bar pub-crawl, shots in every port of call, singing and shouting solidly for four hours. This followed by persuading two or more 'birds' into his bed for some sexual Olympics, Biggsy-style, before snatching an hour or so sleep and then racing back to work to start all over again, outstripped anything that Saddam could muster up.

Since Biggsy had left the Army he'd let himself go. Maybe I'm understating the case ... he'd taken a run and a jump and hurled himself headlong off a precipice into the world of weight gain and hair loss and all the anxieties it brings with it. When he joined the company he was a trim eleven stones and five feet ten inches of human fitness, a tribute to the training skills of Her Majesty's armed forces. Now, in 1997, he was sporting a huge beer gut that topped off his eighteen-stone bulk. But for some reason, the girls loved him. He had more shags than all the rest put together. Biggsy seldom went home without female company. He got bored with just the usual 'shag and go' and even tried to persuade a girl to bring her dog along once. I'm not sure how he got on on that occasion, though.

Having said all that, Biggsy was a really nice guy. He was so proud to work for the company, that he would obey any rule to keep his job. I could kid myself sometimes that I was a strict disciplinarian by berating Biggsy, but the truth was that no matter what I said, this team were heading wherever they chose. Biggsy had one big failing: he hated gays with a vengeance and would gladly castrate any gay man if he were given the chance. This made life a little awkward at times, for the sixth member of the team was very gay …

Mickey, when not fleeing the business end of Nayim's baseball bat (thoughtfully reinforced with nails), was our pub crawl organiser. Outwardly he was anything but camp, but he knew where he preferred to dip his wick and it certainly didn't involve any part of the female anatomy – or, as he made it quite clear, anywhere near Biggsy. This statement didn't mollify Biggsy, who used to positively seethe with disgust and anger whenever Mickey was near. Far from being secretive about his sexuality, Mickey used to taunt the other males within the group – 'Don't knock it until you've tried it.'

To which Mack and Dom would retort, 'Fuck off, you shirt-lifter!'

Amid all the hostilities and baiting, Dom and Mack got on

tolerably well with Mickey, but Biggsy just seethed and steamed at him.

Mickey's birthday arrived mid-season and a lunchtime bash was held in his honour, during which the whole team presented him with a collection of hard-core male porno magazines, showing men with enormous dongs shoving them into other men. Mickey was horrified and delighted at the same time with his gift. His reaction was certainly qualified by the fact that his sister had travelled out from England to see him and was present at the gathering. In fact, she was sitting right beside him. At this time, Mickey was still wrestling with how to break the news of his sexual leanings to his family. He was not overtly happy at the manner in which his birthday gift was presented, but the boys saved the day by making it up to him, chipping together and buying him enough drinks to blow his mind.

So, with this crew assembled, we were ready to face anything. I could lead them through hell or high water, to ultimate success – which equates to more profit for the company – but they had to be trained first. These six big personalities were the biggest challenge I had faced yet in my career. The sales training was no problem, for this lot had the hunger already. The company's system meant that they collected cash for excursions that had not yet gone and that the money was not paid to the company for up to two weeks. During the time that lapsed from collection to delivery, there were a lot of loopholes that could be exploited.

The company thought it probably was not getting all that it was due. So after the outside sales consultant had been eaten up and spat out, I had the honour of telling the group about the new company initiative on collection of monies for excursions. A new, 'failsafe system' had been designed that would eradicate all fraud, maximise company profits, but also help the reps earn more commission in their UK bank accounts, where all their hard-earned money eventually found its way.

This devilish new system was designed to pull in all the money for the company and this new team was to be the first to work under the scheme, the perfect set of guinea pigs. As far as I could see, it doubled the already tedious workload with its truly antiquated abacus-like system and privately I was dreading passing it on to my new team. There was an air of panic in the room as I passed out the mountainous array of forms A, B and C, B2 to C3 and finally D, with summary totals and check-backs. Dom was a veteran of many summer campaigns and he studied the forms closely, while the rather less focused financial acumen of Biggsy and Co asked questions and panicked about the sheer volume of paperwork and change ahead. The questions were coming thick and fast when, after about ten minutes, Dom silenced the team by saying: 'Don't fuckin' worry. I answer any queries as we go along all season. It's easy. I'll explain it to you all.'

He smiled contentedly and sat back, his colleagues calmed and silenced by his reassurance. They huddled together and discussed the new system and its intricacies. It was at this moment that I realised the system might be flawed!!

As I write, the previous system had been abandoned after

two years, but after much scratching of heads, a new system had been worked out by another crack (or is it crap?) team and, true to form, there has been no rep involvement at all. Oh well …

Trained up and ready to roll, the team went off to their respective hotels, ready to meet their clients. Dom, as the most experienced of the team, being a veteran of three summers already in Magaluf, was paired up with the new girl, Paula, and placed in our biggest and potentially most troublesome hotel in central Las Americas, La Carina. The hotel had over a thousand beds and we were not the only company to use it. All the other companies, along with their youth programmes, could be found here, making La Carina their temporary home. In the height of summer this place could resemble an asylum. At one time, the owner of this establishment had great hopes for it. All rooms had television sets placed in them, along with fine furniture. Unfortunately, the youth of that day did not appreciate the efforts of the hotelier to upgrade his establishment. In the very early mornings, after heavy nights of partying and drinking, a television that only transmitted Spanish channels and that they had absolutely no chance of understanding was of no use to them whatsoever. So they occasionally came to the conclusion that these TVs would be better served by being used as projectiles. Over the balconies they went. Some time ago, the hotelier stopped replacing the TVs in the rooms, so sights of flying TVs over Las Americas are becoming rarer.

As far as I'm aware, there have been no recorded deaths or serious injuries from flying TVs. However, it was not an unusual sight to see Dom desperately trying to persuade the hotel manager not to evict another group of lads from the hotel out on to the streets of Tenerife for trashing their rooms. I also believe that a healthy profit was made from the flying TV business as every room that launched one, and there were a few, was charged 100,000 pesetas for the privilege. They always paid, as this seemed a better prospect than spending time as a guest of the Guardia Civil.

Many times, though, groups of lads and girls would let the demon drink get the better of them, bash their rooms up, beat each other up and then upset the lone security guard. He just happened to be a good friend of the local police and, when he called them, they always responded. It was amazing how timid the lads could be once they'd been locked up for the night. I've never had the pleasure of spending the evening in one of Juan Carlos's establishments for lawbreakers, but I hear that they are not the most hospitable of places in which to spend your time. I've seen the bravest of young bucks, who maraud their way around the streets of Tenerife spurting forth with all the ugliest traits of misspent British youth abroad, reduced to tears during their morning-after appearances in Spanish courts.

One wondered what the security guard's brief was when he came to work every night in La Carina. From what I could see, he patrolled the complex to try to keep some semblance of order amongst the inhabitants. He had a mobile phone, a club or an extended truncheon-like device, a pair of handcuffs and not a word of English. In my humble opinion, he was hopelessly overworked and ill equipped. It was the equivalent of being sent to patrol the poll tax riots with a Swiss army knife and being expected to keep order – and then being blamed when a bit of trouble breaks out. Have no sympathy for the hard-pressed security guard, though, for Lord alone knows what his law-keeping credentials are. Several times during the season, I had received reports of the one at La Carina entering rooms that housed groups of unsuspecting girls by means of his master key. You could say he then used his other master key, because if all reports were accurate, and I believe that they were, we just had too many similar cases for them all to be lies, he proceeded to remove his manhood from his trousers and masturbate. You won't be surprised to know that this spectacle did not excite the occupants of the room. Quite the opposite. They usually stood and stared, petrified, and then fled the room to hunt down the marauding masturbator once he had left.

Most reps that worked the youth programme were challenged when it came to speaking Spanish. My team was no different. I don't believe that they had a word of the local lingo between them, so explaining to the police – the men in authority in Las Americas at night – that the security guard had entered a room and proceeded to pleasure himself in the presence of young British females was quite a challenge. Come to think of it, it would have been quite a challenge for my team even in English. I once witnessed Dom standing with a member of the Spanish police trying to explain to him what had happened earlier that evening using a few words of broken Spanish, a lot of hand signs and hip movements. Had I not intervened, and I thought long and hard before I did,

I'm sure that the Guardia would have arrested him or hit him, or both. However, no matter what we said, the police would not believe that this security guard could possibly have done such a thing.

Anyway, quite how the methods adopted by the guard helped him control order within the hotel is beyond me. He was also reported to have beaten up several young drunken revellers and he even chained one of the hotel guests to the generators in the basement of the hotel. Whenever it came to settling disputes with this misguided and, dare I say, alternative bastion of law and order, he had the full backing of the local constabulary heavily in his favour. The management of the hotel also weighed in in his favour, so you can understand why he and others like him – and there were many – prevailed. The solution for any sane-minded individuals, of which there seemed to be few when darkness fell in Las Americas, was to keep well away from these people and not to upset them. If they should burst into your room with a hard-on just let him do his business and let him go.

*   *   *

Reps have to deal with a wide variety of demanding situations in the course of their daily work, and one of the most challenging, and most difficult, is rape.

Paula, our Scouse rep, really came into her own in these situations. I won't say it was a regular occurrence in Tenerife, but in a year you could expect a couple of incidents at least. There are some people who are of the opinion that some of our female guests invite rape. I personally don't subscribe to this view, but I'll give you an example of what was often said, and probably thought, by a lot of people in the Tenerife area.

I regularly visited a French hairdresser out there. He had a family and was a hard-working man. He knew Las Americas very well – he had lived there for close on twenty years and had seen it grow from a small village into the den of iniquity that it is today. He, like many other fathers the world over, occasionally took his children to McDonald's, which is right in the heart of all the bars in Veronicas.

This was also a favourite stop for all the girls and boys on their way to a wild night out in the nearby pubs and clubs. It was a good chance to refuel before the night's revelries. The boys' standard uniform was shirt outside the trousers of any colour, complemented by cool-as-you-like designer labels, surly threatening grins and leering eyes. The girls wore the shortest of skirts and the skimpiest of tops. As much flesh was on show as was legally possible, which left nothing to the imagination.

My hairdresser said, 'These girls, they dress like whores.' I have no opinion on this matter. Youth should be allowed to express itself but, sadly, sometimes there was a price to pay. As evenings rolled on, friends got split up and sometimes wandered off with strangers or even alone. Sometimes, sadly, they ended up getting attacked and in the worst-case scenarios, raped. The next day it was the reps that had to pick up the pieces.

Paula could be the hardest person. She always took abuse from rowdy groups of lads and gave back as good as she got. She could sell with the best of them, but she also had the qualities of a saint when it came to helping a girl through what must have been a horrific ordeal. She could be sympathetic and strong, sensible and firm. I've known her spend a twenty-four-hour stint with a distressed teenager who had been raped, sleep for a couple of hours, and go back to listen and help again. This must have taken its toll on her. I've seen her cry for a while after these testing times. She would talk about her misgivings for the way of life that the business plunges you into, then shrug her shoulders and simply get on with it. This was the most distasteful side of a fun way of life. It was an evil that was a very real part of the everyday happenings in Las Americas and because of the transient nature of the tourist industry, the fear of going to the police and the language barrier, all but the most serious cases ever got beyond the rep. This was sad.

One of the problems of finding places to accommodate youth guests in Tenerife, or indeed anywhere in the world, was that because the clientele treated their accommodation with complete contempt, and frequently trashed their rooms and defecated anywhere but the toilet, the people who owned these places got fed up with them. So it was not surprising that some of the youths ended up in the most run-down, undesirable places that exist on the island. One such place was situated right in the centre of Las Americas' thriving red light district. It was here that I decided to billet Biggsy for the season. As a former member of the armed forces, Biggsy was determined to instil some discipline into his unit and make it the best and most orderly youth establishment on the island. But he faced a tough challenge.

CONFESSIONS OF A HOLIDAY REP

Biggsy's unit consisted of over a hundred separate apartment blocks centred around a small reception area, a bar and a pool – ample enough for all the normal frivolities his guests loved to get up to. His first and most pressing problem was the amount of burglaries, of which there were at least ten every week. All the guests were encouraged to purchase a key for a safety deposit box so that they could lock their valuable passports, money and travellers' cheques away in safety. As ever, when you told young people to lock things away, or not to take drugs, or to wash behind their ears, or to eat more greens, they ignored all the good advice. So, when the thieves broke into their rooms, all the money and other goods would be conveniently lying around for them to help themselves. I sometimes wonder if we'd told them not to hire safety deposit boxes, whether we would have been more successful.

Not that this would have guaranteed their security, for on several occasions, when rooms were burgled, the intruders jemmied the safes from the wall and stole them too. Biggsy was tearing his hair out in frustration. He was selling trips to his guests, booking in his commission, only to find out when some of his clients came to pay that all their money had been stolen. He consulted reception and the hotel management, who seemed surprised at the events and shrugged their shoulders in sympathy and resignation.

For Biggsy, this was not good enough. He wanted action. Upon further investigation, he noticed that in a large percentage of the break-ins, there was no sign of forced entry. Biggsy suspected an inside job. He went back to the management, who protested their innocence. He dared to suggest that their surly security guard, whose methods of law enforcement bore more than a passing resemblance to those of his colleague in the nearby La Carina, just might know something about the events.

He might as well have accused the Catholics of crucifying Jesus Christ. Icy relations were in evidence whenever Biggsy was present in the hotel thereafter. Undeterred, our man decided to stay overnight in the complex to see if he could shed any light on the mystery.

When I saw him the next morning he looked very angry and very tired.

'What's up, Biggsy?' I enquired.

'I just couldn't sleep,' he replied, 'all that bloody noise these bastards make partying all night.'

What an irony I thought … hunter-turned game-keeper, or something like that.

'Never mind,' I said. 'Any luck with the burglaries?'

'No,' he replied, 'but I can't believe it, the apartment next door was robbed during the night.'

He had not heard a thing. His frustration grew by the day, and then he finally reached breaking point after a young couple, who'd gone to bed for an afternoon siesta, awoke to find a young man standing over them actually licking the girl's back. When she screamed, he fled, on foot, with all their worldly belongings, cash-wise, in his jeans pockets. The hotel manager's disinterested shrugs would not suffice this time, and so Biggsy went higher. He sought out the owner and invited him to a meeting in the complex. This time, action was taken. The owner was horrified to hear of the number of break-ins and immediately sacked the security guard and replaced him with another. He told the manager that he'd be going the same way if things did not improve very quickly. By now it was August. It had taken some four months to get action on this problem. I won't say it completely eradicated the thefts, but it did reduce them dramatically. It later transpired that every key fitted every door. It was a kind of universal door-locking system. We never did find out for sure who was responsible, but an inside job seemed more and more likely.

The fact that something had been done was a tribute to Biggsy's persistence, but even he could do nothing about clearing the streets of prostitutes, who liked to tout for business outside the apartment block every night. This minor distraction did not bother the males too much and several times I'm sure they tried to pull one of the girls – as far as I know, without the lure of cold, hard cash. No freebies were entertained, so it seems that some girls can resist the charms of the drunken British male in full flow. The girls though, who'd come on holiday to disco and party their time away, were not amused to find Spanish drivers winding their windows down and accosting them and offering them money for sex as they left the apartments. Much as we tried, there was no way that we could stop this happening. People had to be warned as they arrived not to bother the prostitutes as they go about their business, and to ignore any approach by drivers who were stopping continuously outside the complex to ask for directions to … God knows where.

It made me cast my mind back to the previous year when, at our annual yearly bash with the managing director, she told us to remember that we were working in a sexy industry. I wondered if she meant a sex industry ...

*   *   *

Whatever went on behind the scenes, Tenerife remained one of the most popular destinations abroad for British youth. With all its shimmering neon lights, crowded bars, wild entertainment and pulsating bars, it was tailor-made for revellers to pour themselves into this wild world of partying and playing for as long as they can take, which was usually just a traditional two-week period. They forgot their inhibitions, went absolutely wild and had a fantastic time. For the youth that perused the holiday brochures back in the rainy UK and let his or her imagination run wild, Tenerife was a dream, and the wildest nights in anyone's imagination could come true on what was simply referred to as a bar crawl.

The appointed meeting time was usually 8pm. Nervous youths gathered in hotel bars to meet their respective, though not respectable, reps who would guide them through a truly wild night of whatever they wanted. At 8.05pm, Biggsy descended on his hotel bar, where his group of one hundred paid-up members was waiting for him.

All round Las Americas his colleagues were doing the same. T-shirts bearing the logo 'Pure Energy' were distributed to all present and Biggsy ordered shots of vodka for his entire group to loosen their inhibitions. He then liberated his hotel bar and led the group, who had now become a little more familiar with their new uniforms, towards their first bar. It was a five-minute walk to Valentines, where Dom and Mack were also converging with their groups of a hundred each. Valentines came alive as the DJ welcomed the revellers. A happy hour was announced. The DJ had forty-five minutes to whip the group into a frenzy that they would remember the next day and which would hopefully inspire them to come back looking for more. Biggsy, Mack and Dom were introduced to the throng of youth:

'Let's hear it for Biggsy, the fattest bastard in Las Americas.'

Inhibitions were being shed as the crowd tentatively breaks into a chorus of 'You fat bastard ...'

'Let's hear it for Mack, still waiting for his first shag, and Dom, who's known as Batman 'cause he can't work without Robin ...'

The crowd broke into a rendition of 'Batman, takes it up the arse!' The volume was rising, as the team asked for volunteers for a game called 'Sexual Positions'. This helped further reduce any inhibitions and warmed up the atmosphere. Biggsy, Mack and Dom carefully chose the 'volunteers'. Four nubile females with more than eye-catching figures were persuaded on to the stage, where the game was demonstrated by Dom on the microphone and Mack and Biggsy, in starring roles, alternatively using their co-stars. I won't go into too much detail, but the idea was this. The male danced as suggestively as possible with his female partner, while the DJ played the loudest music he could find. The music then stopped and

Dom, who had his back to the audience, called out a sexual position that could be any of the following: 69; missionary; sideways; or riding the pony! Any couple who was not in the said position was out of the game and had to drink a pint down in one and then retire into the crowd to watch the proceedings develop further.

This went on for as long as the lads wanted and their victims and sorry volunteers were carefully weeded out until the best-looking girl was left. Once the reps had demonstrated the game, there was no shortage of male volunteers to take their places, for they were merely enacting positions that they hoped to be in for real later on in the evening. Then the fun really began. The alcohol was also flowing liberally, oiling the wheels of perversion as the game was played out. As proceedings progressed, the crowd became more vocal. The outcome of this first game left the final couple locked in a daring sexual embrace. They then slapped each other under the guidance of Dom, still on the microphone, who asked them to react as if they had just arrived home to find their partners in bed with their best friends ... mayhem predictably ensued. I thought it was a sick game, but the crowd seemed to love it.

Forty-five minutes rolled into one hour and the crowd was on its way to the next bar, where they met with the rest of the group and the other three reps in the team. The reps encouraged the throngs to try to make progressively more noise with each bar entrance and vocal bedlam broke out amongst the six hundred-strong crowd, all proudly wearing their 'Pure Energy' T-shirts. Biggsy grabbed the microphone and invited four male volunteers to the stage, where they stood ready for whatever came next.

The DJ started up the music for *The Full Monty*, which was all the encouragement the boys needed. When all but boxer shorts were covering the limited amounts of modesty on show, Biggsy asked the DJ to stop the music as he screamed to the girls in the crowd: 'Do you want to see more?'

The question was all too simple; you can guess the next move. Drinks were prepared for all as the throng got ready to leave for the next bar.

The crowd was by now well and truly in the holiday spirit and was up for pretty much anything. This was great news for the bar owners. Normally, the bars in the area didn't come to life until after midnight, but with this crack team of youth reps on hand, the wheels of the party machine were turning long before the normal hour and brought six hundred revellers along with them for the ride. It was a well-known fact that when a bar was full and the atmosphere was – well, what can I say – throbbing, then curious passers-by, looking for adventure, joined the throng as well. The truth is that no bar was left completely empty after the appointed time was up and the majority of the group moved on. However, as good as the team were at whipping up the atmosphere, they were equally good at making sure that they took all of the group with them when they moved on.

When moving on time came around, as it did all too quickly as far as the greedy bar owners were concerned, Dom appointed his troops to various points along the route.

Mickey led, Paula and Tina were at various points along the way, goading the males to follow and whipping them into some sort of sexual Congo chain that involved holding the hands of the person behind you through your legs. After Dom and Mickey had carefully consulted, they announced loudly that Biggsy, much to his chagrin, would be bringing up the rear. Once they were on their way, and Dom had tipped off the next bar that the group was on its way, he went back to the previous bar to 'sweep up'. Any stragglers were quickly assessed as to the level of their sobriety, which by now was usually pretty low. If they were judged capable of making the short journey to the next bar, they were sent on their way, Dom would then have a drink in a considerably quieter bar, where he would collect his reward from the bar owner. They couldn't really refuse, because if they didn't 'look after him', as he put it, he could take the group elsewhere. A brotherly handshake that fooled no one announced his departure for the next bar to rejoin the throng, where Biggsy had, by now, begun a female 'Full Monty'.

Usually the group was made up of about a sixty–forty split in favour of the males, and the sight of four young females taking off their clothes on stage normally left the men in the crowd frothing at the mouth. Biggsy encourages the girls to 'go all the way' and they usually need little encouragement. One of the girls falls and hurts her arm as she is trying to execute a pirouette with her knickers around her ankles. The crowd roars in approval of her acrobatics. Biggsy, realising that she has hurt herself, tries to grab the microphone and call for order so that she can be helped to her feet. The crowd completely fails to understand that this is not part of the show and spontaneously breaks into a chorus of 'You fat bastard' followed by a verse of 'Who ate all the pies?' Biggsy calls on Paula and Tina to tend to the by now tearful female, who is full of remorse for her actions. The girl is helped out of the bar with her friend; Paula is assigned to do the necessary, and the party goes on and on.

By this stage of the evening, people were beginning to pair off. Couples who had just discovered lustful feelings for each other could be seen sucking face and groping at various points of each other's anatomies all over the bars. Biggsy, Mack and Dom were by now eyeing the prey on offer and getting ready to pounce. They had carefully engineered the situation so that they had ample opportunity, if they so desired. Tina usually had the pick of several drooling males to choose from. She was a natural performer and positively thrived on the attention. Paula would have sorted out her target and he would be weakening with every new drink. Mickey, as was normally the case, would have the attention of several adoring females, but would have his thoughts elsewhere. I knew that he had helped several young males extricate themselves from various closets in his time, but he had also confessed to having a fascination for tits. He assured me that he had often taken the opportunity of inviting blissfully ignorant females back to his apartment, so he could continue this fascination and study of said tits at closer quarters.

Sometimes, however, the team had no interest in pairing

off with the punters and just carried on partying when their work was done, at around three o'clock in the morning.

The group was led on relentlessly to the final bar, where they were met by the high-priest of seedy entertainment in Las Americas, Nayim (he of baseball bat-with-nails fame). He had the coveted final bar call and he loved it. He had the job of extracting the last few pesetas from the group's pockets and he was very good at it. His DJ was a bodiless voice, who could relentlessly whip the crowd into a dancing frenzy. Before long, 'Pure Energy' T-shirts were thrown aside as midnight became four, five and six o'clock. It was another crazy night.

All of the pub-crawlers signed up for the full package of excursions and my team was clever in the way the package had been designed. Most of the revellers would not be seeing the business end of a pillow before 5am. This was normal. It was a night that the young holidaymakers' dreams were made of: booze, sex, visual stimuli, music, people and general mayhem made this an evening that a lot of people didn't want to end. But, inevitably, it did and, as this night finished, another day began.

The new day began at about 8.30am, when the next excursion started. A day of frivolities at the beach, jet-skis, parascending, speedboats and games for all. Predictably, attendance was very low. Of the six hundred who booked on, only about a third turned up and this would be looked upon as quite a good turnout.

Nights like the pub crawl evening were commonplace in Las Americas, but an excursion package to excite the youth clientele and get their juices flowing needed a little more imagination than just pub crawls. Good as the crawls were, the young people wanted more.

We put together a package of various days at the beach on jet-skis and nights at various venues around the island with endless supplies of food and drink included in the price. Afternoons were spent at the waterpark. All the families had usually gone home by the time the young hordes descended, so the groups could have a couple of 'no holds barred' hours on the slides without offending any sensitive souls. No package, however, could surpass the adrenaline-pumping mayhem of what has become known as 'The Tudor Night'.

Normally it went like this. People were picked up on coaches from their respective resorts and travelled to a medieval castle (the in-joke is that it was constructed by Wimpy some time in the late 20th century – so truly medieval, then) in San Miguel. Even the name of this area, which shared its name with that of a well-known Spanish tipple, excited our younger clients. Here, they were met by costume-clad knights in shining armour, who guided them across the moat (it was only six inches deep, but it looked pretty impressive). They were then seated in an area with a central sunken jousting arena on a bed of sand, so that they were always looking down on the action. They were fed a medieval feast of chicken and broth, which they ate with their hands, and this was washed down with as much wine as they could drink.

I use the term wine very loosely, because if you ever had

the misfortune to taste it you may well have sought an urgent meeting with the trades description people ... that is, of course, after your even more urgent meeting with the toilet to expel the offending liquid from your stomach. However, all that aside, a fabulous show began with highly trained and skilled horses, horsemen and women performing breathtaking stunts that would have all but the hardest and most cynical of audiences on the edge of their seats.

After about an hour of this truly fine example of man and animal in perfect harmony, the crowd was barely given a chance to catch their breaths before they left the main arena and were led into another large bar area. Another bar awaited them and they were given the chance to dance the final part of the night away as they listened to four black blokes singing Drifters songs. It really was a brilliant night out and most families loved it. When somebody suggested some time ago that it would be a good idea to use the same night for just the youth programme, they had no idea of the mayhem that would ensue once a week during the height of every summer.

Dom and his team picked up their guests on coaches from resorts at about 7.30pm and a crucial part of the night began with their commentary. This was designed to set the scene for the evening ahead, but also to lay down some ground rules for safety and a good time. It was good opportunity to pass on information to the clients before they got too drunk. I have sat on one of these coaches and witnessed one of these commentaries on the way to Tudor Night and I'll share with you just a small sample of the information that is passed on.

'Right, you bastards, shut up and listen!'

The youths generally tended to rise to this level of address with laughs and shouts of drunken derision, for they had already sampled the drinks on offer in the local bars while waiting for the coaches to arrive.

'The chickens are already dead, and they won't fly again so don't try to make them or the knights will get upset. The horses are real, so don't try to run in front of them and don't throw anything at them, or I'll fuckin' throw you out. If there are any vegetarians on board, you can fuck off out the back and eat grass. I'm now going to pass a piece of chalk around the bus and I want you to write the number of the bus on the bottom of your shoes. When you're pissed later on and I find you in the bushes, I'll know what coach to put you on and no fighting or I'll chuck you out. Now, are you all ready to have a good time?'

The resounding answer was 'Yes!' And they did, believe me.

When you first entered the arena during the Tudor Night performance in front of just over one thousand young British tourists, it was a shock. The first thing that hit you was the noise. Your eardrums recoiled at the cacophony of screaming, hormone-laden youngsters. The reps had the idea of dressing certain parts of the audience in different-coloured bibs that corresponded with the colours of the different jousting knights and their horses. This created a competition amongst the revellers, who screamed abuse at ... well, anyone who was not in the same colour garb as they were, basically. Eventually, as the liquid and atmosphere took hold, they screamed at each other.

Now, the chickens will not fly again, but their potential as missiles was great and this potential was soon put to use. Dead fowls were thrown in all directions. The knights did their best to protect their steeds and so the youth resorted to baiting and insulting each other. It was here, at one of these youthful bashes, that I witnessed one of the most curious sights that I have ever experienced.

Each side of the arena was packed with over five hundred young men and women, screaming abuse at the tops of their voices. Chickens, cups, corks and bread rolls joined the insults being thrown and then a curious, tribal-like behaviour ensued. Men and women alike dropped their trousers, pants, knickers and whatever else they were wearing and hoisted up their short skirts to reveal their bottoms, their bare bottoms, in the direction of the opposing side of the arena. This, in itself, was not strange. I have found this to be common behaviour for young, over-excited, drunken British youth. But when five hundred people did this in unison, it really was quite an incredible sight. When the other five hundred youths on the other side of the arena answered the insult in the same way, also in unison, it was even more incredible to behold. This behaviour seemed to go on for some thirty minutes or so – I swear that even the horses stopped to look. Lord only knows what their equine minds made of it all. I could imagine two horses outside the arena in their stable sanctuary looking at each other in disgust and saying, 'Animals!'

Once the jousting was over, and the horses were securely locked in their stables again for the night, the youth were led out to the bar area to enjoy the sounds of The Drifters. I stayed behind on one occasion to witness the mess that the flower of British youth left behind. It was quite considerable, believe me, and several armies of cleaners really had their work cut out for them preparing the place for the next night. Someone told me, and I believed it, that they used to funnel all the dregs back into the bottles to be re-corked. If you ever go to the Tudor Night, drink the wine at your peril.

The potential for these nights to erupt and boil over into an uncontrollable mêlée was vast. The fact that they never did was a tribute to the reps that policed such events. Dom surveyed all from a perch above the crowd and he placed his team at strategic points along the edge of the public seating gallery, the barrier between men and horses. As soon as he sniffed out any trouble, he swooped down and defused it by throwing the offender out. A thoroughly good time was had by all. In my two years in Tenerife, there were very few incidents that took place at the Tudor night.

That said, I recall a few youths being stricken with asthmatic attacks that had been triggered by the horsey atmosphere. And there was one unfortunate fellow who dived into the moat, thinking it was deeper than six inches. He escaped with cuts and bruises – not only physical, but to his pride too – and he is sporting three teeth less as a result of his doomed dive, but he lived.

There it is, just a small recollection of my time in Tenerife. But there are some memories that stay with me more strongly than all the others – enduring and more beautiful aspects of this, the grandest and most diverse of all the Canary Islands. The majestic beauty of Mount Teide, its contrasting rich green landscape in the north compared to the concrete jungle of the money-laden south. The wonderful botanical gardens, the amazing Loro Parque, are simply one more of a host of reasons that make this such a popular destination for European tourists year after year.

These beauty spots held little interest for the thousands upon thousands of the flower of British youth that flocked here in droves every summer, though. Their very different reasons for choosing Tenerife for a summer break have, I hope, been adequately explained in the rest of this chapter.

BENIDORM: SPIRITUAL HOME OF THE PACKAGE HOLIDAY

THE FIRST, AND most important of destinations in the evolution of British tourism. This is where it all began back in the Sixties, and once the fire had started in Benidorm, it really did take off. Before long, giant high-rise buildings were towering out of the earth to hold all the thousands of British tourists who sought out this little corner of paradise. When I was there, the streets were choked with traffic and hundreds of little bars had sprung up selling bacon and eggs and beans on toast to cater for the choosy British pallet. The tiny strip of sand that passes for the beach was wearing away under the constant tread of tourists. It retreated into the sea to try and get away.

Benidorm was ugly. Everything that was wrong with tourism manifested itself here: bad planning, poor roads, old hotels, overcrowding. But try as you might, whatever way you look at it, Benidorm had some serious magic. About sixty per cent of all visitors were repeat business. Not just once or twice, but for some literally hundreds of times. People loved it, and they wouldn't go anywhere else. It was hard to see why sometimes, but this was the mecca of British tourism. I stood on the hill overlooking the resort on my first day in Benidorm at the start of 2001 and thought to myself, *This is it. It really doesn't get any better than this. This is the spiritual home of the package holiday.*

Brits abroad take great comfort in being able to return to the same hotels in the same resorts year after year to try to create that holiday dream, the home from home. You could hear the returning conquerors as they made their way back to their favourite resorts aboard the rep-guided coaches. 'They've changed the road since last year, love. It seems smaller than it was.' This could be the start of a typical conversation, spoken loudly aboard the coach as the seasoned Benidorm visitors found themselves in familiar surroundings. The newcomers, and there always were newcomers aboard these coaches, looked out of the windows of the coach at the busy surroundings and must have thought to themselves, *When does this mess stop, and paradise begin?* Soon, very soon.

Before long, we were rolling into Benidorm and the coach began to discharge its human cargo at their respective destinations. The front of these hotels invariably looked very different to the manufactured sea-view vistas in the brochures, and this had the effect of filling new visitors to the area with suspicion. As an added discomfort, Benidorm had seen the whole area affected by numerous building sites in every available space, either making improvements or building new hotels in the tiniest of gaps. Some said this was an attempt to give the face of Benidorm a much-needed lift. Other, more cynical people said that this was just shrewd owners investing black pesetas before the advent of the Euro. I wouldn't like to comment …

As the first people new to the area were discharged to retrieve their cases and make their way inside their homes for the next two weeks, you could almost hear the people left on board thinking, *I'm glad we're not staying there.* The coach crawled around the traffic-choked streets. One by one the families were despatched and the race to check in at reception began.

Mr and Mrs Been-Here-Before anxiously and loudly sought out 'Pedro' in the hotel bar to renew their lifelong friendship, struck up in a previous visit. 'Pedro, it's us. Mike and Jeanne! We were here last year when you had that rowdy group in!' Pedro, who was really Miguel, and has only worked here for the last two months, was far too professional to look confused, smiled politely and reciprocated the hugs, kisses and handshakes. If he was worth his salt he would flash a look of recognition to his long lost 'friends'. And if he was really good he would already be visualising his tip at the end of every drunken day with these returning conquerors. I think it's a need that we Brits have to be recognised as old friends returning to the fold. It's in the psyche – we love to be loved for what we think we are: empire builders, I think.

I met a hotelier in Benidorm who had worked in the same hotel for thirty years and has many great stories to tell about returning Brits. He talked of people who return year after year and demand the same room in the hotel. And, if it was not possible to accommodate them because 'their' room was taken, they demanded that the people who dared to use that room be moved. They would check every morning to see when that particular room would be vacant so that they could move in at the first available opportunity. One particular man had even had people move into their beloved rooms the day before they were due to go home. I couldn't help thinking that that was a little sad. Sad but true.

Some of the people who visited Benidorm for the first time with their families found that the rooms were not always as big as they thought they might be. Whether this was due to misunderstanding the brochures, or whether it was just down to inflated expectations, who knows, but it was one of the biggest initial complaints. Think of the high street nowadays and it is full of holiday adverts telling you that your children can go free on your summer break. What they didn't tell you was that this could lead to cramped conditions sometimes in the little twin rooms, once the camp beds had been put down for the kids. In such cramped environments, many activities were possible, but anything involving cats and swinging was definitely not on the agenda.

Now I am not saying that this was always the case, but quite often these hotel rooms could test the patience of all who came to share them. What were once the cute little peculiarities of your beloved can turn into the most irritating, nerve-tingling pains in the arse, because of lack of space. Whatever the feelings these rooms gave rise to, and however the occupants viewed the deal – be they returning heroes, pissed-off first-time travellers or stressed and disappointed families – we wanted them one and all at the welcome meeting we arrange especially for them the next morning. Why? Because we wanted their money, or what was left of it, for trips – or more importantly, for our commissions.

During our introductory meetings we became more and more cunning over the years, so that they had become more than just a hard sell. I believe that the guests secretly loved these little get-togethers, because it gave them their first chance to have a good moan at the rep. They liked to have a go about the state of their accommodation or the quality of the flight, or any number of a hundred and one other things they could think of. It also gave them the opportunity to see their very own rep for the first time. Many of our guests would have seen lots of other reps before on their travels, especially those who came back to Benidorm year after year. They would ask you if you knew the reps they had met before on their travels. The chances of this for a new rep to the company were very remote, but none the less, the conversations took place.

'We were here two years ago, so you can't really tell us anything about this place. Our rep then was a fella called Gary. A tall lad with dark hair. Do you know him? Come on, you must know him! Tall, dark, I think he might have been one of them queers, you know, but he was a lovely lad. You must know him, he was here for six months.' The looks of disappointment were plain when the rep said he was not sure if he knew Gary, but he would ask around and pass on your regards. You got used to showing a blank look that disguised the impulse to say, 'Of course I don't know him, you stupid old git. There are hundreds of reps in this company, and I am not in the habit of looking up tall dark men called Gary to discuss the guests who were in the hotel in Benidorm last year.'

Anyway, politeness and good manners were the name of the game, because – as I mentioned just now – we wanted their money. And it was becoming harder and harder to get it as the years went by. There was much competition to extract cash from visitors' pockets in Benidorm. There were myriad entertainment venues to choose from, most of which had free entry and offered a huge diversity of distractions. After witnessing some of these first hand, one wondered how we could compete with some of these acts. For instance, amongst the live lesbian sex shows and the tribute acts to artists ranging from Queen to Chubby Brown, you could find one of Benidorm's legends. Her name is Sticky Vicky. The high point of her act is when she pulls various objects from her vagina, including eggs, bunting and razor blades. She then switches on a household light bulb, with the only obvious means of electrical connection being her clitoris. Quite an act to follow, really. It could leave you a little perplexed about how best to pitch your fun day donkey safari.

One of the strange contradictions about the travelling British public is that, although they were becoming more streetwise about parting with their money for the tour operator-organised trips, they still regularly fell prey to the timeshare touts who adorned the streets like litter in the popular resorts. It worked like this. A crafty Cockney, savvy Scouser or Manc on the make would accost his target Brit with a free scratchcard that offered them a chance to win a fabulous prize. Everyone was a winner, as the scratched card always revealed another lucky draw. The excited Brits were then whisked away to collect their prizes. What this really meant was that they were then invited to be the guest of one of the real timeshare heavies for an afternoon. These were the people who specialised in helping people to sign up for crippling debt for years to come so they could have the privilege of living for a week in an apartment somewhere in the world. Surely not, I hear you say. Where was the evidence for this claim? Well, you didn't need to look any further than the adverts that adorn the walls of the arrivals lounges in every UK airport. Among those promising cheaper holidays for next year, and even cheaper duty free, you would find solicitors' ads promising to help to extricate you from the timeshare deals from hell that you had mistakenly signed up for during your holiday in paradise, the wisdom of which was fading faster than your sun tan. There was a growing business here and therefore, one would think, money was being made. So the next time you are offered a free scratchcard with the chance to win fabulous prizes, think twice, or you may well be on the trail of the timeshare doctors in the UK.

The daily jostle for sun beds was always a great source of irritation for the Brits abroad. For years the beleaguered gentleman-like British tourist played second fiddle to the more cunning and devious forward-planning skills of our European brethren, the Germans. So, because the Huns – one of the affectionate terms associated with our German colleagues over the years (one of the printable ones, anyway) – had the good foresight to reserve their sun beds either very late at night or first thing in the morning, while their British counterparts were either consuming alcohol or recovering from its effects, they were able to bronze their bodies in the best sun traps, which were usually within spitting distance of the pool. Meanwhile, their British counterparts languished with the flies beside the bins, or waited in deep shade for the sun to make a fleeting appearance at 5pm. The Brits, purely due to their gentlemanly tendencies, would not stoop to such underhand measures as to reserve their beds, or so you might believe. I cast my mind back to one particular morning in one of our biggest hotels in Benidorm and an exchange with one of our guests that went something like this:

'It's bloody disgusting. All those sun beds were gone this morning by 7 o'clock. Bloody Germans have put their towels down and reserved all the best places as bloody usual. I've seen a sign in reception that says do not reserve the beds, but they still do it. Can't you do anything about it, eh?'

It was always worthwhile at this point to study the reaction of the miffed Brit when you reply: 'I am sorry to hear that, sir, but there are no Germans in the hotel, it's all British here. And I can't do any more than ask them to remove the towels. But it's very difficult to stop you all.'

'Are you bloody sure?'

'Absolutely sir, one hundred per cent.'

It seems that the Brits had evolved in the package tour business. Not only had we joined the Germans, we were now attempting to beat them at their own game.

The Brits and the Germans have never really mixed well on holiday. Benidorm's money men and planners have recognised this and conveniently separated the two races. In one area of the town, whole areas had been reserved for the Brits, like a little stronghold. The sighting of a German with his hairy-armpitted companion here was rarer than snake's legs. If you ventured to the upper part of older Benidorm in the daylight hours, the sight of a Brit with his varicose-veined wife struggling along on the lookout for a pint of bitter was rarer than a tabloid journalist at a royal garden party. This could be one of the secrets of Benidorm's success. I once sat through an arty tourist seminar in Lanzarote in which a gentleman who was an expert on the evolution of tourism spouted forth for a couple of hours about the beauty of places like Lanzarote, which had rightly challenged the development of mass tourism. For instance, in Lanzarote there was an active effort not to allow buildings to be constructed at more than a certain height, and for all new projects to be regulated so as to prevent the island from becoming the Benidorm of the Canary Islands.

What a load of old bollocks this is. Tourism is the life blood of a lot of places and although many people knock what has happened in Benidorm – think high-rise buildings and congested traffic – I bet they would kill to have the same amount of repeat guests, and even a tenth of its annual revenue. Benidorm is ugly, it's true, but it flourishes and keeps packing the punters in all year round and, after so many years, that can't be bad.

So here I was in the nerve centre of British tourism. I shuddered when I thought of how popular this place was – it must have had millions of visitors over the years. I recalled that when I had started this job, some ten years earlier, this was the one place I dreaded going. I don't know why, because I didn't have a clue what it was like. It was just the name, I think. It conjured up all the old tired and worn-out images of what I thought tourism would be like. That was the beginning of my journey, a journey that I feel I am getting to the end of, but what a place to end. It's a fact: people are so happy in Benidorm that they want to die there. Many older visitors – and let's be honest here, there are quite a few of them, especially in the winter – have actually said that to the reps.

It was in Benidorm that I first noticed how accustomed reps had become to death. When somebody died in a resort, it was sometimes very difficult for reps to deal with. They often had to comfort the bereaved and help the families through difficult times. It could be quite unexpected and very traumatic. Very often, the company would offer counselling to help the rep come to terms with the problem. This is the case in most resorts, but in Benidorm, where death seemed to come almost every day in the winter months, this was seldom the case. Amongst the teams, the resort has become affectionately known as 'Fly and Die'. I once remember speaking to a colleague who was called to deal with his first death in a hotel during his first winter in the resort. The manager told him that one of the clients had passed away. He said he wasn't sure who it was, but whoever it was, they were up in room 689. The rep was very nervous, but realised he would have to go upstairs and try to sort things out. Up in the lift he went to room 689. The door was open. He went over to the bed, where he found not one, but two people lying down with the blankets over them – a man and a woman. Due to the pallor of the two incumbents, he figured that both must be dead, as neither was moving. Then, the woman suddenly sat up in the bed; the rep was so frightened that he wet himself. 'Hello, love, thanks for coming up,' the lady began. 'It's my husband – I think he's dead, but I wanted to stay with him until the doctor came.' She seemed calm and perfectly resigned to the fact that her husband had passed away.

The undertaker eventually came and took the corpse away. The lady carried on with her holiday, which still had eleven days to run. My friend can see the funny side of this story nowadays. But he did get an awful fright at the time. This kind of story was not uncommon. I have known of several cases in which the same thing has happened. I'm sure that when some of the older folks select a holiday from the brochures, they also take into consideration whether they would like to die there. It took me a while to understand this, but it really was true. I think it's quite a good thing really. If nothing else, it saves the company from paying all the costs of repatriation for the bereaved.

Of course, I would never wish to make light of how

stressful death can be to anybody involved. When it comes during a holiday it can be very difficult and painful to deal with. I remember one Sunday afternoon – traditionally my day off – just as I was making my way to the pub to watch the football on TV before retiring to lie on the beach, my mobile phone rang. Normally on Sunday I would have switched it off. I looked down at the screen to see who the caller was. 'Number withheld' shone back at me. *Shall I answer it*, I thought. Nagged by a sixth sense that told me somebody might really need me this time, I answered it. It was our office in the UK. A family was desperately trying to get hold of somebody in the resort, as their fifteen-year-old daughter had just been taken to hospital with suspected meningitis. I thought of phoning one of my colleagues who was on duty that day, but I hadn't ordered a pint yet, and old sixth sense urged me to take this one myself. Very often these suspected cases of meningitis turned out to be nothing more than a flu or a rash. I had no great feelings of dread as I made my way to the hospital. I thought it would just be a case of meeting the family, whose name I did not even know at the time, reassuring them and then returning to the pub to resume my day off.

When I arrived at the hospital, there was no sign of the family. I asked the receptionist if a British family had been in with a young girl who was suspected of having meningitis. The receptionist called the doctor, and I waited five minutes before he came to tell me what had happened. The girl had walked in to the hospital with her family at around midday. She had a rash and a headache. By 1pm she had been diagnosed as having viral meningitis. Incredibly, just forty-five minutes later, she was dead. Just like that. The time was now about 2.45pm. I had apparently just missed the family, who were making their way back to the hotel to pack their cases and go straight back to the UK.

I rushed to the hotel, shocked and feeling quite apprehensive about how I would be able to cope with this terrible situation. One thing was for sure: whatever I was feeling, the family would be feeling a million times worse. I found the father in reception, trying to phone the company back in the UK to get some help. By now I knew the family were called Smith; that didn't make it any easier to find the right words to say to someone in this terrible situation. When I reached the hotel I had no idea what Mr Smith looked like, but when I saw him, even though he had his back to me, I just knew who he was. It was almost as though he was bowed over slightly by the weight of grief drawing in around his shoulders. I approached him and he turned to me. He wasn't crying; in fact, he seemed to be quite business-like, just a little bemused by what was happening.

'Mr Smith?' I enquired.

'Yes, are you a representative?' I nodded. 'We have got to get home. My daughter's just died.' It was one of those awful moments, when you say something although you desperately don't want it to be true. But you know you are going to have to accept it; to give it a name seems the first step along that road. I reached out to shake his hand, which seemed such a wrong thing to do in the circumstances, but I really was lost for actions. I told him how sorry I was for him and his family, and led him away from the reception area. I wanted him to know that I would help him in any way that I could to get through the next few days. He began to cry, and I felt useless, but I awkwardly touched his shoulder and asked where his wife was so I could at least get him away from reception, where a curious group was beginning to gather.

I took him to his room, where his wife was sitting on her bed, quite still and emotionless, staring at the wall. I eventually ascertained that they were travelling with the girl's grandparents, too, who were also in a state of shock. They were all very confused, but the consensus was that they all wanted to get home as quickly as possible. I wanted to help them as much as I could. Grief is a terrible burden to bear at any time, but when you are in a place that is geared up for enjoyment and fun, it makes it a hundred times harder. I quickly made a few phone calls and told the family to pack their bags as quickly as possible. I felt like they were all on the edge, and that if I could keep them busy it might just keep their minds occupied. I managed to secure a couple of flights, but I knew I would be lucky to get them away, as there would be complications about whether the meningitis was contagious or not. But to hell with it, I wanted to help them. We raced to the airport, but there we quickly discovered that the airline would not let them fly.

Selfishly I hoped they might have got on a flight, because I realised that I was going to have to manage this family until they left the resort, and I could see a lot of grief coming my way. I know that sounds selfish, and indeed it is, but I had never dealt with anything quite like this before. The family understood that they would not have been able to take their daughter's body home with them on that flight had they got on the aircraft, but that didn't seem to bother them at the time. Once I had broken the news to them that they wouldn't be able to go home that day, they began to get anxious about what would be happening to their daughter's remains. This was understandable in the circumstances, and so I had to find out what was happening with her. The family were torn between wanting to see her again and trying to remember her as she had been when she was alive. They decided to leave it that day and see how they felt later. The doctor came to the hotel, offered sedatives to the family and told them all that they would not be able to leave the resort for at least four days until they had all been checked to see if they had contracted the disease as well. I decided that I would stay with the family as we had started to bond. So I became their friend and their confidant for the next five days. It was a very difficult few days but also a privilege to be so close to this remarkable family who were so practical in the way they dealt with this terrible situation.

These were some of the most difficult days I have ever spent abroad. I feel almost guilty thinking that I was struggling during this time, as any pain or anguish I was feeling was absolutely nothing in comparison to what the family were suffering, and no doubt still are to this day.

I stayed with them all through their waking hours and tried to help them with two things. I wanted to make sure that if there was anything they needed, I would be the one who made it possible. And I wanted to help them in any way to come to terms with their grief, until they could return home to their relatives and friends. Their moods changed many times during the five days. One moment they wanted to talk endlessly about their memories of their child, and then for hours they just wanted to talk about anything else. Spanish red tape made the repatriation of a body quite a slow process, and it soon became apparent that the family would be returning home alone without their daughter. She would follow a few days later. Understandably this became a terrible wrench for them, and they were determined to see their daughter one more time before they left. The mother asked me to accompany them all to the chapel of rest. I wasn't thrilled about this, but I went along and, as you can guess, it was not an easy day at all for anybody concerned.

The five days seemed to take forever, but eventually we were making our way to the airport to say our final goodbyes. I am not the only rep who has ever found themselves in this situation. Most good reps would do exactly the same thing, but it illustrates how diverse a job like this can be. Laughter one minute and tears the next. Sounds almost pathetic, but it is very true. The mother asked me to do one more thing for them. As they would not be able to accompany their child on her last journey to the airport on the way home to England, she asked me to go to the chapel of rest and accompany the coffin on its way to the airport when her daughter's repatriation was finalised. I agreed. It was a very sad journey. As the plane lifted off taking the family back home, I felt a weight lifting from my shoulders. I never will know how they coped.

It's not so nice to dwell on this side of the job, but it is none the less something that many reps encounter wherever in the world they work. I think some people believe that they are indestructible when they go abroad, but sadly this is not the case. When we see new reps on their training courses at the start of their careers, the fact that they might have to deal with a death during their time in the job is mentioned. It always elicits questions and renders the room silent as the new recruits consider this new possibility. Lip service is all you can pay to this particular part of the job, because in my experience these incidents are never the same, but it really is a tribute to all reps who deal with this kind of thing that they manage to get through it. Like most things that reps end up doing, it is a great learning experience.

A whole wealth of experiences has passed through my life in the years I have spent doing this job – a job that I think is one of the best in the world. And after finally graduating to the mecca – Benidorm – after spending time in the Balearics, the Canaries and Greece, there really didn't seem to be anywhere else for me to go. I found myself considering hanging up my clipboard and trying my hand at something a bit different …

AIRPORTS AND AEROPLANES

WHEN THE GREAT British public lock their doors to go on holiday, it is my common belief that along with the longlife milk, the eggs and butter, some leave their brains in the fridge as well. Well, at least the parts that allow them to survive alone in a hostile foreign climate, miles from civilisation – Benidorm, for example or Ibiza. My belief is held by some of the people who work overseas as representatives in the tourist industry. Our clients arrived through the dispatch doors at their foreign destinations with a sudden attack of amnesia, completely forgetting the name of the location and hotel they were staying in. Then they remembered that they had it emblazoned on the luggage labels attached to the handles of their suitcases. But they had forgotten how to read this information and so had to be helped to do so by their representatives. The latter began the season in May, when they carried out this task as helpfully as possible. But by mid-August they were struggling to be anything less than sarcastic. Or just downright rude.

Apparently this total lack of memory and co-ordination began to take hold long before tourists got anywhere near their chosen resort destinations. I have a friend who used to work as an air stewardess. She gave that prized job up to become a member of the ground staff in a busy regional airport in the UK. This is the job that entails checking in the travelling British public's bags at the local airports. I knew she was becoming restless in this latest venture, so I asked her if she would like to consider becoming a rep overseas in our team. Her reply was quite revealing but, on reflection, not very surprising. 'You must be joking!' she screeched. 'I've packed them off and sent them on their way for two years! I've travelled out with them, helped them blow their noses and wiped their arses, and I'll be buggered if I am going to sit with them for two weeks now and let them moan at me as well.'

Did we let them moan at us for two weeks? Well, it was not really that simple. But then again, it was not too far from the truth. Let's look at it in a little more detail. Once the initial mêlée at the resort airport was sorted out, and the people who had saved hard for the previous fifty weeks to pay for the coming two weeks' sojourn into foreign climes were forced to remember where they had been looking forward to going for the last twelve months, they set off on the first testing leg of their journeys abroad, from the Arrivals hall to the coach that would take them to their chosen hotels.

It was quite entertaining to watch as the typical British family took their first uncertain steps on foreign soil. Cases were piled high on the impossible-to-steer luggage trolley, which was being manoeuvred by a shell suit-clad father, usually with his youngest child, also bedecked in a shell suit, perched on top of the pile of cases. Two screaming and slightly overexcited youngsters, clad in the same fashion-wear, bounced along beside their stressed dad, while the shell suit-clad mum brought up the rear, with baby shell suit in her arms, simultaneously trying to contend with the reams of unnecessary paperwork she has extricated from her oversized travel document holder.

Most foreign airports had solved the problem of steps to the car park by thoughtfully installing ramps. These were a great idea, as they went a long way to helping arrivals negotiate the decline, or incline, to and from the car parks. Unfortunately, these ramps had been cleverly designed with a slight lip at the top and bottom. Quite why these lips existed was beyond me. Maybe Spanish airport designers had a warped sense of humour. For these lips always acted to bring the trolleys to a halt and dispatch the cases and young shell suit on to the unforgiving Spanish tarmac. In some of the more unfortunate cases, this served to create a bottleneck of arriving British tourists at the airport door. Circumspect couples on their first holidays abroad eyed the hold-up suspiciously, glad that they were not the ones to fall victim to this Spanish conspiracy, while the seasoned British travellers waited patiently and took the opportunity to discuss how things had changed since they first came here twenty years ago. The scenes of confusion continued into the car park as the Brits tried to mount the coaches via the driver's door before realising that they 'Sit on the other side of the road here, love.'

We liked to give them all a headstart at this point, so after about twenty minutes or so we followed them out to the park, boarded the coaches and did a namecheck. This in itself could take anything up to half an hour while people remembered who they were, and we changed some of them to the correct coaches, and chased up the odd straggler still struggling somewhere near the Arrivals door. Then off they would go to their respective hotels and apartments to enjoy their well-earned holiday.

The simple act of arriving could throw up a wealth of things to go wrong. For me, the airport was always a dreaded part of the week's work. I would go to any lengths to get out of this particular duty. Which made my next overseas destination, in a summer in the late nineties, somewhat ironic.

*   *   *

After working in the tourist business for the previous few years, I'd spent many hours in hotels, bars, airports, on beaches, around swimming pools, in cars, at meetings, presenting at meetings, training people, motivating people, disciplining, cajoling, even bribing if it helped the cause. All the kinds of pursuits that the tourism employee might well share as they made their way along the road of serving tourists. Many times I'd thought how lucky I was, for there are many of these pursuits that I had genuinely enjoyed and even looked forward to. After all that, I figured it must be time to move up, and so I applied for promotion.

Now, for me, the only pitfall among all of the tasks on the agenda of someone who finds gainful employment in our industry is anything to do with airports. There was a myriad of things that could go wrong. A myriad, i.e. innumerable. Loads and loads. Things that could make your heart quicken and your blood race around your veins, your mouth dry up, your hands sweat, your cholesterol level soar and your life expectancy plummet. How ironic, then, that after chasing promotion for a couple of years, I should be presented with the prize of airport manager. And not just any airport, oh no, but the biggest, the busiest and easily the most troublesome in our entire overseas programme. Welcome to Palma airport.

Were I to have welcomed all our guests individually to Majorca in summer, I would have smiled and shaken hands with over a million clients. That's quite a lot of fun-seeking tourists. I felt like a confirmed vegetarian who has just found employment in the busiest and biggest butcher's shop in the world. Suffice to say that the next six months provided some of the toughest challenges I had yet faced in my career.

News of the troublesome nature of this monstrosity of an airport had, it seemed, reached England and, as is the case in this day and age, the BBC had decided to make a documentary all about it. They announced that they would be following my team around as they worked throughout the summer, simply to observe ordinary folk earning a living. Now, the company I then worked for was very conservative at the best of times and always tended to fight shy of publicity. If you were ever in the corridors of power in the company headquarters, it would come as no surprise to see a sign that said, 'No publicity can ever be good ... so avoid it!' We always avoided cameras and newspapermen like the plague. I was initially surprised, therefore, that the go-ahead had been given for us to take part in this 'docusoap'. Or should I say 'docusoaps'? ITV must have got wind of this, for they decided this would be a good idea as well. They too commissioned a television series. Spanish TV, not to be outdone, also decided to film anyone who looked remotely confused, inquisitive or lost for a few months as well – and that really does cover most people in Palma airport.

The scene was set for the summer. Me, my team of thirteen, two hundred and fifty reps, up to eight film crews and over half a million of our clients, plus all the other companies' million arrivals as well, all vying for centre stage. Just a little added difficulty to spice up the working day.

I had always believed, and had always said to anyone who would listen, that airports were a nightmare. Lost luggage, delays and confused people reading illegible information, usually placed at impossible angles designed to crick the strongest of necks, were some of the reasons that have brought me to this conclusion. Normal, otherwise rational people seemed to change into bloodthirsty devils or mindless hooligans hell-bent on revenge when confronted by problems at airports. They sought out representatives of their holiday companies to threaten and sometimes even carry out unspeakable atrocities on said reps. All of this has

241

done nothing to dim my cynical view of these places. However, on hearing of my imminent rise up the company ladder to the lofty perch of airport manager, I decided to try to adopt a positive approach.

I bought one of those books that promote positive mental attitude as the answer to all problems. I began reciting a mantra: 'I love the airport – no, I really love the airport.' I could be heard muttering these words at any time of day or night during my vacation back in my father's house in the UK. This was a subliminal attempt to change my view. So much so that my father asked me whether I would like to go for Sunday lunch at our local airport, just to satisfy my ramblings.

I was almost beginning to believe that mantra, until I set eyes on Palma airport. I immediately changed my mind. No man, at least no one man, could possibly love something so big. It was just not possible. Palma airport was huge. Isaac Asimov's book cover illustrators could not have dreamed this place up. It was simply humungous. It also sported several fine examples of Spanish engineering genius (to understand the true meaning of this, see 'inefficiency' in the dictionary). Long walkways that converged into each other, no signposts whatsoever, a duty free shop outside the departure gates, disabled lifts that were too narrow for wheelchairs and ramps that would be steep enough to test the stamina of Olympic shot-putters. These were just a few of the imponderables on offer at Palma airport. I was positive that many more would reveal themselves as time wore on. The future was going to be bright.

The first meeting of the season was not, as I thought, with my team or any of the dignitaries at the airport, but with the producer of the TV series that would track my team during the course of the summer. She had a team of about five or six camera crews, who would be following us while we worked. They promised never to intrude too far into sensitive areas and not to interfere with the day-to-day operations. They would simply watch and film. They needed to suss out the team to look for potential 'stars' to follow for the season and they wanted me to put the team at their ease and to encourage any would-be stars to step forward. As it turned out, this was not going to be a problem as there were one or two in the team who already had stars in their eyes.

As the TV team was going to be following us pretty much every day, they would be living on the island, so the company took it upon itself to find accommodation for the entire group. At our initial meeting, the offer of 'basic accommodation' seemed to be no problem for the crew. After a couple of weeks in the Majorca sunshine, however, they changed their tune. I've never heard such a cacophony of moaning in my life. No air-conditioning, no mini-bars in the rooms, no maid service, too much noise, no food at four in the morning from the local shops ... I hesitate to use the term 'prima donnas', but ... well, perhaps it was not what they were used to at home.

The crews worked in twos and would concentrate on different people in the airport, or focus on families who'd been picked out in the UK before departure and would be followed through the whole experience. The crews mostly turned out to be nice people, though after working with them for a few weeks, I did begin to wonder if having an unusual name was half the secret of getting to work for a TV company. There was a right mixture of wonderful Christian names: Dolphus, Celeste, Cordelia and a few more that escape me for the moment. I thought about my own name and considered applying for a job. But not for too long.

It was not unusual to see the company's personnel being pursued around Majorca by a couple of microphone- and camera-wielding individuals during that summer. Eventually, the TV crew became just another part of our lives, but they did piss off one or two of our guests on the odd occasion. Naturally I was curious to meet my team. They had had a particularly hard year previously, and some of them were still shell-shocked after the opening year of the new, high-tech terminal. That had coincided with the worst yearly performance of our company airline. ATC (air traffic control), lack of crew and technical faults had, it seemed, all conspired to destroy morale and heartily damaged the reputation of this outpost in the Balearics. I knew my task would be a challenge, when I was introduced to one of our big suppliers at the start of season function. His eyes widened as he grasped my hand in a firm grip, looked me up and down and said, 'Pobrecito', which translated means 'Poor thing!'

On my first morning at the airport, I met Miriam. Our paths had crossed previously at a conference, which companies throw from time to time. Airport supervisors, of which Miriam was one, were different animals in my book. They spent their working lives outside the mainstream, outside of the everyday hustle and bustle of the resort. For whatever reason they become neglected and taken for granted as they battled their way through the season in what was, if I am honest, the single most important part of the operation. As we were so often reminded, you never got a second chance to make that all-important first impression and our guests always remembered the last thing that happened to them. Even if they had a wonderful holiday, mess it up at the airport and that would be the thing that stayed with them. The problem was, the airport could be a stressful place to spend your life and not many people were too keen to spend their time in, as it were, the front line of front lines. Those who did, tended to become dedicated to the cause, protective of their domain and bitter towards any outside interference. They loved the airport and treated it as their own – either that, or they failed miserably and were quickly replaced.

Miriam was totally in love with Palma airport. It was her territory and I was seen as an outsider, threatening to interfere and change it. I was afraid that she might treat me with contempt, make me feel unwelcome and unwanted. I was not to be disappointed. Miriam showed me around the airport like a homeowner who is deep in negative equity and reluctantly showing the new owners the corners of her soon-to-be-repossessed house.

'This is the ramp we have to use and you will have to use it very quickly if you want to get anywhere in this airport, so you're gonna need a lot of stamina,' she barked at me in her Brummie accent, like a female Jasper Carrot.

'This is where the coach drivers' boss sits, if you can ever find him – and believe me you'll need to find him, especially when three flights are coming through and you ain't got no coaches for the guests. Loads of other things go wrong here that you'll need him for,' she chirped. 'How's your Spanish?' she added.

'Oh, I get by,' I replied. 'I've worked hard at it.'

'Well, it won't be any good to you here,' she sniffed. 'The drivers only speak Mallorquian.'

I could see that I was going to have my work cut out for me. Miriam's broad five-foot-two-inch frame, topped off with its nest of bright red hair that bore testimony to her Irish parentage, marched me quickly round the main entrance of Palma airport. Then she left me to 'explore' on my own for a while. She would get back to me in two hours to take me off to a meeting with the rest of the team, who were apparently dying to meet me. I bet they were.

Miriam was back at the appointed time to take me into Palma to meet the thirteen members of our team in a hotel in the centre of town. Several new members had been recruited, as a number of people from last summer had had enough and got themselves easier jobs in places such as torture chambers. Of those thirteen, only twelve had turned up. The thirteenth, Jean, was 'too busy' and couldn't make it. Miriam introduced me as the new boss, 'our airport manager'. I had never heard the word 'manager' delivered with so much contempt. The team eyed me with a tired, resigned look. I was just another false dawn in their eyes. They knew I couldn't make the planes run on time, any more than I could stop the tide from coming in. I was determined, though, to make the season more enjoyable. I decided then and there to start as I meant to go on. I took them all to the bar and bought them a drink and we had a chat.

There were some interesting characters all right. First there was a Swedish guy known as Benny – he did tell me his real name, but it was far too complicated to pronounce, let alone write. He looked like he'd just stepped out of Abba: six foot tall, blond hair, blue eyes and a perfect blond beard. He was an instant heart-throb and his laid-back approach initially made him the ideal man to deal with irate British holidaymakers waiting for late departing planes. When the people from the TV saw Benny, they instantly spotted star potential and decided to follow him at every available opportunity. I was confident that this would only give us good press, for every time I spoke to him he was chilled out and seemed happy with the world in general. Many times I walked into the airport during a troublesome delay and anxious queues of guests were milling around the desk demanding answers from Benny:

'When's the flight going to land?'

'When's it going to take off?'

'Will our cases be on it?'

'Will they have the duty free on board that I want?'

'Will I be sat near bloody children?'

'Can we all have window seats?'

Benny remained his usual calm self. He never completely

opened his eyes, or so it seemed to me – they always seemed to be at half-mast, so he looked sleepy and tired. I never worried about the cameras following Benny as he disappeared time and again into the 'lion's den', known as the Departure lounge, to placate another load of angry guests awaiting the arrival of the flight to Newcastle, already three hours delayed.

Some time towards the end of July, though, I was lucky enough to see some of the footage of the cool, calm, laid-back and affable Swede dealing with our British clients. It was not what I expected. Benny's affable and friendly demeanour had, it seemed, evaporated. He was angry, impatient and, at times, downright rude. The cameras loved it. Benny treated the irate guests with sarcasm and contempt. His personality as I knew it resembled a hippie in a weed garden. He had now become a hyena in a butcher's shop.

'What time is our flight going to take off?'

'Do I look like the bloody oracle?' he barked.

'We're not seated together, why not?'

'I don't know and I don't care. At least you've got a seat, so shut up and stop moaning,' came the stern reply.

Benny was never challenged by the guests because he was so tall and threatening, but he was clearly not the kind of person to instil calm into a stressful situation. Needless to say, Benny's forays into the Departure lounge swiftly became limited to return flights to Sweden only.

Then there was Jose. On the face of it he was a nice guy. He came from Portugal and was residing in Majorca for a while with his girlfriend. Well, that was the story the first time I met him anyway, but it changed many times during the summer. Jose looked, for want of a better way of putting it, foreign. He had dark skin, with an oily complexion, thick, greasy black hair, which topped off his slight, five-feet-five-inch frame. He was one of those people who liked to invade your personal space – i.e. he would get about an inch from your face every time you spoke to him. You could smell his breath, and I can tell you that Jose had a real taste for garlic. I wouldn't have been surprised if he took it with his Cornflakes every morning. It was strong, believe me. Sometimes he got close enough for you to see some of the work his dentist had ahead of him. Needless to say I tried to keep most of our face-to-face meetings to a minimum. Jose would not have looked out of place as an extra in the film *Gandhi*, so I wasn't surprised when his nationality changed to Indian halfway through the season. We arranged a charity football match in June against the airport staff, at which time Jose became a Brazilian for a while. Towards the end of his stay, he became South African. By this time, nobody either believed him or cared. Jose left us to become an actor, quite fitting really as he'd done an excellent job playing the part of a confused character all season. I wish him well, wherever he is.

There were also the stalwarts amongst the team. The girls who'd worked at the airport for years and had seen it all before. These people are the people who keep it all going. Women like Beryl, who'd been working for the company for some fifteen years, from rep to the office and finally to the airport, where she'd found her niche. Beryl worked through all the delays without ever moaning; her experience and her know-how set her apart from the rank and file. But she was not alone; there were others who were just as important: Linda and Jan. June, a thirty-something mother of two, who'd been living in Majorca for some years, was also part of the team. She was blonde and buxom, with a bubbly personality; an absolute must for the TV cameras.

Palma airport was laid out on four different levels. Level one was for Arrivals. It's about half a mile long, with several lifts, a number of unusual coffee bars and car hire offices etc. At the very end of one side of the airport, you could find our Arrivals office. It was staffed twenty-four hours a day and was always busy, the focal point for all activity. Bus drivers, reps and airport staff were always milling around making enquiries. It could be quite a stressful place to work.

On the second level, we had Departures. This had a similar layout to the ground floor and we also had an office there, which could be equally busy but we had the added advantage of being able to send the guests off to the Departure lounge before their flights depart.

Most airport tickets will have a standard text informing you to check in two hours before your stated time of departure. I never took this too seriously because it was usually just a precaution to get people there and stop any last-minute panicking. Getting there two hours before departure in Majorca, though, was an absolute must.

The walk from the check-in desks to your gate could be anything up to three-quarters of a mile, and with very few signs to help you on your way, this could be a difficult task.

We lost many people between the check-in desk and the gate during the summer. Planes were held up as passengers were searched for all over the vast, wide-open spaces of this aviation station's corners. I would not have batted an eyelid had a herd of wildebeest passed by the desk in migration. The only wild beasts we did see were returning youths leaving the island early for a number of reasons – having been thrown out of apartments for drunken behaviour, split up with their friends or just running out of money. Whatever the reason, it was not uncommon to arrive at work early in the morning to find four or five youths asleep on the floor outside the Departure office in the hope of getting a standby flight home. One particular morning there was a youth asleep on the floor who'd pissed in his jeans and then gone to sleep on the spot. What a sad way to make your departure. When he woke up and we eventually got him a standby flight, we let him go for free because Beryl didn't want to take his sodden money, which had been stewing in his pockets all night. And people wonder why money smells the way it does.

I was more than a little perturbed one Thursday afternoon when I arrived in the Departure lounge to see the desk surrounded by a number of angry clients whose flight had, as we say in the business, 'gone tech'. This excuse covered any number of problems, from lack of crew, to faulty toilet or dodgy engine. The clients wanted answers and they were becoming increasingly angry with us as our updated information outdated and contradicted the last thing we'd told them.

One woman got herself into such a state that she managed to engineer a panic attack and promptly collapsed in front of the desk. We called an ambulance that, judging by the amount of time it took to arrive, must have been on another island. The different television crews from the BBC, ITV and the Spanish TVS were on the scene much more quickly and were positively licking their lips at this spectacle. The poor lady could only see cameras and microphones inches from her face as she tried to regain consciousness. It was like a shark attack. June, who was on duty at the time, decided that this was her chance for stardom. She immediately loosened her blouse, put on her make-up and attended to the woman, with Dr Benny in close attendance.

The mob around the desk smelled blood; as I gave them the news that they would have to stay an extra night on the island, I was mighty glad that I had a desk between us. Angry clients, delayed aircraft and missing luggage are enough to have to deal with on their own, but add TV to the equation and you can quickly descend into farce, which is exactly what happened that day. Eventually, the ambulance arrived for the woman, but on seeing the TV crew she decided that she felt better and would like to give an interview. I was not impressed and neither were the ambulance drivers, who were determined to get what they came for. A curious tug-of-war developed, with the drivers trying to persuade the woman into the ambulance and the TV crew trying to keep her out, while June and Benny in the middle pouted for the camera. What a shambles.

So that was the second floor and Departures, with its long,

orderly rows of check-in desks. If you ever find yourself in Palma airport waiting to check in for a return flight home, take a look around you at those other check-in desks. There were one hundred and seventy in all. As you stood in the endless queues, with your suitcases inching forward, you might find yourself wondering why only a few of the desks are open. You would be on well-trodden ground for, during my time in Palma, I just could not figure out why so many of the desks always seemed to be closed. I think that the designers must have just kept on drawing desks until someone said, 'Stop, we don't want that many!' I believed that if all the desks were open, it would have made the whole check-in process unbelievably quick. But that would have been too simple.

One thing the design had allowed for was the separation of nationalities – well, the major nationalities using this airport anyway. At the right-hand end of the airport you had the arriving and departing British. At the far left-hand side, as far away from the Brits as is possible, you had the arriving and departing Germans. In the middle, you could find all the nationalities that the Spaniards, when they designed the airport, thought would be OK to leave and arrive together, i.e. the Spanish themselves and smatterings of French, Swedes, Russians and a few more Scandinavians. On the face of it, this separation idea was a good one. When mixed together in hotels, resorts and particularly around swimming pools, the Brits and the Germans do not always make the best of pals.

The separation was certainly not made in order to

distinguish one nationality from another, because I can tell you that, from my experience of working in airports in this business around the world, the British traveller stands out like a beacon. On arrival, we were usually completely inappropriately attired. We were the only nation I had seen who travelled to the sun in heavy coats and hats, with far more luggage than we would ever use. In a lot of this luggage, you'd find that we usually brought food – yes, food. We travel to a foreign country to sample the sun and the lifestyle and we bring our own beans, bread, sausages and untold other goodies. The manufacturers of British suitcases have also cunningly designed most of them to look exactly the same. Most of the travelling families waited anxiously around a conveyer belt for cases that look just like those of the family standing behind, who even now were pushing their trolley into the ankles of the family in front. The great British public had managed to overcome this problem by sticking pieces of fluorescent tape to their cases for ease of identification. This also made it fairly easy to identify the Brits on arrival.

And we were just as easy to spot on departure. After two weeks in the hot sunshine, cultivating their tans, the Brits set about their return journeys clad in attire that was only suitable for the beach. You could usually pick them out in airports, the ladies in their bikini tops and skimpy shorts and the gents in a pair of shorts and little else, save usually for a football shirt, normally that of a team such as Manchester United or Newcastle, in their hands. This they would don as they mounted the steps of their inbound aircraft. You wouldn't believe that on ninety-nine per cent of occasions they would be returning to the wind or rain, or both. I think that they had worked so hard on their tans that they were determined to show them off, no matter what. The fact that people stared at them upon their return to the UK had more to do with the fact that they were dressed so skimpily, in near sub-zero conditions, than anything to do with their beautiful tans.

One other thing that made an awful lot of Brits stand out was the fact that an awful lot of them were drunk. Sad, but true. This was probably why they could become so nasty when faced with delays, as they often were. Not only did they have the inconvenience of waiting, but they also had to contend with the possibility that they may have to recover from a hangover if the delay continued. Either way, there was never a problem spotting a British package holidaymaker at the airport. It would not be unfair to say that we were the most inappropriately dressed nation in Europe.

As I said previously, Palma airport had four floors ... well, strictly speaking, there were six. The top two were used for office space. At least, the top one was. The fifth ... well, to tell you the truth, I never saw the fifth floor. I tried to gain access to it once, but it must be where UFOs are stored or something, because you just couldn't get in there. Maybe it didn't really exist. It might only have existed as a number inside the lift, who knows?

Then there was floor three. Nothing surprising about floor three, really. It served merely as an access point to the Departure hall from the car park. Just why this couldn't have been made directly from and to the second floor and the real Departures, was beyond me – and most people, incidentally, who used floor three for quick access to Departures, only to find out that they had to return to floor two anyway …

I could only guess as to the purpose of floor four. It was either meant to be a national car park, the next indoor basketball stadium or perhaps even a venue for concerts. It currently lay on top of floor three, with no obvious purpose. But then that was the beauty of Palma airport – it was the great unknown.

I did find one very good use for floor four. One busy Thursday morning, I arrived at work in the Arrivals hall to find the usual chaos of the biggest arrival day of the week. Our girl on duty, June, was ensconced in our tiny office. Surrounded by microphones and cameras, by now she was a regular focus of attention for the TV crews. This morning was quite an unusual day, as the star presenter from England had arrived and was practising at being an airport rep for the company. June was milking the opportunity to show her the ropes on national television, the guests, watching all this from the confusion of the Arrivals lounge, were becoming more and more frustrated at the attempts of the TV people to deal with their queries. As politely as I could, I tried to persuade June that, perhaps, her duties lay elsewhere at that time. The crew, however, were more persuasive and, predictably, even more confusion than normal reigned. The obvious place to retire to rethink one's strategy was the fourth floor. Henceforth it became my favoured spot whenever I needed to retire and muse on how to deal with the latest piece of madness.

It's difficult to convey just how vast the airport really was without resorting to primitive terms such as 'bloody massive' or 'a monstrosity', but I can't really find a better or quicker way to get the message across. Flights were regularly delayed because passengers who had booked in had become lost on the way to the gates. Some we never saw again, so just what happened to them, I'm not sure. Their luggage was offloaded and stored in the airport and that was that. Either they got on flights to different destinations or simply got lost in the 'Palma Triangle'. What? I hear you say. The 'Palma Triangle'? This was a new phenomenon that I'm convinced must have existed, for even reps that set out to make the journey from Departures to Arrivals disappeared regularly. They usually turned up again, safe and sound, at their homes some time later, but they never made it to their intended destination. Yes, Palma was a great place to go missing, and many of our team took the opportunity to do so when work became a little too testing.

Meeting the challenge of dealing with the great British public abroad – travelling, delayed, aggressive and pissed off – was, in itself, enough to keep me busy. But there was more to come. As if I didn't have enough on my plate, the Spanish unions, of which there are many and many powerful ones too, decided that they would add to the difficulties.

The bus drivers decided, in May, that it would be a good idea to go on strike for more money. Every arriving passenger at Palma airport had a transport requirement when they first set foot on the island. Approximately ninety-nine per cent of the guests arriving used a coach company laid on by their tour operator. So when these people decided to go on strike for more pay, the consequences were quite serious, to say the least. Take Saturday, for instance. There was a flight movement every sixty seconds. Everything had to run like clockwork and the traffic had to keep moving or, eventually, the airport would have become full of arriving passengers who were stuck, with no way of getting out of the Arrivals hall. There was another problem: all the guests who were scheduled to leave the island had to catch coaches to the airport to connect with their return flights. Planes cannot leave empty. The upshot is that, without the buses, eventually the airport would come to a complete standstill and this could have very serious consequences, not only for Majorca, but for all the other Balearic Islands as well. Eventually, the knock-on effect would filter down everywhere. No joke!

The drivers' unions were well aware of this. They made their pay demands and they were not going to take no for an answer. As the proposed strike day drew nearer, all tour operators eyed the negotiations with great concern and began to make precautions to dig in. The coach company that we used had already come to an agreement with their owners, so we had reason to believe that our passengers would still be ferried around regardless. These hopes were quickly dispelled when we were informed that pickets were massing on a nearby island to fly in at a moment's notice should the strike go ahead. Word somehow got back to the

UK press, when some insignificant minion blabbed to the English newspapers. They took great pains to explain to the travelling public just how miserable it would be trying to get in and out of Majorca this summer in the face of Spanish bully boy union tactics. The news hit the *Daily Mail* and quickly spread; it was quite amusing to see some reps' words quoted in a national newspaper, though. I wonder who they were?

Anyway, tension was high as the day of the strike drew nearer and our guests were becoming agitated as to how it would affect them. The long-serving members of the team had seen it all before and were convinced that the bosses would give in at the last moment and the strike would be called off. Wiser minds thought differently and realised that this time the unions were deadly serious. The strike was due to begin at midnight on Friday and plans were being made to utilise every taxi on the island and to get all of the Saturday departures to the airport before midnight, so that we would have one less thing to worry about.

It seemed that all tour operators had the same idea, so space was becoming a problem. By eleven o'clock, one hour before the deadline, the airport resembled a refugee camp. Thousands of people were bedded down on lilos, with emergency blankets, sprawled across seats and lying on the floor. It seemed that every available square inch of floor was utilised, as the passengers squeezed in. It really was an incredible sight. It wasn't long before the bars ran out of food and drinks. We'd sent out to the nearest super-market for supplies earlier in the day but these were quickly disappearing too. Soon the toilets broke down and began to leak; the stench of excrement and sweat coupled with the inevitable sound of screaming children as well as drunk and angry adults filled the air. Outside the airport, every other available space was also being utilised. What was rumoured to be an emergency morgue, alongside the main terminal, was now a very lively waiting room full of Germans. The old terminal building was also being used as all other nationalities crowded in as well. Even the fourth floor was being employed to help us out. One thing was clear: if the strike went on for more than a few hours, then things would quickly deteriorate and we would not have been able to cope. At twelve, the strike began. As if by magic, all the coaches disappeared and hundreds of baseball bat-wielding thugs appeared, who obviously made up the paramilitary wing of the coach drivers' union. Any doubts that we may have had regarding whether or not our drivers may have been able to work through were quickly dispelled as thugs smashed the windows of a coach that was slow to leave the car park. The heat and the strike were most certainly on.

The unions were allowing us to use taxis to take the guests out of the airport and we had contracted, at great expense, about fifty for this purpose. As fast as they moved, though, they were always going to struggle to cope with the sheer numbers of arrivals once the second flight had arrived. One company took the decision to hire a minibus to ferry guests around. This seemed like a good idea until the pickets stopped the minibus, beat the driver up and set the bus on fire. Things were getting heated. By now the pickets had massed at the entrance to the airport and were chanting slogans, to anybody who wanted to listen, about how they would win or die. It really was very intimidating; we struggled on.

Some of our arriving guests waited up to three hours for a taxi before they could leave the airport. By 8am, the bulk of our arriving flights were in and most had managed to leave on time, but the team were exhausted and it was clear that we could not go on for much longer. We then got the news on the radio that the strike was over ... the bosses had folded and normal services would be resumed. I have often cursed coach drivers as they meander ahead of me on the highways at twenty miles an hour, but that morning, when the first of our coaches pulled up at the airport car park, I could have kissed the driver. The pickets dispersed as quickly as they had arrived and eventually the crowds thinned out.

The coach drivers had held the island to ransom and they'd shown us just how powerful they could be. Bully boy tactics had triumphed and guests were held in contempt. Let's hope it never happens again, or at least never when I'm there. I was exhausted when I drove home – so much so that I fell asleep at the wheel and crashed into the back of a coach! I wasn't injured and, mercifully, neither was anybody on board, but it did seem like a bit of divine retribution ...

One thing about working at Palma airport is that because you are so busy, the time seems to pass very quickly. Before you know what's happening, you're halfway through the season. By mid-July, things were settling down and I was beginning to get used to the ways of working in Majorca, when one morning I received a phone call from my boss, who explained that one of my colleagues on the mainland of Spain had fallen pregnant and was about to go on maternity leave. Would I mind going over to cover for her until the end of the season? I asked for some time to think this over and about thirty seconds later I gave her a considered reply: 'When would you like me to go?'

Three weeks later, I was firmly settled in the north of mainland Spain as the manager of a new team. The season was coming to an end, the reps were firmly bedded in and all looked rosy for me. After Palma, this was heaven, or so I thought.

This new posting took me to a part of Spain that's quite unique. It was right in the middle of the Catalan heartland and these people are not renowned for their friendly welcome to outsiders. They are, largely, very successful business people. The tourist industry is thriving and with many different nationalities from around the globe descending on the Catalan capital, Barcelona, you don't tend to come across as many Brits on tour as say Benidorm or Mallorca.

This means that in plain facts and figures you go from Mallorca, with its 105 flights a week, to the positively pedestrian 12 weekly arrivals all flying in and out of my little airport. I just couldn't wait to start work here. It would be like a return to sanity after the madness of Palma.

On the first available 'flight day' I went along to the airport to observe the operation first hand. It worked like a dream. The airport was situated in a remote little town about ten miles from the main resort. It was easily manageable with its two storeys – one for arrivals and one for departures. Once the guests had checked their luggage in on the ground floor, they head up to the first floor where they passed through the departure gates. There they could find a reasonable sized bar and a duty-free shop, where they could while away the time and have a drink or two if they desired, before they departed.

The manager of the airport was a little old fellow of a very jolly and friendly nature called Juan. He had worked at the airport for years and was a very friendly and accommodating man. He had done every job in the airport from working in the control tower to cleaning the toilets, to actually checking in the passengers for their journeys home. He was always smiling, happy and creating a very good working atmosphere for excellent customer service to thrive.

I had a spring in my step as I returned to my office in the main resort. The rest of the operation seemed to be functioning quite well, so I thought I could work out my time here just overseeing things and trying to relax after the excesses of Mallorca. It was like a dream come true, and when I discovered how close we were to Barcelona –an hour drive away – I thought it might be a good chance to soak up a bit of real culture, maybe even go and see Barcelona FC play. Now I will freely admit to being a bit of a Philistine when it comes to beautiful architecture and fine art, but even I couldn't help but gaze in awe at some of the amazing and fantastic sights, such as the Sagrat Cor, with its awe inspiring grandeur. The place is just amazing and it's got some great shops and bars to get pissed in. Moreover, because it's a big city, the chances of you ever seeing anyone you know is practically zero, so you can do pretty much anything you want (within reason, of course).

It's not really a downside, but still worth mentioning, when the season starts to come to an end around September-time the air gets a little colder and the area becomes prone to the odd thunderstorm. The storms help to clear the atmosphere but they can be quite fierce at times. There was one typical September evening in my first few weeks at the new resort when I decide to retire to my bed sometime around midnight. There was a storm brewing in the area but as I retired to my room I thought nothing more of it, as I slipped into a contented slumber.

I don't quite recall what the subject of my dream was on that fateful September day, but I do remember that it was something to do with being home in the UK and being very contented. For some reason, the house was quiet save for a phone ringing somewhere in another room. The dream went on, but that bloody phone was getting louder and louder…. I was snapped back into reality with the cold realisation that the ringing was not in my dream but my phone screaming at me from the bedside table.

One thing about this job that never changes, wherever you work in the world, is that as the manager you are on 24-hour call out. You can be woken up at any time in the day or night to deal with a number of problems, ranging from death to complaints about feathered pillows. Mercifully, these occasions are few and far between so it's not really much hassle, but you tend to keep one ear alert for the shrill ring of the telephone calling you back to reality.

What now I thought, as grabbed the intruder and pressed the answer button.

'Sorry to bother you Cy,' said the calm voice of a colleague, who in my sleepy state I did not recognise. 'A plane has just crash landed at the airport.'

My first thought was that it was just a wind-up from one of my old Mallorca buddies.

'Fuck off!' I said, 'I'm tired.'

There was a brief silence at the end of the phone and then a rather more urgent retort.

'Cy, I am not joking, there has been a crash at the airport and you have got to go to the resort office immediately and get the resort organised.'

Something in the tone made me realise that this was serious.

I jumped back into reality very, very quickly. My first jumbled thoughts were that if this really was a plane crash then it must be very serious. It's a nightmare scenario and subconsciously I felt sure that there would be deaths.

'How many are dead?' I asked.

'We don't know yet.'

Within ten minutes I was on my way to the resort's office. My feet left the ground and I knew they wouldn't be touching it again for a while.

The truth was dawning on me; there really had been a plane crash. One of our seemingly indestructible jets had fallen out of the sky. The crash had happened about midnight or some time soon after, and I was in the office by 3am. I had no idea of what I would be facing, or whether there had been any casualties; I didn't know any of the details of what had happened. I rounded up the office staff as quick as I could and, to their credit each, every single one of them was in the office by 5am ready to offer help in any way that they could.

I have been faced with many different and challenging incidents over the years, and you never really know how you will react until you live through them. There is no company handbook to tell you how to react in the face of unusual circumstances because they are all very different, but somehow you just instinctively know what the right thing to do is and you go into autopilot – no pun intended.

I worked for a fantastic company and in the face of these horrific events the top brass, and a positive cavalry of senior managers, offer support and help to their customers and staff in any way they can. It's very reassuring. But, as the resort manager in those first few hours after a major incident has occurred, you are the one on the spot until reinforcements arrive. In those first few hours, the team were looking to me for leadership and it was my biggest test to date. By 5.30am, the press had got hold of the story and were beating a path to the office door hungry for some kind of comment from us. I was, by now, getting some sketchy details from the airport that the plane had broken up on landing, was lying in three pieces in a field and one person had been killed, although this was not confirmed.

The press were given a firm 'no comment' from us in the

office, but this did not dissuade them from camping outside and accosting anyone who tried to get in or out. The phones were starting to go berserk, ringing every time the receiver was replaced. The company was mobilising every rep and manager it could get hold of from nearby islands or resorts near enough to get people to us.

I caught a glimpse of the news on the office TV and the true enormity of what we were facing struck home. A TV camera had somehow managed to get near the stricken aircraft and film the wreckage. The formerly majestic 757 lay stricken in a field broken into three pieces. The commentators were saying that it was a miracle that there had not been multiple casualties, and looking at the TV pictures I couldn't see any reason to disagree. News was also filtering in that there hadn't been any casualties and incredibly everyone on board had survived the impact of the crash.

Thankfully, we found out around 8am the next morning some of the passengers had been released from hospital, but the press were anxiously pursuing them for any comment on what had happened, or what they were planning to. It was bedlam. I received a call from my boss who had flown in from the Balearic Islands and was making his way up to us with 90 extra reps to help in any way they could. The plan was to put one rep with every party 24 hours a day to monitor their individual needs.

Although there were many cuts and bruises, everyone apart from one elderly lady had been released from hospital and had made their way to different hotels in the resort, where armies of reps waited to look after their every need.

The companies headquarter in London had by now also realised the enormity of the situation and Sara, the managing director, was on her way out to see the scene for herself and to offer her support where possible.

Some, in fact most of the people who had survived, had nothing with them at all, save for the clothes they stood up in, so there was an immediate need to get them basic survival bits and pieces. I was despatched to the bank to draw out as much money as I could. The company were understandably desperate to avoid any repercussions from irate customers who were recovering from the shock of surviving a crash landing, so I was under orders to get every penny I could lay my hands on and look after the guests no matter what it would cost. At £35,000 the bank ran out of money, but the managing director was said to be arriving with another £8,000 in her bag. Even this would not be enough. There had been over 230 people on board the aircraft and we were going to give them around £500 each, and pay for any extras that they needed, such as glasses, tablets and clothes. It was going to be a massive operation but the needs of the shocked survivors where at the top of our list of priorities.

By 10am, the office was buzzing with extra staff that seemed to have been mobilised incredibly quickly and, at times, it almost felt like there were too many people helping out. Money was flowing freely, and for the first time I began to realise how vast the company I worked for was; money and people seemed to be appearing from everywhere. Our suppliers, such as hoteliers and coach companies, were very supportive as well and soon they were lending us millions of pesetas. The survivors were shocked and afraid, but definitely glad to be alive.

It was quickly realised that we were going to need much more than just well meaning reps to help out, and before long trained counsellors were on their way out to help, too. As the team in the resort grew, so my role diminished and I quickly became a bit-part player. I was given the job of accompanying the managing director as she made her way around the resort. I acted as her driver, translator and guide. I'd met her a few times before at various meetings and conferences and also, of course, during my stint at Palma. We got on quite well, in a sort of boss-serf kind of way. She was very much in touch with the staff on the ground, and I really felt that she had our interests as well as the guests at heart. We got on well enough and this was one of the reasons why I had been assigned the job of accompanying her.

I took her to the airport and when we arrived there was a real sense of disbelief among the staff that something like this could have happened to them. I met Juan, the airport manager in the arrivals hall, and he looked and seemed exhausted. His normally all encompassing smile was weak and unconvincing. He had not slept at all the previous night after pitching in and trying to help amid the confusion and mayhem that ensued in those few hours after the crash. He escorted us to the office at the rear of the airport where we found the pilots of the stricken aircraft waiting to be interviewed by the Spanish police. They were piecing together what had happened in the time immediately leading up to the crash.

We were seated in a small stuffy office with a couple of guys from the airline, who had gone out to look over the plane with the investigators from the planes manufacturing company and some people from the Spanish air traffic control. Mobile phones were constantly buzzing and intruding on the conversation as we tried to make sense of what was happening. We got word from the resort office that some of the people who had been involved in the crash desperately wanted to get hold of their hand luggage and their suitcases that had been left on the plane. We did what we could to get these items back, but the crash investigators were adamant that absolutely nothing could be removed from the wreckage until they had completed their investigation – and that might be some time. Eventually, the pilot and co-pilot were allowed to talk uninterrupted to the managing director of the airline who had flown in from Corsica.

The pilot looked like one of the archetypal World War 2 heroes; a typical old-school pilot I thought. He may have been around 50 years old, although some of the papers had him down as younger, but on that day he looked more like 85; tired, drawn and drained from the terrible events of the night before. He still had his bloodstained uniform on and his head had been cut open, but he kept a stiff upper lip in the face of the rounds of gruelling questions. He slumped in his chair and took a cup of coffee in his shaking hand. It emerged that all he wanted to do was to get home to the UK to see his wife and family, but the authorities wanted him to stay around until the investigation was complete. He looked close to despair as this news sunk in.

His co-pilot was a younger man and some six feet tall. He didn't look as drained by the ordeal. He was still in his uniform, too, but he was smart and alert, and if he was tired after the events of the night before he did not show it, as he shook hands and made small talk. If the pilot represented the old-school then this younger man was definitely of the new regime – smart, professional and almost cold in his approach.

By now the company had got on to a lawyer and they were challenging any right to detain the two men, but it would be some time before the issue was resolved. The company had already ordered a plane to come and collect the pilots from the scene, but the Spanish were digging their heels in, determined to keep them at the scene. The battle was on.

The pilot it seemed just wanted to talk about what had happened and we were willing and sympathetic ears to his needs. There had been rumours already that during the storm the airport had been closed to incoming flights, but the pilot assured us that this was not the case. Incoming aircrafts had been advised to divert to Barcelona, but it was still left in the hands of the pilot whether or not to attempt a landing. Besides, the weather at Barcelona, scarcely an hour's drive away, was not any better and a Dutch flight had landed just half an hour prior to the crash-landing. Therefore, there was nothing unusual about attempting to land at the airport that evening. The pilot rightly believed he was not taking any undue risks.

As he sat there in the tiny cramped office explaining what had happened his voice was quiet and reflective. At times he would stare into space, no doubt running through the previous night's events in his mind. His emotions were understandably close to the surface and I got the impression he was torturing himself inside, going over and over the night's event. If he was blaming himself then he was doing so unnecessarily because back in resort the passengers were calling him a hero. The pilot insisted that he was the last person to leave the aircraft. Only after he had checked that everyone had made it off did he make his way to safety. Then in the terminal building, still injured, he went to speak with the passengers individually and try to reassure them. The passengers all maintained that the captain was a hero and I am inclined to agree with them. It must be every pilot's nightmare. You can practice for these things as much as you like, but you can never be prepared for the reality and horror of such a situation when it occurs. For a man who had just been through a life changing experience, he was remarkably calm and collected.

It emerged some time later that contact with the ground had been lost during the final stages of the landing, as the thunderstorm raged. The realisation that they were about to crash was not lost on the two pilots, as they allegedly bid each other farewell just before the impact. The plane apparently landed front wheels first and broke into three parts, losing the engines before the craft came to rest in a field. Text book crash apparently. The passengers were saved by the fact that the engines fell off before the craft came to rest and this prevented any risk of fire on board. Many of the locals referred to the sight as a miracle. It is easy to see why.

The fact that the engines came off also meant that the plane lost all power, so the only way to communicate on board was to shout. Apparently the staff at the rear of the plane were unaware that there had been a crash until they heard their colleagues at the front shouting, 'off, off, get off', to the passengers. As passengers slid down the emergency shoots into a muddy wet field in the middle of a thunderstorm, they must have been very confused and afraid. The immediate reaction was to get away from the plane in case it caught fire. They ran towards a light that turned out to be the terminal building. The terminal staff were unaware there had even been a crash and were alarmed to see groups of terrified British tourists coming across the runway shouting about a plane crash. Incredible really.

A couple of days after the crash, many of the guests wanted to go home but understandably not everyone wanted to fly. Coaches were laid on to take those guests back to the UK on a 36-hour journey. Counsellors, doctors and nurses accompanied many people home to make sure they were OK. It was a traumatic time for all concerned and some people, I'm sure, will never fly again. Who can blame them?

As the stricken plane lay in the field, the first action of the company was to paint out the logo on the tail and body. I found this a bit cynical but I suppose necessary. It would be bad publicity, I suppose. It certainly kills the old belief that there is no such thing as bad publicity. Not in the airline business anyway, it would seem.

A couple of days after the crash, I got the chance to have a look onboard the aircraft. As I travelled out to see it, the first thing that struck me was how it had managed to land in the only place where there were no obvious obstructions – 20 yards either side of it and it would have hit trees. I don't even want to think what damage this would have caused.

As I approached the aircraft from the rear, the sun was shining again and the only evidence that the field had been under attack from a fierce thunderstorm was the deep groove in the field that looked like a river bed, which had been created by the impact of plane. It seemed like the earth had acted as a natural brake to slow the jet down.

The rear of the plane rested at a 30-degree angle, and although the logo had already been painted out, it was clearly recognisable with its blue tail pointing up to the sky in defiance: proud and unbroken. The fuselage had cracked and broken out of line just behind the tail and debris was sticking out from the gap, like entrails protruding from a once proud beast slain in battle. The right hand wing pointed at an angle up to the sky, while the left wing rested on the ground, at one with the dried mud. A second crack appeared some 30ft in front of the wings and you could see into the body of the plane itself. It looked dark and disordered and was suggestive of the panic that must have ensued on the night of the crash.

I walked round to the front of the craft to look at the cockpit. As the plane had crashed into the field so the wheels had buckled and broken, and they now lay embedded into the bottom of the plane. This meant that you could see right into the cockpit because it was eye level. The inside of the cockpit seemed as if it was just waiting for the captain to jump in and fly it away again, but this image was quickly dispelled when you saw the large hole that had been broken into the floor of the aircraft like an unsightly wound. Because the craft was so low and dug into the earth, it seemed very small, quite unlike ones usual image of such an impressive piece of engineering.

There was an eerie silence as we surveyed the wreckage. One of the company's flight attendants was tenderly rubbing the fuselage and openly crying as one of her colleagues comforted her. It was quite a moving scene. We were all being reminded that we were not invincible and the risks we warn our guests about every time they board an aircraft are very, very real indeed.

I boarded the aircraft at the rear and was shocked at the scene that confronted me. Oxygen masks hung from the ceiling, seats were crushed against one another and there was debris everywhere. It was a scene of utter chaos. I couldn't help thinking how on earth anyone came out of the crash alive. It was, and still, is incredible.

That whole event was very traumatic for many and no doubt lives were changed for ever that night. They say that what doesn't kill only makes you stronger. Well, there a lot of stronger people from that experience, but it could have been so much worse.

HOME
AND AWAY

AFTER ALL THE DRAMA at the airport, it was good to escape to the ski slopes again, where the only concern about things falling from the sky related directly to snow, or the lack of. Bliss!

It all began with me forgetting to bring a handkerchief on to the ski slopes. Forward thinking, I knew to make a list of everything I might need for the day ahead – it was a regular ritual. Gloves: check. Hat: check. Ski pass: check. Lip balm: check. Money for drinks: check. I just forgot to pack the hankies. Now, as I headed down the red run passing the beautiful alpine scenery all around me, I couldn't concentrate on any thing other than my nose, or rather the contents of my nose, which trickled down on to my sensitive upper lip, straying in and out of my line of vision. I should have stopped there and then and dealt with the problem, but I choose to wipe it with my sleeve and wait until I could attend to the offending hooter at the bottom of the slope.

Such was the excitement and exhaustion on arriving at the

bottom of the slopes some minutes later that I forgot to attend to my runny nose. The temperature in the Tyrol on that particular day never got above -6 degrees and dropped considerably lower as the day progressed. My nose dried up. I had no more runny embarrassments and I almost forgot that I had neglected to pack my hankies earlier that morning.

I attended the ritual après-ski drinks in the bar at the bottom of the nursery slopes later in the day. It was always a good chance to catch up with the customers and see how they were progressing and lay the foundations for a night out later on, and perhaps even test the ground to see if there might be a chance for a bonk with one of the girls from home. After all, the uniform was supposed to double up as a pussy magnet, but as the season progressed I was slowly finding out that the uniform didn't act as a magnet, nor did it double up as a plastic surgeon – once an ugly bastard, always an ugly bastard. It would seem a ski uniform can't make up for what is yours by birth: your looks.

As is so often the case with après-ski, one drink becomes two and before long it starts to get dark outside and the temperature drops. Inside the packed bar, though, the temperature rises and eventually your body begins to warm through. Soon my nose began to thaw and itch. In an absent moment, I gave it a quick rub with the back of my hand and it throbbed in disapproval. I then recalled how I had forgotten to bring my hankie earlier in the day and made a mental note to not forget the vital tissues in the morning. The festivities continued, the night passed by and my nose issues were temporarily forgotten. I could never have guessed that one act of forgetfulness could cause me so much distress in the weeks to come.

On waking up the next morning, I discovered that every time I breathed in my nose was whistling with the effort. It sounded like a steaming kettle with every inhalation. I swiftly got up to go the bathroom to blow my nose and clear the blockage. There is no doubt that high in the mountains, where the snow falls and settles so liberally and beautifully, that the air is fresh and dry and will thaw neglected nostrils. I was about to learn a painful lesson. My nose was red on the outside and dry and raw on the inside. I felt like I had been given a coat of tarmac from the inside and it had been a thorough job. I was in agony and no amount of blowing or careful excavation could relieve my discomfort. As my knowledge of skiing, and the kind of equipment you might need to become a successful skier, was quite limited, I had predictably not packed any Vaseline and had no idea that it would be useful. In hindsight, I now know that a necessary item to add to the check list is Vaseline, and lots of it. This was just the start of my nasal agony.

My sidekick and confidante throughout that first season was a man named Mike Martin. He was a seasoned ski rep of some two years on the Austrian programme. We quickly became very good friends both on and off the slopes. He was an excellent skier who seemed to glide across the slopes effortlessly with style and grace. He transferred this style and panache to the bars of the Austrian resort at night and seemed to glide home with a different beauty every other night. In short, he was everything I was not. Whilst I carved up the slopes in a surly, awkward and brutal manner, he made gentle incisive cuts across the hills with the blades of his skis, like a surgeon on call to the errant slopes. He charmed the girls into bed, whilst I retired alone after nights of wrestling with inappropriate chat up lines like a door-to-door salesman with nothing to show for his labours. Smooth operator though he was, the thing that really impressed me about Mike was how he could tell I was suffering from a troublesome nose just from seeing me attempt to ski. Not that he was the best advert for a perfect nose, Mike sported a fair sized hooter himself and had earned the name of Concorde in the Alps, but then I suppose if you are sporting a huge nose you know only too well the consequences of not taking good care of it.

'Sore snout Cy?' he proclaimed as I winced towards the ski lift one cold January morning. 'You want to try some Vaseline up there you know. It's this dry air. Let me have a look.'

I arched my head back and he gazed from a respectable and safe distance into my cavernous inflamed angry nostrils. He winced at the sight before him. 'Gosh, that looks sore,' he proclaimed. 'Get some Vaseline up there,' he repeated, 'that'll sort it out.' Our friendship was cemented, so to speak, by that act of mercy and good advice.

Not realising that Austria had also entered the modern era at the same time as the UK and also embraced the new consumer culture and the miracles of modern simple medicine, I sent a letter home to my mother with strict instructions to send me some Vaseline with her reply. Some weeks later, it miraculously appeared and not a moment too soon. I pushed great mounds of the stuff up into my swollen, rock solid snout that by now resembled a bright red, angry bulbous mass. Within a couple of days, my boulder-like nose had relaxed and I eventually found some relief. Once the swelling had died down and my vision was clear, I found that the local supermarkets had pots of Vaseline on sale all over the store. I could have stopped my suffering earlier but my ignorance had prolonged my nasal ordeal. It was too late to save me from the predictable nickname Rudolph, as well as hours of piss-taking at the expense of my nose.

Whilst penning these first few lines regarding my nose, I feel I have to qualify the need to go to print on such a snotty subject, which on the face of it would seem a trivial matter – on my face though it was anything but trivial. A pain in the nose can become a real pain in the arse. I speak from bitter nasal experience. I've had the misfortune of having my nose broken on no fewer than three separate occasions during my short career as an amateur boxer. Believe me when I say that it is painful and all consuming. Once you've had the misfortune of suffering pain in the nasal area, and understand how the pain can be all consuming, you do every thing in your power to prevent any more pain. I have been careless in this appointment. The number of breaks is ample proof of that, but to be afflicted by the pain from drying up is careless to say the least. Apologies for those who don't share my passion but be warned: always pack hankies and never forget the Vaseline when making for the slopes.

Nose aside, one tries to forget the minor inconveniences as best as possible and instead enjoy the chance to ski and get paid for the privilege. Not only was the skiing fantastic, but you couldn't fail to recommend the great nightlife on offer in Soll. It was a bit like being in San Antonio, but all the punters were knackered and had more money than the average drunken fun-seeker in Spain, which meant they got drunk without the night ending in a bust-up! Mike and I would often cruise the bars like all self-respecting reps on the look out for single girls to pass the night away with.

One such night springs to mind instantly. Mike and I were relaxing and drinking in the Austrian bar, which on that particular day was the latest favourite haunt of the ski punters. A beautiful blonde haired girl had wandered into the bar some two hours earlier with her tall dark haired, and frankly not so beautiful, friend. It's important to get the facts right here, and although this may sound cruel, the dark haired girl was simply ugly: I believed I was in with a chance.

We noticed them immediately. So too did every other male in the bar. All eyes were on the blonde. We however had the advantage, we were wearing the ski reps uniform and they immediately noticed us. Well, I say immediately, it was after we had sidled over into their general view and bought them both a drink, which I might add we paid for. This was a rare thing in those days. Any how, I think they noticed Mike before they noticed me.

It soon became clear that the beautiful blonde only had eyes for Mike. I guessed this after he came up for air after another session of tongue wrestling with the beauty. He gave me the thumbs up like a submarine engineer returning from the torpedo room. I was busy distracting her taller friend, who on closer inspection was uglier than I first thought. Her long dark hair hid a pockmarked face that bore the scars of persistent and determined acne, presumably from her youth, a parting reminder of an age that by the look of her had been some time ago. She was a good 12 inches taller than me and a good deal bulkier than my own respectable 13 stone. She was quite a considerable size but after a few beers I felt I was up to it. A band, a group of regular resort musicians, was playing in the corner of the smoky bar, adding to the atmosphere. They did their best to stoke things up by goading the crowd into cheering us on and announced that this was the first time we had got anything close to a snog all year long. The girls, to their credit were unmoved. The blonde continued to snog Mike, and her dark haired friend kept winking playfully in my direction.

After a timely visit to the gents to amongst other things attend to my throbbing nose, Mike asked me to leave the bar with him and his beau to accompanying the taller friend. Blondie wanted to go back to Mike's room but wouldn't leave the bar until her friend was fixed up. Mike is a good mate and I felt I couldn't let him down, so off we went. We left the bar with the band playing 'Teenager in Love' in our honour, a dubious privilege under the circumstances. The freezing night hit us all. In stark contrast to the loud smoky atmosphere from inside the bar, the temperature outside had plummeted considerably. The freezing weather sharpened my senses and had the added effect of sobering Mike and I up, making the reality of things all the more stark. The girls, it seemed, had been consuming alcohol since they had stopped skiing earlier in the day, which was about 9.30am.

With the time now close to 10pm, it meant that the odds didn't go in our favour. The blonde girl's slurred speech, and her more amorous attempts to get Mike's salopettes undone, confirmed my suspicions that the cold air had only helped to heighten the affect of alcohol on her.

By now, my companion had decided that she really liked me. She tucked me under her arm and I heard her say, 'Do you know you whistle when you breathe? I think it's kind of cute.' I didn't even try to answer, as I we trotted behind Mike and the staggering blonde.

We were headed for Mike's apartment, which was only a 15 minute walk away, and we seemed to be on track. I barely had time to consider what the hell I was going to do with the giant leading me down the street, when Mike seemed to stumble ahead of us and sit down on the street. From a distance, it looked as if he and blondie had decided they couldn't wait any longer and elected to get down to business right there and then on the kerb. It was only as I got closer and managed to get my head clear of the armpit of my new friend that I could see what was really happening. Mike's sense of self-preservation had served him well as he tried to extricate himself from the clutches of his beau who had begun to vomit. The ensuing attempt to avoid the hot surge that was coming from her mouth had led him to fall beside her on the pavement. She hung on to him as she retched uncontrollably; the ensuing tussle had seen them tumble to the floor.

My new partner who had been whispering sweet nothings into the top of my head for the last 15 minutes detached herself from me and ran to the aid of her suffering friend.

She stepped over Mike and seated herself beside her buddy and began to vomit too, presumably in sympathy. What a good friend I thought to myself. I couldn't at the time, and still can't to this day, name a single companion of mine who would vomit in sympathy with me. Probably just as well. It's times like these that you can feel excluded from a very close friendship, but I'm glad they left me out of this one.

I looked over at Mike who was doing his best to move away from the vomit as quick as he could without ruining his uniform or his image. He was a not a happy man and the night had definitely not quite gone to plan. We looked across at each other and shrugged. If we left them there to vomit in harmony, we could probably get back to the bar and try again, but there was always the possibility that they might freeze to death. We were both in full uniform and once again the company's guardian angel was hovering above us telling us to avoid bad press and cover up all evidence. We decided to phone for a taxi. After a wait of 15 freezing minutes the taxi driver refused to take them home. We had no option but to walk them back to their hotel to safety.

By now the girls were full of slurred but no doubt sincere apologies. The freezing weather had served to sober them up and as a consequence the grim realisation of what had just happened began to hit home and embarrassment set in. We took the long walk to the hotel in silence, Mike and I leading the way and the girls a short distance behind.

When we reached our destination, Mike just couldn't resist a quick peck on the cheek with his would be beau; he was no doubt regretting a missed opportunity. Unfortunately for him, the blonde girl still in a tipsy state mistook his courteous peck on the cheek as an invitation for a full on snog. Mike misjudged the situation and, before he could adjust, Blondie stuck her tongue in his mouth. Ugh. He was still spitting some 30 minutes later as we made our way home. Ah, the joys of ugliness.

There is a belief that reps have a life of sex, drugs and rock'n'roll, and no doubt there is a lot of that going on, so I can't leave this subject without a small reference to this wilder side of the life of a rep. I'll spare you the blow-by-blow accounts, but I'm sure you can join the dots!

I was recently reading an account of a reps time working in Spain for club 18 to 30, and he was saying that he thinks he slept with something like 50 girls in one season. That's quite some going for any normal person in their lifetime, but for any rep working in the youth hotspots for just a few months that's quite a slow season. My mate Biggsy's count was well over 90 one season – and he had a long-term girlfriend! He just wouldn't go out unless he could pull someone and take them back for a good seeing to.

Shagging just becomes part of the way of life. The boys are proud of the girls they have slept with and will boast about it, the girls on the other hand can be a little more discreet. It's something that I have always found intriguing. Guys can shag themselves silly, tell everyone and wear their conquests like medals. The girls, however, are a different matter entirely. They sleep with a few guys and they become slags. It doesn't seem fair really. This attitude, though, is not confined to the world of repping, it seems to present worldwide. It's probably why girls have managed over the years to be discreet, while the lads are as loud and crass as can be. Make no mistake, though, while the lads have got the reputations, the girls have managed to find a way to have fun as well. Hats off to the girls I say. Lads blab, girls smile knowingly.

So, what can I tell you about the sex lives of reps from my era? Well without resorting to breaking confidences, or sporting my medals, I can tell you that it all goes on: sex on the beach, sex in a club, group sex, paid sex, all kinds of sex, and the reps are at it whenever they can get it. It's great fun. I think when you take a job you have various priorities: money, job satisfaction, caring for people, lots of things really, but when you take a job as a rep your top priority is probably a little different...

I remember being inspired watching some reps years ago when I was on a youth holiday with my mates. The reps cared not a jot for our welfare, but they were shagging all of the girls in sight and we didn't have a look in. From that moment onwards, I wanted some of that action. Sure, I thought, I could do a better job on the welfare front but I also wanted the kind of magnetic attraction that they had with the girls.

I think most reps, when they accept the job, think about the customer service aspect of things and how they are going to meet new people, but more importantly they think about how they are going to shag everyone they can, and some – not all – do. Certainly no one does the job for the money because the pay is shit. Make no mistake, you'll never get rich being a rep but you will certainly get rich experiences, especially of the sexual variety.

Sex is almost like a currency abroad. I remember, after being promoted and negotiating contracts with coach companies and excursion suppliers, going through the usual round of monetary examinations and then being whisked off to the local brothel, where the owner of the coach company put his gold credit card on the counter and said, 'Give this man anything he wants. Make sure he gets looked after.' Of course, I limited myself to another pint of lager and left... honestly!

There is one curious condition that grips reps at some stage in their repping career (normally it's at the end of season) and that's called panic shagging. By the end of season, in both the summer and winter resorts, the girls are looking gorgeous and the blokes are full of confidence, drinks are flowing and there is a sense of relief to have reached the end of a long arduous season. There are no guests and your guard is down. As the night passes, you find yourself talking to one of your colleagues, time flies by, and the next thing you know people are leaving and you are left alone with a person you would never have dreamed of sleeping with. You look at each other, and next thing you know you are in bed together in the throes of wild passion. It seems like it was meant to be – the most natural thing in the world – and then you wake up the next morning and think, Oh my God... what have I done? She, too, is thinking the same thing. That is panic shagging! Shag the guests and there is no comeback, but shag your colleagues and you have to face them for god knows how long, and that is one of the consequences of panic shagging.

THE LAST
RESORT

GETTING ON AND off planes during my time working for tour operators overseas was as normal as getting in a car to go to work. I just got used to it over the years. Now, in the Autumn of 2001, as I boarded the plane for the last time on company business, to return to the UK and begin a new chapter in my life, I felt a little melancholy. I had many memories of ten great years in so many different destinations. Originally I only joined for six months so I could have a paid holiday and bonk all the girls I could find. Whatever happened to that idea? Now I was heading for London, doubtless to find some changes since I had last been there.

I was sure that I was going to find it a challenge to fit back in to life in England. I viewed it as going to a new resort. After years of packing and unpacking suitcases I wanted to put some roots down. I'm sure there comes a time in everyone's life when we feel this way, although I suspect that it comes a lot sooner for some than others. There are, of course, the things I would miss about my time abroad – obvious things, like the weather and the lifestyle, the siestas, and the do-it-tomorrow, devil-may-care attitude of the Spanish and the Greeks. I would also miss all the free drinks … it really was going to take some getting used to, this paying-in-a-bar thing that the British insist upon. The good things about being back in the UK were that I wouldn't have to work weekends any more, and I wouldn't have to pack my suitcase again, except to go on holiday. What bliss. I didn't have to be on call again twenty-four hours a day, living in fear of being summoned to the Costa del miles away to placate an angry lynch mob complaining about the sub-standard rooms they received for their sub-standard prices. I was going home. My first stop would be at the head office to see whether they could offer me gainful employment in the metropolis.

As I approached head office, I could spot the new reps waiting to go off on their training courses. They looked young and nervous. They reminded me of wartime evacuees, setting off for their new lives in the country, their cases all packed and ready to transport. I passed them by and ventured into the building, seeking work in my new resort. One thing became very clear, very quickly. Anybody who has worked in the UK for the company, and has never worked overseas – and there are many – believes that time spent working overseas in one of our many resorts is a holiday. They couldn't get their heads around the fact that it's bloody hard work; it's more than a job, it's a way of life. After a few rounds of interviews, during which I managed to re-establish my credentials as a hard worker with more than just a sun tan on my mind, I managed to set myself up with a job. And that was me sorted, ready for my new life here in the UK. Pretty simple really. I decided to venture out for a celebratory drink.

When I left this country at the start of the Nineties we seemed to be looking forward to great things in the future. The new millennium, not so far away, was carrying us on a wave of optimism to a new beginning. The internet was just starting to grip people's imaginations, though nobody was really sure of how that was going to affect our lives. I think that thirst for the future has gone now. It was like a passing fad for new fashion, and it has been replaced by another new fashion – a fashion for anything that is old. I was to find this in many places, but the first place I became aware of it was a pub called Molly Malones for my drink. I chose it because it screamed from every sign outside that it was Irish, and I thought I might get a nice pint of Guinness inside. It was obviously quite a new pub. I seem to remember that the last time I had been back in London this place had been a bank. *Well, it's always good to see the demise of the banks*, I thought to myself, *and what better thing to replace it with than a pub? Great idea*. But when I walked in the door, it just looked so wrong. New but desperately trying to look old. There were old Gaelic signs, such as 'Caed Mille Failte', emblazoned all over the walls, and all the seats were painted to look older than they really were. There was an old plough on the ceiling, hanging precariously to give it an authentic look, and there were even fake groceries behind the bar to add to the impression that you had just walked into an old Irish pub. It didn't work for me. The decorations simply gave themselves away as fake and new. Further investigation revealed that this pub was not unique. There were, it seemed, loads of them all over the place.

It's not just the pubs, though. I was horrified to see people wearing flares again. Surely we learned our lesson the first time round. Even Raleigh are thinking about bringing back the chopper bike again. Cars too are being designed to look old again; the new Jag looks suspiciously like the old model, and there's a Chrysler car that is becoming ever more popular which looks like it could have been taken straight from an old Humphrey Bogart film. The TV has joined in too. There are so many programmes about loving the Seventies or the Eighties, and now even the Nineties it seems. People seem to look for a comfort in the past that they can't find in the present. We seem to have become obsessed with looking back. I suppose that may sound a bit ironic coming from me, considering that I have just reminisced about the last ten years of my life. I am all in favour of looking back, but where the hell are we going?

If you drive on the motorways nowadays, the answer is obviously nowhere. There is no such thing any more as rush hour; it seems that it's almost impossible to drive anywhere without being involved in mind-numbing traffic jams, all day long every day.

Gyms as well. Bloody gyms! The whole country is obsessed with them. You have got to be a member of one, or preferably a member of one that has not even been built yet, because it's cheaper to sign up for full membership before it opens. I have tried to join a gym since I came back home, but I honestly find the monotony of running nowhere too much like what I do in the daytime – i.e. driving nowhere.

One thing that remains the same is the attitude of banks. They still write you shitty letters when you go ever so slightly overdrawn, and they still charge you for them. One day somebody might invent something that gets rid of banks altogether. That would make me very happy indeed.

And there are always new and better ways for financial organisations to relieve you of your hard-earned cash. Everywhere now I see adverts for people urging us all to consolidate our debts into one manageable amount. This is fraught with suspicion for me. I think the idea is, you clear all your credit cards into one crippling debt, and then you have the clear credit cards to run up even more debt with all over again. I am sure that in ten years' time the adverts will be reversed: 'Take your one crippling debt and break it up into lots of manageable monthly amounts.'

The mobile phone now runs our lives. This, sadly, is also the case in Europe. But here in the UK we have gone one step further, in that children as well as adults are now totally obsessed by these bloody objects. How the hell did we ever manage our lives without the damn things? Who knows, but it looks like they are here to stay.

Oh, and I nearly forgot another of the changes that have taken place over the past decade, one that took place in my own line of work: the demise of duty free. Duty free used to be something that you looked forward to when you went on holiday. You got the chance to buy cheaper goods as you left from your departure airport. You felt privileged because you could only get to this shop if you were flying, and it was only available in the Departure lounge of the airport, Now, duty free is available in the Arrivals hall as well – how novel. The most curious thing is that duty free doesn't actually exist any more. How can something vanish only to be replaced by even greater amounts of goods to buy?

Of course everything changes in time. You know you are getting old when you look in the mirror only to see someone looking vaguely like your father staring back at you. The grey hairs have now invaded my head in their legions, and somehow I just couldn't cut the mustard as a rep anymore. My image is moving into a new era of parenthood and responsibility. After some arm-twisting and the gift of a ring with a hefty diamond attached, Beth, my long- suffering girlfriend, agreed to become my wife. She has now given birth to our beautiful daughter, Charlotte. I will do everything I can to dissuade her from becoming a holiday rep, and I fear the day she brings home her first boyfriend and tells me he works overseas for a tour operator. I think not.

So here I am in the last resort. Sometimes in your travels as a rep you make friends that you think are going to be for life, yet here I am back in the UK and I can hardly remember some of the names of the people I worked with back in my first year. A rep's experiences pass in the blink of an eye. Holidaymakers are becoming more and more demanding as well. The threat of TV coverage can strike fear into the hearts of reps and holiday companies alike, and the guests use it whenever they fear they might not get their way. When I was working in Spain, I once told the owner of the hotel I was working in that *Watchdog* were coming to film. He genuinely thought I was referring to some sort of pet programme for dogs. Nowadays

Watchdog is as well known around the Costas as the line 'A small beer, please.' Oh the times they are really a-changing.

The biggest revolution has been in travel. Changes were taking place before I left the UK, but they have definitely gathered momentum since. The world is no longer the vast place that it used to be. We can now hop on and off planes and go anywhere in the world at relatively cheap prices – this is good: travel can be a great education. And I only speak from personal experience. I know that I am different as a result of seeing a bit of the world. I appreciate how rich in culture Europe really is, but I also appreciate the good things about the UK.

Believe me, Britain is a great country to live in. We are free; we all get the chance to earn fairly good salaries; we have places to go and things to do. When you watch the news in this country, however, you could be forgiven for thinking that we were living in hell. It seems that we are constantly moaning about one thing or another: the trains, the air we breathe, the crime rate, the government, our wages, our health service or our teachers. I am not saying that everything is perfect – far from it – but why do we have to moan about everything all the time? I remember when I was a kid, on *News at Ten* every night they used to have a spot that was called 'And finally …', which provided a chance to look at the lighter side of life and laugh at some of the things that go on in the world. It seems that this spot is now reserved for a bit of self-mutilation. More doom and gloom for the nation. I think the UK is still a great place to live. Let's tell each other now and again.

Me? I'm glad to be back.